BARTOW'S HEALING HANDBOOK

NEW REVISED EDITION

YOUR PERSONAL GUIDE
FOR
HEALTH AND WHOLENESS

by

DONALD W. BARTOW

LIFE ENRICHMENT
PUBLISHERS
CANTON, OHIO

Published by Life Enrichment Publishers
P.O. Box 20050, Canton, Ohio 44701

Life Enrichment Publishers offers special discounts for bulk pur-chases of its products to be used for fund-raising, premium gifts, sales promotions, educational use, etc. Book excerpts or special editions can be produced to specification. For information contact the Special Sales Department, Daring Publishing Group, 913 Tuscarawas Street, West, Canton, Ohio 44702. Or call 1-800-445-6321.

Library of Congress Cataloging-in-Publication Data

Bartow, Donald W.
　Bartow's healing handbook / by Donald W. Bartow
　　　p.　　cm.
　Includes bibliographical references.
　ISBN 0-938736-28-0 (v. 1) :
　　1. Spiritual healing.　2. Spiritual healing--Biblical teaching.
I. Title.　II. Title: Healing handbook.
BT732.5.B363　1991
234'.13--dc20　　　　　　　　　　　　　　　　　91-17920
　　　　　　　　　　　　　　　　　　　　　　　　　　CIP

10　9　8　7　6　5　4　3　2

Printed in the United States of America.

TABLE OF CONTENTS

III
WHOLENESS A TO Z

IV
WHOLENESS

Author Don Bartow is unusual by anyone's standard. A uniquely inspired pastor serving congregations since 1948, he set new standards wherever he went. As one of the very first pastors of any mainline denomination to hold healing services in public, he caused quite a stir in 1959 among the conservative cadres who held that such "miraculous" 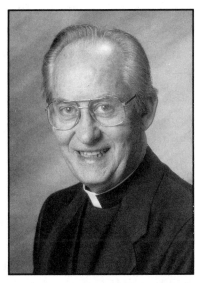 events were best served behind the traditionally private veil of the church's sanctuary, or worse, this great gift was completely ignored. But Pastor Don Bartow had felt personally called and deeply stirred by God to provide *anyone* who felt the need to witness this special and gracious blessing of healing the opportunity to come to services to see for themselves the wonderful gift of *wellness*.

By 1970, the energetic young pastor had personally served in the healing of hundreds of Christians in need of physical, spiritual and emotional healing; suddenly he felt strongly moved yet again by the Holy Spirit to further broaden his message of public healing into other mainline denominations. He founded his Spiritual Healing Ministry - the response was stunning; the needs of thousands of suffering men, women and children nationwide were filled as he assisted hundreds of churches both great and small to begin and maintain healing services open to all to behold the miracles at hand.

As the call on his services steadily grew through multiple appearances on television (700 Club, 100 Huntley Street, TBN, to name a few), Don Bartow became internationally known as one of God's true healers. An early riser and tireless worker in the name of Jesus Christ, Don Bartow has authored multiple books, audio cassettes, and has held dozens of successful seminars, conferences and retreats throughout the country, all devoted to promoting wellness instead of sickness.

"God does not intend for you to be sick! Jesus does not want you to suffer! Ask His help! Just ask - and *believe*!" is his message.

Pastor Bartow retired from his pastorate in mid-1991 when he decided to devote the remainder of his life to the one great mission of healing among God's Children. Asking for loving guidance, and within weeks of his retirement, God led him to acquire a huge facility - a former church that had fled a dying neighborhood for the more eloquent suburbs - where he instituted the Total Living Center (TLC) in Canton, Ohio. This complex of offices, meeting halls and sanctuaries now serves as the nerve center for his healing ministry. It is not a church. It is a center that feeds the poor, counsels the troubled, ministers and guides the young, and sends forth calls to those bearing missionaries' hearts to spread the word of God's Grace through healing.

INTRODUCTION

Dear Friend,

This HEALING HANDBOOK has been written with several goals in mind:

1. To present the Good News that wholeness of body, soul, and spirit is a worthy goal which the Lord, Jesus Christ, wants each person to receive.

2. To inspire individuals and congregations to believe Jesus heals today!

3. To proclaim illness does more than afflict the body or soul - it also affects the spirit of a person.

4. To provide a helpful resource to help everyone understand the biblical, theological, and practical facets of a healing ministry.

5. To inform and inspire Christians to strive to live a lifestyle of wholeness and healing.

6. To challenge all Believers to fulfill the commission Jesus gave to His followers to teach, preach, and heal (Matt. 10:7-15; Mark 6:7-13; 16:15-20; Luke 9:1-6; 10:1-20; John 14:12).

7. To alert Believers that healing is not an option nor an adjunct to the program of a local church, but the central message of the ministry of Jesus and should be for His Church.

8. To provide guidance to help churches begin and/or maintain a vital ministry of healing.

9. To warn of the grave consequences of neglecting the message of healing for those in need of hope and healing. Jesus frequently and fervently encour-

aged His disciples to heal. He also pronounced harsh judgment upon those who hear the message of wholeness and who reject it (Matt. 10:7-15; Luke 10:9-16).

Today there is great interest in the Church and the Body of Christ concerning the healing ministry. There is also much confusion and many honest questions. I have endeavored to impart to you what I have learned and understood in over thirty years of my life and ministry while proclaiming and practicing the ministry of healing.

The Lord Jesus healed when He was on earth and He still heals today. I pray God will richly bless you as you read this book and most of all that you will become a doer of the Word and enter into the fullness of His blessing.

May we labor together and follow the pattern the Lord Jesus gave of bringing healing and wholeness. To Him be the glory forever and ever. Amen.

In His Victory,

Pastor Dow Bartow

I John 2:17

I

WHOLENESS LOST

BODY   MIND   SPIRIT

The complete answer as to why humankind lost God-given wholeness and became diseased is not known. However, there are many things which are known and which can be proclaimed.

1. When Adam sinned against God, death, sickness, and disease entered the world (Gen. 2:17; Rom. 5:12).

2. Through sin, Satan gained power over humans. He seeks to often exert this power through illness. He seeks to destroy everyone through sickness, disease, and death (Job 2:7; John 10:10). His goal is to keep us from effectively worshipping and serving God, because he knows his time to do so is limited.

It will end when Jesus returns to reign. But in the meantime, we can learn to live in this world victoriously through the power of His resurrection and the power of the Holy Spirit.

BODY

1

MY PERSONAL PILGRIMAGE

WHY I BECAME INVOLVED IN THE HEALING MINISTRY

"Lord, I will conduct healing services until the day I die, even if I have to do it from a wheel chair."

This was a promise I made to the Lord in the latter part of 1959. It was a sacred promise and made in light of what had been happening in my life.

It seems appropriate for my first HEALING HANDBOOK to begin with a presentation of my own pilgrimage in the area of healing. In this journey, I came to devote practically all of my resources to spreading the message of God's healing power.

In the late fall of 1958, I began to feel sick. The symptoms were those associated with some type of flu. I was weak, ached all over and just didn't feel up to par. Naturally, I felt in a few days I would be over this condition and life would go on as usual.

However, I continued to worsen. Visits to the doctor did not reveal any serious problem. I ended up in the hospital for three days of extensive tests. The report from the specialist and the family physician was they could not find anything pathologically wrong with me.

By this time I had developed pain which was with me 24-hours-a-day. Each morning upon awakening I would hook my right leg over the edge of the bed and pull myself to a sitting position. Then I would wrap my legs in elastic stockings to keep them from swelling and plunge into the activities of the day.

Believe me, the plunge did not take me very far from the shore of misery. By mid-morning I was so worn out, I could barely continue the other necessities of the day.

When told that even specialists could find nothing wrong with me, I became even more disturbed. I sought to maintain some semblance of humor, but life was becoming very dismal for me.

I said to the doctor, "If there is nothing wrong, how do you explain the constant pain? How do you explain the swollen legs?" The doctor had no answer. She still insisted my problem was not of the body. Her viewpoint was it was the result of stress, being over-worked, and being too involved in the parish.

The following Sunday morning I tried to convey to the congregation the report of the physicians. I did the best I could, but after stressing the over-involvement portion, I found myself blurting out to the congregation, "In other words, you make me sick!"

The laughter reinforced what I already knew-- that I was among friends and I was loved by those people. However, the problem worsened.

In mid-April of 1959, I was driving to a banquet in Bellevue, Ohio. It was while traveling along to fulfill this commitment on the banquet circuit that I felt the Lord spoke to me.

"I want you to start holding healing services." I was startled and replied, "Lord, you want me to start holding healing services?" "Yes." It was as if the Holy Spirit and I were conversing.

"How can I conduct healing services considering the shape I am in?" I never recall His answer to that very logical question. The feeling simply persisted that I should start holding such services.

You must understand...I had never read a book concerning healing services in a local parish. I had never attended a conference to discover how to do it. I did not have a friend in the pastorate conducting such services. This was in 1959 and very few churches held healing services--especially mainline denominations!

It seemed to me God was imparting the fact that I should hold them during the week. I asked, "Lord, how can you get anyone to attend a healing service?" Sure, we had our regular Wednesday night prayer meeting. The four of us enjoyed it! And the four included me and my wife. So how in the world was I going to get more to attend a healing service during the week?

Interestingly enough, I felt the Holy Spirit tell me, "Give them something to eat." Then, strange as it will sound to you, I can still recall the debate concerning the details of the meal. The conversation while riding in the car was as real with the Lord as it has been with anyone throughout my life.

It is amusing to me now, but very serious at the time when I consider the debate I gave the Lord in arriving at the cost of a meal. I felt it should be at least a dollar per person. Yet, the Spirit seemed to hold out for only 35 cents per person. My contention was this would not even cover the cost of the food.

Finally, I felt cornered by the Spirit and had no way to go, but the road of obedience by conducting healing services. Therefore, I had to come up with a very reasonable and logical way of getting out of this ridiculous request on the part of the Lord.

I responded with what I knew was my perfect way out of the whole situation. "Lord, if I live, three weeks from tonight I will conduct my first healing service." This was great because I was certain I would not live for three more weeks! I was in bad shape and getting worse. Like some other pastors I know, and certainly like some lay people I know, I would rather die than hold a healing service! Isn't this strange? But I was very sincere about this matter. I did not want to hold healing services.

I went home and on Sunday announced the first healing service for May 6, 1959. We would meet at 6:00 in the evening for a meal to feed the body, then study the Bible around the table to feed the soul. We would then go to the sanctuary for the healing service, and feed our spirits.

Do you know...I lived. I held the service and we were on our way! There were eight people at the first service and six came forward for the ministry of laying-on-of-hands with prayer. We already were having more than at the prayer meeting.

Food, needs, and curiosity continued to help increase attendance. We went from 8 to 12, 20, 30, 40 and 70 people at the services. We discovered eating

together was great. In fact, our church had something to eat almost every time anyone got together
for anything! There were the Wednesday night
meals, other potlucks, food at home gatherings, and
so forth!

One of my favorite exaggerations was to comment
about the disturbance at the Sunday morning worship services when people opened their sack
lunches. In fact, eating became such a vital part of
the fellowship in our church that, being a writer, I
wrote an appropriate song, "God be with you, Till we
EAT again.

Interestingly enough, people began to be healed!
However, I got worse. There was still no solution to
my problem, but I knew I was getting worse. I had
concluded I would be dead by age 33, the age of Jesus
when He was killed. (I was becoming convinced the
good die young--I have lived long enough now to
disprove this theory.)

I told my wife, Mary, my epitaph was to read, "I
told you I was sick!"

After several months of one of the most successful programs we had ever started in the church, I
decided to end the services. Sure, people were coming in larger numbers than any mid-week service I
had ever conducted. Sure, people were being helped.
Sure, the congregation had responded in a positive
way to the emphasis upon healing. However, I was
not healed. In fact, I was much worse.

My unilateral decision was to announce at the
next service that it would be our last. My shallow
conclusion was: if I was not healed, no one was going

to get healed at our church. Talk about being selfish--
I was to the nth degree. It was me or no one.

It was while in that frame of heart the Holy Spirit
spoke to me and said, "Do you proclaim a perfect
plan of salvation?" My response, "Yes. I do!" He
probed deeper with, "Are you perfect?" "No," I
blurted out. "That's right. You are not the One who
saves, Jesus Christ is. You are only the one who
proclaims the good news that Christ saves." I agreed
with His conclusion.

Then, penetratingly the Spirit continued to prod
me. "The same thing is true of healing. You are not
the Healer, Jesus is. You only proclaim His desire
and power to heal. Jesus does the healing." How
graphically I could see the logic of these insights!

It was in the light of this revelation that I made a
sacred vow unto the Lord. "Lord, I will conduct
healing services until the day I die, even if I have to
do so from a wheel chair." I had been caught by the
wisdom of the Holy Spirit, the love of the Father, and
the ministry of my Master, Jesus Christ. There was
now no turning back regardless of outward conditions or inward feelings. I must be about my Father's
business and surely it was the same as that of His Son
during His earthly ministry.

A great truth dawned upon me at this time. I
realized in a dramatic fashion that I AM CALLED
TO BE A PROCLAIMER AND NOT AN EX-
PLAINER! I do not fully understand, but I can be
fully obedient. This I have sought to be through the
years. I continue to proclaim the Good News of
God's healing power even though I still do not un-

derstand all of the facets of illness or wellness. I walk by faith and seek to proclaim the fullness of His message that the Kingdom of God is at hand.

It is a thrill for me to write that a funny thing happened on my way to the wheel chair. Shortly after this encounter with the Spirit and my resolute position of holding healing services until my death, I was marvelously healed. Truly I am in much better shape today than I was as a 30-year-old young man.

Jumping ten years ahead in my story to the spring of 1970, I was mowing the backyard one day when I received a vision from the Lord to take the message of healing to all the churches of the land.

(The Lord speaks to me dramatically in the strangest places: He called me to start a healing service while driving in a car. He gave me great insights concerning leadership in the congregation when I was dipping backed-up sewer water in my basement. He filled me with His Holy Spirit when I was sitting on top of my dresser in my bedroom talking to a friend. He gave me a prayer language (tongues) while I was jogging in the streets of Sharon, Pennsylvania. I often say it seems the only safe place for me is the sanctuary.)

While mowing the lawn the Lord gave me a vision of the many churches of our land and their need to hear the message of healing. I said, "Lord, do you know how many churches there are in this land?" Jesus replied that He knew all about them and where each was located.

Realizing I was incapable of this task, I remonstrated with, "How can I ever do this task?" It was then the Holy Spirit gave me three distinct guide-lines:

First, I was to gather around me those who believe healing is for our day. They would undergird my efforts with their prayers and support.

Second, I was to begin writing concerning prayer and healing. My first book was published by World Publishers, but dealt principally with church admini-stration. It was in May of 1970 I wrote my first article about healing and started to mail it to a few hundred people.

Third, I was directed to preach and teach con-cerning healing. There would be cassettes and other teaching tools prepared and used to advance the message of healing, especially within the mainline churches of our land.

All of the income from any and all of these three areas was to be used to advance the message of healing. I have sought to faithfully fulfill the above three areas. I have not done it perfectly, but I have certainly done it persistently.

The bad news is that I have not yet done the task as completely as perhaps I could have. The good news is that through mailings, speaking engage-ments, radio and television appearances, etc., I have reached over 250,000 churches of our world with the message the Lord heals today.

I continue to reach out with the message of heal-ing with my books, speaking engagements, cassettes, and many other resources. It is a joy to report many more churches conduct healing services today. One of the greatest joys is to proclaim the Presbyterian

Church USA (my denomination) has put in its Constitution that every church should hold healing services! (See W-3.5400 section of the Directory for Worship of the Presbyterian Constitution.)

The dozens of conferences at Westminster Presbyterian Church in Canton, Ohio alone have been used by the Lord to reach thousands of pastors and lay people with the message of healing. Pastors from large and small congregations and from all the major denominations, plus independents have been present at the conferences and returned to their congregations with the message of healing and hope. The main goal of the conferences has been to help congregations to begin and/or to maintain a vital ministry of healing. We have no way of ever knowing how many have been touched through this portion of the ministry, let alone through all the other conferences, seminars and retreats in which I have participated throughout the nation.

I have kept my vow unto the Lord. I still conduct healing services and by His grace I will do so until He says my mission is completed. Upon the completion of my mission in this life, I know I shall go on to the perfect healing of the resurrection. Jesus is my strength and my salvation. I believe with all my heart that the Lord is my healer.

My prayer is this HEALING HANDBOOK will be another tool used by the Lord to advance the message of His presence and power in our midst. Jesus is the Lord that healeth. Amen!

MY PERSONAL HEALING PILGRIMAGE TIME TABLE

The following is a time capsule of my journey of seeking to know and serve the Lord. Special emphasis is put upon those incidents which are related to the ministry of healing:

May 3, 1928--Born near Shawnee, Ohio.

1938--First time to attend a church and to hear the message of salvation proclaimed. Accepted Christ as Lord and Savior and felt called to be a Pastor (was ten years old).

September 1946--Entered college.

September 1948--Became student Pastor of three churches in Wood County, Ohio.

April 1, 1949--Baptized in the Holy Spirit.

September 1951--Began serving three churches in Hancock County, while attending Seminary.

1954--Anointed Perry Alspach and witnessed my first great physical healing through prayer. Perry had an incurable skin disease that was instantly healed.

June 1954--Ordained to the Gospel Ministry.

June 1955--Assumed a Pastorate in Toledo, Ohio.

Late Fall 1958--Became very ill.

Spring 1959--While still very ill, felt led to begin holding public healing services.

May 6, 1959--Conducted first healing service.

1960--Made sacred vow unto the Lord to conduct healing services until the day I die even if I have to do it from a wheel chair.

1960--Shortly after the vow to hold services, I was wonderfully healed.

August 1, 1966--Assumed Pastorate at the Westminster Presbyterian Church in Canton, Ohio.

January 4, 1967--Began holding weekly Healing Services each Wednesday night at Canton Westminster Presbyterian Church.

Early Spring 1967--Wrote first book, "Creative Churchmanship."

April 1970--Had a vision while mowing my lawn that I should take the message of healing to all the churches of the land.

May 1970--Wrote and mailed my first Spiritual Healing Article.

May 20-23, 1974--First Healing Conference held at Westminster Presbyterian Church.

1981-Published "The Adventures of Healing."

1981--Published "A Ministry of Prayer."

1983--Appeared on Trinity Broadcasting Network (TBN) in Los Angeles.

February 1, 1984--Experienced the strange phenomenon of having my spirit leave my body and relate in a very moving way with the Spirit of the Living God.

February 6, 1984--Opened the United States Congress with prayer.

February 9, 1984--Appeared on the "700 Club."

May 1984--Observed the 25th Anniversary Year of conducting healing services.

1985--Published the daily devotional book, "The Ministry of the Master."

October 1985--Co-hosted "100 Huntley Street" for a week.

1986--Had achieved the goal of reaching approximately 250,000 churches concerning the message of healing for our day.

1987--Started to make use of Electronic Keyboard music at the Wednesday night meetings.

1988--Added the K-700 Technics Keyboard to the electronic music part of the Wednesday night service.

June 6, 1988--Appeared on the Heritage (PTL) Network.

August 13, 1990--Wrote a letter to the congregation announcing my retirement from Westminster Church effective July 31, 1991. This date completes 25 years as pastor at Westminster.

April 5, 1991--Signed option to buy the Total Living Center facility.

May 8, 1991--Held the first healing service at the Total Living Center.

2

DO PHYSICAL HEALINGS OCCUR TODAY?

A question I am often asked is, "Do physical healings occur today?"

My answer is, "They certainly do." There are not nearly as many as we desire, but there are many healings: physical, mental, and most importantly, spiritual.

Perhaps the main reason this question is asked is because many feel the church's ministry of healing deals only with the mind and the emotions. They basically believe a person may be helped psychologically, but not pathologically.

I have witnessed many physical healings. The following are a few of them.

RARE SKIN DISEASE

Perry was a 76-year-old friend of mine who suffered for years with a very rare skin disease. It left him bedfast, in constant pain, and defeated emotionally. The disease completely covered his body and his flesh looked like scales. A puss-like substance oozed from his body. His wife would change his briefs four or five times a day. When Perry would go to the rest room, his skin would fall off like dandruff and the vacuum sweeper would be used to clean it from the carpet.

Perry's wife phoned me to relay Perry's desire to be anointed with oil. Myself and two other men went to their home and I anointed Perry. This was late Saturday afternoon.

Early Sunday morning, a phone call from his wife requested us to stop by the house prior to church. We stopped to see Perry. He was sitting on the edge of the bed pulling off his skin and throwing it in the waste basket. The flesh which remained was perfect. He spent all day Sunday removing the old diseased skin and ended up with skin almost like that of a young child.

ARTHRITIS

One of the women who attended a conference at our church had severe arthritis in her hands. They were swollen, her fingers drawn, and she lived in constant pain.

The Lord gave an instant healing after prayer. The pain, the swelling, and the stiffness left immediately and never returned.

WHIPLASH

"It's different, it's different!" Joy exclaimed as she rose from a kneeling bench in the chapel of a Baptist church in Detroit.

I was leading a conference at this church and some of her friends had brought Joy for the ministry of laying-on-of-hands with prayer. I ministered unto her with a brief prayer. She stood up completely healed!

It was later in the afternoon the report came to me of her spectacular healing. It was then I learned of her desperate condition.

Some years previously she had been involved in an auto accident. She received a whip-lash injury which got progressively worse regardless of extensive medical treatment.

She walked with a shuffle, suffered frequent and severe headaches, had endured years of deep depression, and three times attempted suicide.

The moment she was ministered unto, the pain left and the depression disappeared. She was baptized in the Holy Spirit and spoke in tongues. The Lord certainly blessed Joy! She was changed from a discouraged, disgruntled, and defeated Christian, to a victorious and witnessing dynamo for Christ!

RIGHT HAND RESTORED

An auto accident had left a lady with her right hand practically useless. This was a special curse to her because she was an accountant and did much writing. This was becoming increasingly difficult for her.

Long and arduous physical therapy had only restored partial usage of her hand. She attended a healing service at our church. You can imagine her joy when the next morning she awakened to discovered her afflicted hand completely healed!

THE SHOE STORY

I will never forget Anna's stunted leg.

About a dozen of us were assembled in the chapel at Westminster Church. Anna had come from another state with relatives to our healing service. Her problem was the short leg. A built-up shoe had helped her through the years, but it was still a problem.

A lady of our church and I knelt in front of Anna and I removed her shoes. As I held up her legs for all to see the difference in length and began to pray, the short one grew about two-and-a-half inches. Now they both were of equal length! We all rejoiced!

After several moments, a sister-in-law remarked, "Now, Anna, you are going home with the same condition you have had for 73 years. You will be walking lopsided!" We smiled as we realized with a built-up shoe, Anna would again be lopsided!

I will never forget Anna's response. She said, "Oh no, no!" Then she went to the front pew of the chapel where she had been seated for ministry and picked up what all of us presumed to be her purse.

She opened up this supposed purse and took out a pair of ordinary shoes! She went home level! What a night for all who witnessed this tremendous display of faith.

CANCER, CANCER, CANCER

Chuck had been a long-time member of Westminster and on several occasions served as an Elder on our Session. The years had taken their toll, physically.

Pneumonia forced him to go to the hospital. Tests confirmed more serious problems. It was discovered he had lung cancer, brain cancer, and leukemia. This, in addition to the constant back pain which had not been helped with two operations. His efforts to combat the constant pain had led to addiction to prescribed drugs. In addition, he had high blood pressure which could not be kept under control even with medication. His family was told to prepare for his death.

I ministered unto Chuck as he lay in the intensive care unit, really unaware of my presence. The Lord reached out and touched him with a great healing.

Chuck left the hospital with no back pain, easily controlled blood pressure, no brain cancer, no lung cancer, and no leukemia! He continues to serve in our church and he praises the Lord for His grace and goodness in granting this healing.

BRING THE CHILDREN

I was ministering in a Presbyterian Church at Richmond, Ohio. A lady brought an eight-year-old girl forward and mentioned she suffered from back pain. She wanted relief from the back pain.

I inquired about her legs and was told one was about four inches shorter than the other because of a rare disease. I asked if I might pray for her legs also. The Pastor and his wife and about 125 people present watched intently as I began to minister unto her. Praise the Lord, before our very eyes the leg extended to within a quarter of an inch of the other--it grew four inches!

I found out the next night the little girl was scheduled for rather radical treatment in the near future at one of our nation's leading medical centers. They were going to restrain the growth of the good leg. How wonderful that she was spared many agonizing treatments and many days of confinement.

DOWN'S SYNDROME

Mike and Beth were devastated with the news their newborn, third child had Down's Syndrome. She had the physical characteristics: the flat face, thick tongue, short fingers, muffled cry, difficulty eating, and her blood cells showed 53% had the extra chromosome present in Down's Syndrome children. Their kind physician had spent over an hour explaining the future of a child such as little Michelle.

Beth and Mike requested that I anoint little Michelle. My response was, "I am most willing to do this. However, I do not want to do it simply to comfort you as parents, but to have us believe for the reversal of the Down's Syndrome problem. I do not want to make any false promises, but at the same time, we do not sell short the arm of the Lord to heal."

I anointed Michelle on Tuesday and again on Wednesday. Wednesday night, as I promised Beth, all present at the Healing Service prayed at exactly 7:22PM and Beth and a friend did the same at the hospital. Thursday morning when Michelle was brought to her mother, it was obvious to us that we had received our miracle! She was different in appearance, strength of body, and on her way to normalcy.

Later, tests by five experts in the area of Down's Syndrome revealed Michelle to be normal or above normal in all areas! A later blood test revealed a dramatic reversal of the blood count (18%) which confirms the Down's Syndrome condition. She was three months old when the report of the change in the blood was received. That same day, her doctor said although she was only three months old, she had the development of a five-month-old baby! God had done it again!

CONCLUSION

Space prohibits further examples in this book. However, I have witnessed many more. I often say to individuals, "Any one of the above would have made my years of emphasis upon healing all worthwhile!"

May I say that all the physical healings in the world will not convince some people of the desire of the Lord to heal today. Just as in Jesus's day, there are many who want only to worship tradition and perform the liturgy. They do not desire to permit the power of the Lord to flow in and through them. This was the condemnation Jesus made of the Pharisees.

However, there are many who hunger for the good news that Jesus heals today. I feel called to proclaim this good news and to encourage others to do likewise. I believe the words of our Lord Jesus,

"Verily, verily, I say unto you, he that believeth on me, the works that I do shall he do also; and greater works than these shall he do; because I go unto my Father," John 14:12.

"...they shall lay hands on the sick, and they shall recover," Mark 16:18.

3

EXERCISE AND HEALING

There is abundant evidence that physical exercise is essential to our total well-being.

The type, degree, and length of physical exercise will vary with age and capabilities. Some people can train for the Olympics, while others confined to wheelchairs are greatly limited. However, everyone must have a degree of exercise.

Our body is important. It was created by God to be the container of your soul and spirit. The body was created first and then the living spirit was placed in the created body (Gen. 2:7). What good is a body if the spirit is absent? It is of no value and we dispose of it with some type of burial. What value is the spirit without the body? It is of no value in this world. When the spirit departs there is no way a person can exist in this world and even the body becomes useless. You are a triune person and all three facets of yourself are important.

The Word verbalizes what experience verifies again and again that the body is mortal. It does not last forever (Gen. 2:19; Job 21:26; Ps. 104:29; Eccl. 3:20, 12:7; John 11:39). The life of the body is frail and short-lived (I Chro. 29:15; I Sam. 20:3; Job 7:6; Ps. 39:5, 78:39, 103:14-16; Is. 38:12, 64:6; James 1:10, 4:14; Heb. 9:27; I Pet. 1:24).

Your body is precious in the sight of God and should be properly cared for by you. It may serve for only a brief period, but it still is sacred (I Cor. 6:15; I Thess. 5:23). Several years ago I wrote a poem which I feel conveys the importance of the body and at the same time conveys the brevity of physical life in light of the eternity of the spirit.

THE ETERNAL FLOWER

Many gardens fair adorn the land
With fragrance sweet and beauty grand.
From lowly seed appears the green,
Which forms a part of earth's fleeting scene.

And thus the body is the seed,
Which serves a vital, short-lived need.
But the spirit within, the eternal flower,
Is nurtured forever by God's power.

You must always seek to keep your body in proper control and in proper perspective. Our tendency is to spend so much time, money, and energy on the body and neglect our soul and spirit.

Isn't it interesting many believers cannot wait for Sunday's service to end so they can make it to a restaurant to eat a big meal they don't even need? Isn't it intriguing more time is spent caring for one's hair than for one's spirit?

Paul realized the natural tendencies when he wrote urging believers to put on the Lord Jesus Christ (Rom. 13:14).

Even though the body is temporary and must be kept under control, it is still necessary to care for your body. One of the ways to do this is through proper exercise. Even though Paul says bodily exercise profits very little (in view of eternity), it is still exceedingly important (I Tim. 4:8).

I can't devote the time or space to list all the varied forms of exercise for different individuals. Books and magazine articles about exercise are too numerous to mention in this brief chapter. They can be secured at any library or bookstore.

One exercise I would like to discuss is walking. Almost anyone is capable of walking a little extra every day for exercise. Research and experience have shown it is an effective contributor to greater health of body, soul, and spirit.

WALKING SUGGESTIONS

First, you should walk vigorously a minimum of 30 minutes at least three times each week.

Second, you don't need a fancy walking track. Practically anywhere will do. Do avoid walking near busy, air-polluted highways. Discover the merits of walking at:

- your neighborhood mall
- your neighborhood school hallways or gym
- your local streets
- your city walking paths

- inside your own home
- your YMCA or health club

Third, wherever you walk determine the area which must be covered to equal a mile. It might be twice through the mall or 140 times around your recreation room.

Fourth, use some creative way to determine when you have completed a mile. It is amazing what some have come up with, and you can develop your own idea. Consider some of the following:

One person put clothespins on a line near his walking area. Each time around he removed a pin. Ten pins represented a mile. He placed 30 on the line prior to the walk. He didn't have to worry about how far he had gone. He knew when the pins were all gone three miles had been traveled or any fraction thereof according to the pins remaining on the line.

A woman used a Chinese Checker board and placed marbles on the board representing her desired miles. Each one for her represented a 20th of a mile. It was fun for her to see the marbles disappearing from the board as she covered her desired distance.

Another lady used a peg board with sticks in it. Each represented a quarter of a mile and she removed one each time she came by the board. It added a little spice to the walk and left her free of worrying if she had covered the desired distance.

Some simply determine how long they want to walk and watch their time. A fast pace for 30 minutes or more does wonders.

Some individuals appreciate using a rebounder, stationary bike, treadmill, ski machine or even the currently popular stairmaster. Any and all mechanical devices which enable you to exercise are worthy. The only precaution is that it not be too strenuous for you. If it is within your physical capability, then whatever does the job for you is acceptable.

The time of day appropriate for you is a personal matter. However, most people have discovered it is better to walk early in the morning. The sooner in the day the better. However, keep in mind the most important thing is to do it!

Frequently a person will be more consistent in exercising if it is done with one or more friends. The discipline brought to one another serves as an encouragement. Don't hesitate to invite others to help you do what you know you should do and what your friends know they should do.

Many have discovered their period of walking takes on added importance if they use a portable cassette player with earphones. Pleasurable symphonies, motivational talks, contemporary Christian music, preaching tapes, scripture tapes, and gospel music will add to the joys of your body, mind and spirit.

Also, especially if you are walking alone, it is a wonderful time to worship and quietly listen to God.

Simple and consistent exercise should be the goal of every believer. Whatever, whenever, and however you exercise, do so sanely and sensibly under the care and direction of your physician.

You have only one body. Exercise it!

4

VICTORY OVER CIRCUMSTANCES

Is perfect physical health necessary for a victorious spiritual life? Many would have you believe this is true.

It is wonderful to have a healthy body. However, victory is not just physical. Real victory lies much deeper.

"If I had good health..." is the "If Land" of many people.

This "if" is often used as an excuse to neglect Spiritual Laws. This excuse causes failure to fully develop a person's God-given potential. A physical malady is really no excuse for one's incomplete commitment unto the Lord. The truths of God's Word help us to face ourselves. They help us to triumph in the face of adverse circumstances.

Great achievements have often been the fruit of individuals who were physically handicapped. They didn't have perfect physical health, but they had great spirit. They may not have always felt well, but they felt called to great things.

Someone has aptly stated, "Ninety percent of the work in this world is done by people who don't feel well."

Consider what some have done even though burdened with physical affliction.

MICHELANGELO

He was deathly sick off and on throughout his entire life. Severe money problems often plagued him due to abandonment by his sponsors. Yet, he created monumental paintings and sculpture.

TCHAIKOVSKY

His beautiful and moving music gives no hint of the multitude of his problems. He was hopelessly neurotic, fearful of people, terrified of thunderstorms. He even had a fear that sometime his head would fall off while he was conducting.

ELIZABETH BARRETT BROWNING

This most capable poet was an invalid.

BEETHOVEN

He never heard his last works played. He heard the sounds in his mind and put them on paper. Beethoven became stone deaf. Yet, he even wrote Missa Solemnis, which many feel is the most beautiful mass ever written, during his soundless days.

COLE PORTER

Most of his songs are known for their bright, cheery, lifting style. However, most of his adult life he suffered from osteomyelitis.

GEORGE GERSHWIN

He wrote popular and classical music until his death. Yet, he suffered from a brain tumor.

PATRICIA NEAL

She suffered three near-fatal strokes and had to learn to walk and talk again. Further, her young son became hydrocephalic resulting from a bus accident. One of her daughters died. In spite of these tragedies she sprang back to be honored for her acting skills.

CONCLUSION

One of the special traits each of the above possessed was the ability to forget their handicaps. They may have stumbled, but they never stayed down (Phil. 4:13, 19).

5

THE HANDS OF JESUS

Hands fascinate me. They are miracles of perfection. They are versatile, powerful, beautiful. The hands serve worthy or unworthy purposes according to our desires. The heart determines if they will be used to cradle a child or commit a murder.

We use our hands to greet a friend, feed ourselves, ward off an attacker, express approval or disapproval, wave good-bye, type a letter, change a tire, read Braille, and a thousand and one other things. The hand in and of itself is unaccountable for its actions and yet is involved in almost all of our overt acts.

The 27 bones in the hand are more than 25% of the bones of the body. There are five bones in the palm, fourteen in the digits, and eight in the wrist. The average person will flex the fingers and make use of the hand over 25 million times in their lifetime.

One of the most unique aspects of the hand is the finger-tips. The fingerprints appear in the fourth month of development and no two are alike. Everyone is a person in his/her own right as far as fingerprints are concerned.

These marvels of nature are enhanced further when you realize one of the largest areas of the brain, known as the motor cortex, serves the hands.

The Bible reveals to us the relationship of the hands and the release of the power of God. Jesus often touched and/or laid hands on individuals as He imparted wholeness to them.

THE HANDS OF JESUS

The hands of Jesus were instruments of help to many people. They were hands of labor, peace, blessing, sacrifice, hope, promise, power, and healing. Jesus did not hesitate to use His hands to impart healing. Why should many in the church be so fearful of the ministry of laying-on-of-hands? Our insights and interpretation of the scriptures need to sharpen to the point of obedience in this area.

Please consider the following specific references to the touch of the Master's Hand. I hope you will be inspired and informed!

1. The leper--"*And Jesus put forth his hand, and touched him, saying, 'I will, be thou clean.' And immediately his leprosy was cleansed,*" Mark 1:41; Luke 5:13.

2. The ruler's daughter--"*While he spake these things unto them, behold, there came a certain ruler, and worshipped him, saying, 'My daughter is even now dead; but come and lay hand upon her, and she shall live,'*" Matt. 9:18; Mark 5:23.

3. Peter's mother-in-law--"*And he touched her hand, and the fever left her: and she arose, and ministered unto them,*" Matt. 8:15; Mark 1:31.

4. The deaf--"*And they bring unto him one that was deaf, and had an impediment in his speech; and they beseech him to put his hand upon him. And he took him aside from the multitude, and put his fingers into his ears, and he spit, and touched his tongue,*" Mark 7:32, 33.

5. The blind man--"*And he cometh to Bethsaida; and they bring a blind man unto him, and besought him to touch him. And he took the blind man by the hand, and led him out of the town; and when he had spit on his eyes, and put his hands upon him, he asked him if he saw ought. And he looked up, and said, 'I see men as trees, walking.' After that he put his hands again upon his eyes, and made him look up; and he was restored, and saw every man clearly,*" Mark 8:22-25.

6. The infirmity--"*And he laid hands on her; and immediately she was made straight, and glorified God,*" Luke 13:13.

7. At Nazareth--"*And he could do no mighty work, save that he laid his hands upon a few sick folk, and healed them,*" Mark 6:5.

8. The multitudes--"*Now when the sun was setting, all they that had any sick with divers diseases brought them unto him; and he laid his hands on every one of them, and healed them,*" Luke 4:40.

Incidents 2, 4, and 5 are of special importance because Jesus was asked to lay-on-hands.

This request would not have been made if He had not been ministering in this fashion. They were requesting of the Master what they knew He did. They had seen Him lay-on-hands for the sick.

If Jesus practiced the laying-on-of-hands, how can we as His followers neglect to do so?

6

ACTION OR ALIBIS?

Each of us is called to "act" upon the promises of God. There are hundreds of promises in His Holy Word. Our response toward these promises should be like Paul's:

"And being fully persuaded that, what he had promised, he was able also to perform," Rom. 4:21.

This verse sets the pace for the way we should act upon His precious promises. Trusting in His promises is a big step toward our victory. The following are just a few of the promises, which have been given to all believers:

"And we know that all things work together for good to them that love God, to them who are the called according to his purpose," Rom. 8:28.

"Jesus said unto him, 'If thou canst believe, all things are possible to him that believeth,'" Mark 9:23.

"Therefore I say unto you, 'What things soever ye desire, when ye pray, believe that ye receive them, and ye shall have them,'" Mark 11:24.

There are far too many people unwilling to really believe God's promises. They choose to wallow in the stagnant pool of "If Land," and are thoroughly convinced if things were different now, or if they had been different, life would be great.

How foolish to let your life be determined by the "ifs."

Which of the following "ifs" do you use as an excuse?

If I had a good education...

If I had enough "pull"...

If I didn't have a wife and family...

If I only had a wife and children...

If I had money...

If I could get the right job...

If I had good health...

If I only had time...

If times were better...

If other people really understood me...

If conditions around me were different...

If I could live my life over again...

If I did not fear what "they" will say...

If I had been given a fair chance...

If I just got a break...

If other people didn't have it in for me...

If I were only younger...

If nothing happens to stop me...

If I could only do what I want...

If I had been born rich...

If I could meet "the right" people...

If I had the talent some people have...

If I dared to assert myself...

If I didn't have to keep house and look after the children...

If I only had somebody to help me...
If I lived in a big city...
If I were only free...
If I could get away to the country...
If I had the personality of some people...
If I were not so fat...
If I could just get a break...
If the boss only appreciated me...
If my family would get off my back...
If I could only get out of debt...
If everybody didn't oppose me...
If I had married the "right" person...
If people weren't so dumb...
If luck were not against me...
If I lived in a different neighborhood...
If I had a different pastor...
If the people in the church were really spiritual...
If other people would only listen to me...
If I didn't have to work so hard...
If my wife really understood me...
If my husband would really listen to me...
If God would really show Himself to me...
If I win the lottery...

The list of "ifs" is endless. I would encourage you to depart from "If Land" and dwell in the land of God's certainties.

May you view every alibi as a temptation of Satan. Resist it and live victoriously!

7

THERE ARE NO FAILURES

The following witness by a physically afflicted individual is dynamic: "I am lame, and I recall at the age of 15 I prayed (in church) for a physical miracle to make me walk straight like other people. My prayer was not answered in this way. Instead God gave me a fierce desire to avoid letting my lameness keep me from leading a full, rich, active life; spent as far as possible in helping others. I have done this!"

This person has grasped the real meaning of spiritual healing. So often when healing is under discussion, the question arises, "What about failures?"

The question itself is indicative of the individual focusing primarily on the physical. Further evidence that most people think only of the physical is seen when a group is asked, "Have any of you ever seen a miracle?"

Most will answer, "NO." Those who answer, "YES," will give an account of a physical healing they have witnessed or experienced. This emphasis upon the physical is natural. The physical can be easily seen and discerned.

Even the biblical accounts are usually concerning physical healings. They were the ones which impressed those who beheld the healing power of our Lord.

MAN MORE THAN PHYSICAL

When there is no apparent physical healing, some people are ready to cry, "God has failed me."

Pause for a moment and consider. What really is healing? A person is more than a physical being. Every individual is also a mental and spiritual being.

The following diagram will help you to see that the person coming for healing has a multitude of problems and needs. The circle represents the WHOLE person. The numbers represent the many facets of the life of the person.

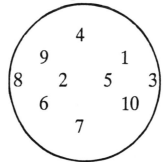

Each number in the circle represents an area of disease or difficulty in the life of the one receiving prayer.

The individual receiving Laying-on-of-Hands with prayer may have: 1. Terminal cancer. However, this person also comes with...

    2.   fear of death

    3.   financial worries

    4.   concern for family

5. guilt of past sins and present doubt
6. worries of what will happen to his/her wife/husband and children if he/she dies
7. despair as he/she questions, "Why me?"
8. fear of losing his/her job
9. almost unbearable pain
10. physical weakness

This sick one is more than a person with a physical disease called cancer. This person has a multitude of problems. When there is no evidence of physical healing, some people are ready to forsake God.

This is undue emphasis upon a single factor of life. An individual may not be cured of cancer, but yet receive help in one or more of the other areas of deep concern.

The person may be healed of the cancer. However, the point is, when one comes for healing, he or she is always helped and cured in some area.

Sincere prayer on the part of yourself and others is imperative. There are no failures for those who sincerely seek the Lord and His healing touch. The approach of a complete ministry to an individual brings healing into proper focus.

There are physical healings beyond explanation. We call them miracles. Even more miraculous are the healings of mind, emotions, marital problems, etc. No one should ever say upon receiving the ministry of Spiritual Healing, "Nothing happened." Jesus is reaching out to bring to you life abundant. This is your wholeness!

MIND

8

YOU ARE WHAT YOU THINK

Many Americans are weight conscious and carefully watch what they eat so as to maintain proper weight, lose weight, or in some cases, to gain. What we eat is important. However, what we think should be of greater concern to us than what we eat.

The real self is spiritual. Our relationship to God and others is determined to a large extent by what we think. The Bible plainly teaches our thoughts affect our entire life.

"Keep thy heart with all diligence; for out of it are the issues of life," Prov. 4:23.

"For as he thinketh in his heart, so is he..." Prov. 23:7.

"...Wherefore think ye evil in your hearts?" Matt. 9:4.

I learned the hard way how thoughts can affect one's health. They can have a bearing on your general well-being.

As a child of about eight I was at a family reunion. In my presence an uncle said to my father, "Bill, Donald looks sick."

Now, I felt fine, but this remark centered attention upon me. The thought flashed through my mind, "Well, if I am ill I will be noticed. I will be an ill-looking child to the best of my ability."

My health was excellent until I was approximately 30 years old. Then this pattern of thought which had been more or less dormant from my childhood days began to bear fruit.

A serious illness had come upon me and I was getting progressively worse. Further, I saw nothing but more trouble for the future. This latent thought of desiring to be ill came to my conscious mind.

It was difficult for me to share with another believer that perhaps unconsciously I desired to be ill. However, I shared this with my wife and it meant a great deal to me. You are what you think had really come home to me. I had been unconsciously feeding wrong thoughts into my mind and body for many years. I was now reaping the harvest of something I didn't even realize I was doing.

The Lord used this confession to enable me to be delivered from the power of this evil thought. The power of the past had been broken.

I was grateful He enabled me to replace the negative thought with the positive one of His desire for wholeness. Each of us needs to constantly believe the Lord desires wholeness of body, soul, and spirit. Thanks be unto Jesus for the health I have enjoyed for many years.

In your mind, are you convinced and willing to accept that the Lord desires wholeness for you?

Or are you often thinking, "My situation or illness is too hard for the Lord." The way you think deep within will have an effect upon your health and total well-being. The Apostle Paul knew the power of proper thinking when he wrote, "*Finally, brethren, whatsoever things are true . . . honest . . . just . . . pure . . . lovely . . . of good report, if there be any virtue, and if there be any praise, think on these things,*" Phil.4:8.

One who has been greatly used to teach healing has said, "Any hurt bottled up within you will cause a condition that will get steadily worse until it is released. Worry, fear, anxiety and tenseness are all major causes of diseases that get beyond the power of science to make right."

9

FEAR--OBSTACLE TO HEALING

It is my firm conviction every believer and every congregation would be blessed beyond measure if they would accept what the Lord has in store for them.

If this be true then a very fair question is, "Why do so many people neglect the things of the Lord?"

Another important question is, "Why is healing from the Lord shunned by so many people?"

Many individuals neglect the healing ministry because they cannot surmount the apparent obstacles.

There are several common obstacles which effectively block the power of the Lord in an individual's life. They will also prove a stumbling block to the healing ministry of a congregation.

THE UNKNOWN

The first obstacle I mention is false fear. Fear is always lurking its ugly head to discourage Christians. Many people are left powerless with unwarranted fears. One of these unwarranted fears in the healing ministry arises from the fear of the unknown.

Many feel all healing of the body should be in the hands of the medical doctor, and mental illness left to the psychiatrist.

They fail to appreciate these persons of science are instruments of God's healing. They do not understand the living, present, power of Christ.

FEAR OF OTHERS

Another fear hindering the healing ministry is, "What will others think if I become involved in the ministry of healing?"

Many Christians have been "brainwashed" to the point of thinking they must please others instead of God. The early Christians had to make a decision as to whom they would serve (Acts 4:19). You must do likewise. Jesus said we are called to fear only the living God (Matt. 10:28).

Believers cannot wait until all have accepted the healing message before proclaiming Jesus Christ as the Great Physician. In fact, only a few in any one congregation may really believe this. However, remember, the church has always moved forward on the faithfulness of the remnant.

FEAR OF MEMBERS

Pastors and lay persons often say, "But our congregation is not ready for the message of healing." My answer is everyone in the congregation will never be ready. The few who are ready need to be encouraged and used as God's instruments of healing.

Think for a moment! How many of your congregation are ready for tithing? What if you were to suggest there be no more contributions made to your church until every member agreed to tithe? You say, "How ridiculous!" Yes, but is not this the same logic we use when we neglect to emphasize the message of healing because some may not understand or are unwilling to accept it?

Cease to fear the unwilling and go on for God with the ministry of healing as a part of your congregational life.

WHAT WILL THEY THINK?

Another fear is, "What will others think when I tell them Christ can heal and I am afflicted myself?" Satan used this fear on me for a long time.

It was in 1959 I felt led to begin public services of healing. At the time I was gravely ill. My legs were wrapped in elastic stockings each morning to help keep them from swelling throughout the day. I could not turn over in bed without hooking one leg over the edge of the bed to help pull me over. I was in constant pain and very weak. It was in this afflicted state that the Lord led me to begin the healing services.

After holding the services for a few months Satan attacked by saying, "How can you lay-on-hands for others to be healed when you are so ill yourself?"

This almost defeated me. I am grateful the Holy Spirit came to my rescue at that moment. He asked, "Do you proclaim a perfect plan of salvation?" My instant reply was, "Yes." He asked, "Are you perfect?" My reply, "No! Christ alone is perfect. It is He I proclaim."

It was then I clearly saw the truth. The healing message is not dependent upon my good or bad health. It is like the message of salvation which is not dependent upon my perfection. Christ is the Healer. It was at this time I perceived the tremendous truth that I was called to be the proclaimer, not the explainer.

Now I was able to rebuke the inward fear and tell the Lord, "I will hold healing services until the day I die even if I must do so from a wheelchair." I hasten to say a funny thing happened on the way to the wheelchair. I was marvelously healed!

Emily Gardner Neal in her book, "The Healing Power of Christ," beautifully writes of her call to the ministry of healing, in spite of continued physical affliction. She tells what her affliction has taught her. "I was to learn what it was to be stripped of pride, ...I was to learn patience, ...I was to learn a new compassion for all who suffer,...I was to learn through experience the validity of what I have so long taught..."

A WELL-CHARTED COURSE

You need to realize involvement in the ministry of healing is not a step into the unknown.

In fact, it is pursuing the teachings of our Lord and the efforts of the devoted through the centuries.

If you are hesitant because of the fear of the unknown, please consider the following:

1. There are many healings recorded in the Gospels. Jesus Christ who healed then is "...*the same yesterday, today, and forever,*" Heb. 13:8.

2. The history of the early Church--the Book of Acts, contains many instances of healing (Acts 3:6-8).

3. During the first three centuries of the Church healing miracles were common experiences. It was not until the church became "popular" that it became "powerless."

4. Throughout the centuries there have been many individuals greatly used by the Lord in a ministry of healing. Through the ages, those willing to believe the Bible means what it says have experienced God's healing power.

5. Hundreds of congregations are today witnessing this power from God. The healing ministry is being discovered as very much a part of the total ministry of a local congregation.

6. There now exist many wonderful books in the area of healing. More are being produced all the time.

All of the above witness to the fact that we do not have to travel in the land of fear of the unknown.

The course has been well-charted for you. There is abundant proof of God's desire for your wholeness. There is abundant proof His Church should be a healing Church.

Any fear which hinders your involvement in the Ministry of Healing is a false fear. Cast it aside. Do not permit it to hinder you from exercising great faith in the Lord's healing power. He can and will heal!

10

MISUNDERSTANDING-- OBSTACLE TO HEALING

Misunderstanding of the nature and place of Spiritual or Divine Healing is one of the greatest obstacles facing this ministry. If this obstacle is to be overcome, much effort is needed to interest and inform individuals and local congregations. I offer the following as steps toward removing the obstacle of misunderstanding.

SERMONS

The pastor sets the pace for this vital ministry. A series of messages can introduce and explain healing to the congregation and occasional messages can keep them current on the subject.

MISSIONS AND CONFERENCES

Individuals interested in healing should be encouraged to attend missions and conferences concerning healing. The local congregation should assume all or part of the expense of those from their church who are delegated to attend. It is especially important the pastor attend such activities to be informed and inspired.

VISITING SERVICES

There are always new ideas, insights, and enthusiasm to be gained through attendance at a service elsewhere. This is a good way to introduce individuals to the need for and possibilities of such a service in your own parish.

HEALING SUNDAY

Most churches have several special Sundays throughout the year. What is more important than one which emphasizes healing? Illness and problems are common to all individuals and families. They need guidance on how to best meet their problems. Guest speakers, informed Sunday School teachers, lay witnesses--can all help make this Sunday most valuable.

ARTICLES

The parish letter, Sunday bulletin, or monthly newsletter are sources of information. The pastor or lay member of the congregation can write concerning healing. The Articles in this book may be copied and used in any way most helpful to you and your congregation. Proper acknowledgment should be made regarding any portion of this book which you may reproduce.

READING

Healing materials should be in an easily accessible place. Periodically, attention can be called to good books, magazines, and other resources which will help individuals understand the message of healing. A healing library should be developed over a period of time.

CLASSES

Many schools have presented a course in the area of healing. Some have used guest leaders for these courses. Many communities have had healing as one of the courses in their united School of Religion. Six to thirteen weeks can easily be devoted to this vital topic.

ENDORSEMENT

The success of a healing ministry cannot be attained simply through the pastor's leading, or through enthusiastic endorsement by one or two lay people. It must have the endorsement and support of the local governing group. Congregations today need leaders who will emphasize that God heals today through physical and spiritual means. It is not an option for you and for me. We can overcome every obstacle.

11

RESENTMENT--OBSTACLE TO HEALING

Resentment is one of the biggest obstacles to healing that I know. There are literally thousands of Christians suffering the consequences of resentment toward their spouse, relative, pastor, church, business associate, neighbor, or other situation or person.

It is impossible to estimate the nervous disorders, emotional problems, and physical ailments resulting from these resentments.

OBSTACLES

There are many reasons resentment is an obstacle to healing. I list a few of them.

1. It blocks reception of God's forgiving spirit in your life.

2. It brings a haze across your life which throws all individuals and situations out of focus. Resentment will tarnish all of your situations and decisions.

3. It continually pours the poisons of negative and destructive thinking into your body, soul, and spirit.

It is no figment of the imagination when someone says, "He gives me a pain in the neck." The bitter fruit of resentment is often manifested in the physical body. This is vividly illustrated by the individual who told a guest-speaker that during his message he resolved a long-standing resentment toward his mother. The exciting thing to him was the moment he had resolved the resentment in his heart, he lost the pain in his neck and shoulders! This pain he had endured for years in spite of an abundance of medical treatment for it.

ANSWERS

I would like to present some practical guidelines for removing resentments.

PRACTICE THE PRESENCE

I strongly encourage you to constantly seek the presence of the Lord. The use of devotional literature, moments of silence, confession, worship, etc., will all help you. The following Bible verses are worth your careful consideration: Mark 11:25; Luke 17:4; Eph. 4:32; Col. 3:13.

SINCERELY PRAY

Resentment can be helped a great deal by sincerely praying for the one you resent. Pray for specific blessings for the person. Lift the individual to the throne of Grace. Consider all aspects of the person or situation which are annoying you and commit them unto the Lord.

THE LORD'S PRAYER

I suggest you frequently pray the Lord's Prayer. Especially open your life to the portion which says, *"Forgive me my trespasses as I forgive _____."* Actually say the name of the one or ones you resent.

LEARN FORBEARANCE

Each of us falls far short of perfection. William Cowper spoke to all when he wrote:
> *"The kindest and the happiest pair*
> *Will find occasion to forbear;*
> *And something, every day they live,*
> *To pity, and perhaps forgive."*

BE REAL

Realize the "real" person is one who does not harbor "little" or "big" resentments. There is no virtue in defending yourself and saying, "I'll never forgive." This only produces more stress.

FORGIVE NOW

Plans to forgive someday are not enough. You must be willing to forgive now. At least be willing to let the Lord help you remove your resentment.

SPEAK KINDLY

Don't continue to speak ill of the one whom you resent. Kind words will serve to reduce harsh feelings within your heart.

TANGIBLE ACTION

The Lord may direct you to write a letter, confess to a person, make restitution, or have a heart-to-heart talk as a tangible act on the road to forgiveness. Remove the obstacle of resentment today! It can be done. Do it now!

12

VICTORY OVER NERVOUS DISORDERS

Nervous disorders have reached epidemic proportions. It is estimated that at least one of every five in our nation will experience a nervous disorder serious enough to require medication, hospitalization, and in some cases confinement to an institution.

SYMPTOMS

There are several symptoms which indicate a nervous problem existing or developing. Some of them are: despondency, continual fatigue for no physical reason, undue shyness, headaches, depression, unable to sleep or eat, undue apprehensiveness, irrational fears, fixed ideas, obsessions, destructive attitudes toward self and perhaps toward others.

CAUSES

There is no one cause of nervous disorders. The following are among the contributing factors.

The mad rush for wealth

The restless desire for change and variety

Our incessantly noisy environment
Chemical dependency
Overworking to make ends meet
Strain from unrelenting tensions
Over-indulgence of food, drugs, alcohol, sex
Search for meaning or purpose in life

INNER STRENGTH

Does the Spiritual Healing Ministry have a message for the emotionally disturbed? Indeed it does! It brings to them the message of hope and the Source of healing.

The Lord will help you prevent a nervous collapse or to be healed of one. The secret is the inner strength He gives to you, through the person of the Holy Spirit--God can dwell in you!

Many in our age, spiritually speaking, are like a tin can from which all the air has been pumped. It collapses from the normal pressure of the atmosphere. So many people are simply collapsing from the pressures of society because there is nothing within to sustain them. Remember, "*For God hath not given us the spirit of fear, but of power, love, and of a sound mind,*" I Tim. 1:7. Try the following suggestions to overcome your nervous disorder:

CONFESSION

Don't try to go it alone. Seek some trusted friend and discuss your fears, real or imagined, which are practically paralyzing you. Also, confess any guilt which may be upon your heart. This will remove the negative and make room for the positive. It will make more real your confession to God.

BELIEVE

Believe what? Believe you are a child of God! Do not rely upon your feelings, but rely entirely upon His promises. Consider, "...*whosoever calleth upon the Name of the Lord shall be saved,*" Rom. 10:13.

Believe the Lord is with you this very moment. Don't expend time or energy wondering if He will be with you a month, year, or decade from now. He is with you now! (Psalm 23:1).

VISUALIZE

Seek to picture yourself as whole. Picture the wholeness you will have instead of the affliction you now have. This is not an escape from reality, but a journey to reality. You must get your eyes off of your problems and focus on the Problem Solver--Jesus.

THANKFULNESS

Begin now to develop the spirit of thankfulness toward God and people. Verbally express thanks to members of your family, to your friends, co-workers, etc. Above all give thanks to God for His many blessings.

RELAX

The spirit of quietness is essential. A few minutes a day for you to permit your body and mind to slow down will do wonders. Claim His calmness. "*Be still and know that I am God,"* Psalm 46:10. Talk with the Lord and give Him your problems. He'll take them.

13

OVERCOMING THE FEAR OF ILL HEALTH

Fear is the curse of the world. Especially the fear of ill health.

You should fight this fear as you would the black plague. It should be tuned out of your life. It can only entangle you in a web of affliction and despair.

Someone who had overcome a disease-ridden life gave the following advice: "Tell those people who are always sick that unresolved problems of fear, hate, jealousy, insecurity and other upsetting emotions can cause physical illness. I know because they kept me a semi-invalid for years."

I want to present some general characteristics of exaggerated fear of illness.

I. WILD IMAGINATION

Wild imagination is the art of looking for one dreadful disease or another, running from physician to physician. The mind becomes geared to the morbid belief one has a dreaded disease.

II. HYPOCHONDRIA

Hypochondria is a style of life which accents illness. It gives birth to the ingrained habit of being illness-centered. Much of your conversation and most of your thoughts deal with illness.

Relentlessly you pursue the "fads" for cures and speak disparagingly of physicians and counselors who even hint that your illness may be emotional.

III. SELF-CODDLING

Abnormal fear of ill health will often lead to self-coddling and overprotection of one's well-being. This may lead to your refusal to properly exercise. Further, it helps cover up your laziness and failure to assume rightful responsibility at home or at work.

IV. INTEMPERANCE

The fear of ill health with its many manifestations provides for many the perfect excuse for over-indulgence. It may be in alcohol, drugs, etc.

SOLUTION

If any of the above are part of your life, may I suggest the following:

1. Know who you are fighting. It is the evil one, Satan. Illness is not of the Lord (Acts 10:38).

2. Believe the Lord wants healing and wholeness for you. Really believe this. Do not simply verbalize this thought (John 10:10).

3. Learn to pray. "...*Men ought always to pray and not to faint,*" Luke 18:1. Every person at one time or

another fears ill health. Destroy this fear through prayer.

Do not fertilize the fear with discouragement, or negativism. Learn to commune with the Source of Healing, Jesus Christ. May you courageously face your tomorrows with Him.

Remember--"Courage is fear which has said its prayers."

4. Discipline your mind to think health. Rebuke thoughts of ill health.

The body is equipped for wholeness. All the resources at its command rush to our defense when we are attacked by disease. There is overwhelming evidence disease may originate with negative thinking. A change of thinking in most cases is more important than a change of pace or climate.

14

OVERCOMING THE FEAR OF DEATH

Christians often say or sing the words, "Because He lives, I too, I too shall live."

Yet many Christians possess a morbid fear of death. They are almost paralyzed with the fear of dying. This fear is often manifested in one of the following ways:

I. DWELLING ON DEATH

Some develop a mental habit of dwelling upon thoughts of death. Even minor illness is perceived as a major issue.

II. LETHARGY

Unbridled thoughts about death will affect every area of your life. You will become a problem to yourself and to others. You may enter a state of despondency and/or depression.

Friends may credit this to outward circumstances when in reality it is because you are inwardly plagued with a fear of death.

III. UNREASONABLE ATTITUDE

Many individuals who have a great fear of death develop an unreasonable attitude toward the ordinary risks of life.

They may refuse to ride in an automobile, plane, or train. They may become very suspicious of food prepared by others or purchased from the stores. Also, they may become suspicious of even the natural and harmless actions of others.

IV. UNBELIEVING SPIRIT

Fear is the result of an unbelieving spirit. It is your failure to appropriate the power of His promises.

The fear of death results from the unwillingness to believe Jesus Christ can deliver the Eternal Life He promised.

CONQUERING THE FEAR OF DEATH

There are several steps which I feel will help you conquer the fear of death. They may appear simple, but they are powerful.

1. Sincerely believe Jesus wants you to enjoy life. An abundant life is God's desire for you (John 10:10).

2. Really believe you are born and reborn for eternity. God is not dead, nor does He sleep. Jesus not only spoke of the reality of eternal life, but He demonstrated it. The tomb is empty! (Mark 16:9; Matt. 28:9, 16; I Cor. 15:6, 7; Luke 24:15-31; John 20:19, 24; John 20:26-28; 21:1-24; Acts 1:2-9).

3. Face the reality that life in this world will end for you. Every person is a terminal case. Longfellow wrote, "The young may die, but the old must." The Bible states, "*It is appointed unto man once to die...*" (Heb. 9:27).

The Christian's death should be seen as ultimate healing! It is not the end, but rather the beginning! It is to be faced with faith and not feared.

4. Develop a lifestyle of service to others. You are called to be a worker with God (I Cor. 3:9).

The mind busy with the concerns of others does not have time to dwell upon death. It is too busy living.

The constant thought of death has misery as its companion. Thoughts centered upon a meaningful life in Christ always have joy as a companion.

5. Realize occasional thoughts of death are natural. Christians should seek to believe Jesus will be right there with us in the valley of the shadow of death, just as He promised in the 23rd Psalm.

Constant dwelling upon death is devastating to you and yours. Dispense with the fear of death. Live victoriously unto Christ!

15

OVERCOMING THE FEAR OF CRITICISM

The critical spirit can be crippling. Many a child, relative, employee, loved one, friend, or co-worker has been hurt by undue and often unwise negative criticism.

DEFINITION

The dictionary defines critical as: *1. Inclined to find fault or judge with severity. 2. Occupied with or skilled in criticism.*

The critical spirit seeks to deprive others of their rightful possessions or unique personality.

Thus, a thief criticizes those from whom he steals, a politician speaks disparagingly of an opponent, a neighbor puts down the family next door. Each seeks to be exalted through cutting down others.

It is because of these unfortunate realities of life that many people develop an unhealthy fear of criticism. You need to realize the seriousness of this fear and to consider its unhealthy consequences.

SELF-CONSCIOUSNESS

A fear of criticism will lead you to become very self-conscious. You will discover it difficult to meet strangers, launch new projects, remain poised in strange situations, or even to maintain a good body posture.

UNSTABLE

The fear of criticism is often what leads to a lack of firmness in making decisions. It will leave you hesitant to develop definite convictions. You will be more inclined to side-step and almost always agree with others without careful examination of their positions. You become a double-minded person and thus unstable in many areas of your life (James 1:8).

LACK INITIATIVE

The fear of criticism will stifle your initiative. Even wonderful opportunities will not be embraced because you fear what others may say if you fail, or even if you succeed. A fear of criticism is often the reason for a general lack of ambition, mental and physical laziness, undue suspicion of the motives of others, always having an "excuse" for your shortcomings, and accepting defeat or quitting.

OVERCOMING

The Good News is you can overcome the fear of criticism. Consider:

1. Do not expect all people to speak well of you. Some individuals have become so negative that they

have honed it to a fine art. Jesus warned against wanting all to speak well of you (Luke 6:26).

2. Remember, many often found fault with Jesus Christ (Matt. 9:11, 12:2, 15:2; Mark 2:7, 7:2; Luke 15:2, 19:7; John 6:41).

3. You are to fear God and not man (Matt. 10:16-39).

4. Develop a meaningful life of private and corporate prayer. Jesus said, "...*ought always to pray and not to faint*," Luke 18:1. He often spent time in prayer (Matt. 26:41; Mark 1:35, 6:46; Luke 5:16, 6:12, 9:18, 22:41; Eph. 6:18; I Thess. 5:17; I Chr. 16:11).

5. Really believe the Lord is your judge and not people. Prayerfully consider Matthew 10:16-42.

6. Keep your eyes on your successes instead of your failures. Thank God for the individuals who encourage you. Seek to die to self, and to live for God and others. You can be unshackled from the fear of criticism. You can be free in the Lord! (II Cor. 3:17).

16

RELINQUISHMENT

Relinquishment is one of the keys of a victorious Christian life. It is essential to the victory you desire now and in the future.

SURRENDER

Relinquishment is defined as "renouncing or surrendering a possession or right," or "to let go."

In the spiritual sense it is getting rid of self-will. It is the deep conviction that God's will and wisdom is best for us.

NOT RESIGNATION

Relinquishment is not resignation to blind fate. It is a commitment to a living faith.It is an awareness God cannot be manipulated or His will bent to yours. However, at the same time it is realizing God is the Creator and sustainer of all life. He is the Giver of every good and perfect gift (James 1:17).

There are too many people who want others to be surrendered to the Lord, but are unwilling to make their own surrender. They are like the person who said,

"Take my WIFE, and let her be;
Consecrated Lord, to Thee."

The victory does not come in having your wife or someone else surrender. It is your own life you must surrender unto Him.

HOW TO RELINQUISH

There are some positive and tangible steps which I suggest will help you relinquish all things unto the Lord:

1. The first point to keep in mind is relinquishment is commitment to a Person. It is not a belief or a program. It is to Jesus Christ.

You cannot lean on people. They are not divine, all wise, or all powerful. People will ultimately let you down.

It was because God's presence was with him the Apostle Paul could say, *"...I have learned, in whatsoever state I am, therewith to be content,"* (Phil. 4:11).

2. Relinquishment comes when you commit to the concept that God has a purpose for your life.

You must accept in your heart that in the midst of all the mysteries of life God has a purpose and plan for you. His purposes and plans may be entirely different from your present aims or goals. However, you must accept that He knows what is the very best for you. The Lord Jesus imparted this truth when He said, *"If ye then, being evil, know how to give good gifts to your children, how much more shall your Father which is in heaven give good things to them that ask Him?"* (Matt. 7:11).

Glen Clark wrote, "God's plan for me is a perfect part of a larger plan. It is designed for the good of all and not for me alone. It is a many-sided Plan and reaches out through all the people I meet. All the events and people who come into my life are instruments for the unfolding of this Plan."

3. Relinquishment releases spiritual power in and through you. You come to really know it is "*Not by might nor by power, but by my Spirit says the Lord of Hosts,*" (Zech. 4:6).

The struggling self saps spiritual power. You will drown in your own self-pity and selfishness. Seek to rely on the Lord's promises. He is the answer to your problems.

Many hours after his boat had capsized, a young man was rescued. Why? He had not panicked, but floated most of the time. He let the water support him. Otherwise, within a few frantic minutes he would have exhausted his strength and drowned. Relinquishment frees us from floundering in self's waterhole. You can float on God's power and promises. "*...Not my will, but thine be done,*" (Luke 22:42).

17

WORRY AND SPIRITUAL HEALING

Is there a cure for worry? This generation is trying to eliminate it. We are seeking to eliminate worry through insurance, social security, guaranteed annual wage, advances through medicine and technology, etc.

Yet, a recent survey revealed one out of five adults has or will have a nervous breakdown or serious nervous disorder.

The message of Spiritual Healing is you can "kick" the worry habit.

NOT OF GOD

The plain and persistent teaching of Jesus is we should not worry. He imparts the beautiful truth that our heavenly Father is tenderly caring for you (Matt. 6:25-34).

Further, St. Paul assures you of the Lord's ability to meet your every need (Phil. 4:19).

NEVER HELPS

Worry will not help your situation. In fact, worry is irrelevant to the solution of your real situation.

An analysis of worry in a large segment of our population revealed that:

1. 40% of an individual's worries were about past events or actions,
2. 50% of the worries concerned the future,
3. only 10% concerned current circumstances.

What a waste of energy! Great is the wisdom expressed in the statement, "I never live with my yesterdays." It fits so well with Paul's statement, "...*forgetting the things which are behind...*" (Phil. 3:13).

The psalmist comforts us about the future when he writes, "*My times are in Thy hands...*" (Ps. 31:15).

AFFIRM GOD'S PRESENCE

Affirming the Lord's presence will help you to replace the trivial with the important. It will lift your spirit from the transient unto the eternal. It will enable you to concentrate upon the One who controls all instead of upon the things which seek to control you.

William James has well said, "The essence of genius is to know what to overlook." You should not overlook what the Lord has given you. "*For God has not given us the spirit of fear, but of power and of love, and of a sound mind,*" (II Tim. 1:7).

BE ACTIVE

Idleness is the devil's tool. Self-pity and withdrawal are often Satan's chosen instruments for furthering the worry habit. Kick the worry habit by actively seeking to do the following:

1. Deliberately discipline the mind to think on the Lord's promises.

2. Admit your weakness in the area of worry. Discuss this hang-up with a friend and together turn it over to the Lord and leave it with Him.

3. Regularly attend Spiritual Healing Services (hear God's word) for help to keep your eyes upon the Problem Solver instead of upon your problems, (real or imagined) about which you worry.

4. Discover opportunities and become involved in areas of practical service. This may be community work, helping a school, changing vocations, going to work full or part-time, etc. Seek the Lord's wisdom and guidance concerning your involvement and follow Him.

5. Realistically face each situation which you encounter. If there is something you can do, seek wisdom as to how best to do it. Then do it!

If you can't do anything about the individual or situation because of distance, lack of ability, or other reasons, then put it in the Lord's hands and let it stay there.

The prayer of serenity is worthy of your consideration and use.

"God grant me the wisdom to accept the things I cannot change, courage to change the things I can, and wisdom to know the difference."

6. Don't worry about not worrying. You can "kick" the worry habit. Do so today! Amen.

18

STRESS

Stress is one of the most prevalent characteristics of our day. It seems all of us are living under a great deal of stress all the time.

Do little things upset you as never before?

Do you feel overly worthless and doubt your own capabilities?

Are you plagued with unexplainable anxieties?

Does practically every situation look hopeless to you?

WHAT IS IT?

Stress may be defined as that condition or state when you are ill at ease. It is when the body is not in a state of healthful equilibrium. It is the rate of wear and tear on your body.

A BANK ACCOUNT

I like the way Dr. Hans Salye likens each life to a bank account. He says your vitality has been inherited. You cannot add to it, but you can take from it. Stress accelerates withdrawal of one's vitality.

CONSEQUENCES OF STRESS

Among the many consequences of excessive and prolonged stress are headaches, high blood pressure, stomach trouble, general feeling of tiredness, irritability, withdrawal, or a change in personality.

STRESS CHART

Dr. Thomas Holmes and Dr. Minoru Masuda of the University of Washington in Seattle have given much time to the problem of stress and its consequences. They conclude that good or bad changes in your life affect your body. They developed a Stress Chart to rate the amount of stress caused by events in your life. As you review their Stress Chart and appraise your life, keep in mind they are presenting only a guideline. The degree of stress and accompanying reactions will vary much from person to person and the Stress Chart can only present a statistical average. Events of the past year or two should be used to comprise your total score.

1. If your score is between 150-199 you are in a mild life crisis.
2. If 200-299 you are in a moderate life crisis.
3. If over 300 you are in a major life crisis.

Stress Chart

Rank	Life Event	Mean Value
1	Death of Spouse	100
2	Divorce	73
3	Marital separation	65
4	Jail term	63
5	Death of close family member	63
6	Personal injury or illness	53
7	Marriage	50
8	Fired at work	47
9	Reconciliation with mate	45
10	Retirement	45
11	Change in health of family member	44
12	Pregnancy	40
13	Sex difficulties	39
14	Gain of new family member	39
15	Business readjustment	39
16	Change in financial state	38
17	Death of close friend	37
18	Change to different line of work	36
19	Change in number of arguments with mate	35
20	Mortgage over $10,000	31
21	Foreclosure of mortgage or loan	30
22	Change in responsibilities at work	29
23	Son or daughter leaving home	29
24	Trouble with in-laws	29
25	Outstanding personal achievement	28
26	Mate begins or stops work	26
27	Begin or end school	26
28	Change in living conditions	25
29	Revision of personal habits	24
30	Trouble with boss	23
31	Change in work hours or conditions	20
32	Change in residence	20
33	Change in schools	20
34	Change in recreation	19
35	Change in church activities	19
36	Change in social activities	18
37	Mortgage or loan less than $10,000	17
38	Change in sleeping habits	16
39	Change in number of family get-togethers	15
40	Change in eating habits	15
41	Vacation	13
42	Christmas	12
43	Minor violations of the law	11

WARNING SIGNS

Along with the Stress Rating Scale you may want to consider the following to determine if you are now living under excessive stress.

Do you notice undue tenseness in your body-- tense head or neck muscles, excessive fluttering of eyelids, clinched fingers or toes, irregular or shallow breathing?

Do you find yourself being suspicious of friends and bothered even in familiar places and situations?

Are you having trouble getting along with others of your family and/or friends?

Has life lost its meaning?

Do you have high blood pressure?

If any of the above are part of your life, it may well be you are under excessive stress.

Hypertension is one of the most prevalent diseases of our day. It may be because of your natural tendency toward high blood pressure.

However, it may be caused to a large extent by the pressures of your life. You would be wise to have your physician check your blood pressure and to follow his advice if control measures are needed.

The most important thing we can do to relieve stress spiritually is to learn to trust that all of these stressful situations are in God's hands. We must seek to believe that "*all things work together for good for those who believe in God and are called according to his purpose,*" (Romans 8:28).

SPIRIT

19

HEALING OF THE SPIRIT

HEALING OF THE SPIRIT

A healing, like all other facets of life, is not received to be used selfishly, but to help others. We are made whole of body, soul, and spirit to help others to come to this wholeness.

One of the most puzzling things to me in the area of the healing ministry is the reaction of individuals who are healed physically or emotionally. The healing may have come through surgery, medicine, therapy, and/or prayer.

It is a mystery to me, for instance, why...

...when someone is healed the person so often fails to really give the Lord the credit,

...an individual who has been healed often times does not continue to attend the healing services and faithfully bear witness as one whom the Lord has touched,

...often the person healed does not really become a faithful follower of the Lord and an ardent participant in His Church,

...so many are willing to accept His gifts, but are hesitant to accept and to confess Him as the Giver,

...many say they believe God heals in diverse ways including doctors and medicine, but react negatively if someone gives the Lord credit for her/his healing.

AN INSIDE JOB

It was while prayerfully dealing with the above puzzle I came to realize unless a person is truly changed on the inside, their outward lifestyle will not change a great deal. The only healing which can produce profound change in a life is a "spiritual" healing.

In the light of this insight I began to search the scripture and to appraise the ministry of healing. The following insights have proven helpful to me and I trust will be of value to you.

PROPER EMPHASIS

The message of healing is essential to the proclamation of the full gospel. However, it must be noted that sometimes the emphasis upon healing leaves the impression that only physical healings are involved.

I have even been accused of neglecting the Spirit because of my emphasis upon the availability of total healing. This accusation falls short of the message I seek to convey.

WHOLENESS

The wholeness Jesus proclaimed included body, soul, and spirit. We must be careful not to neglect any one of these areas. He healed the body. He also forgave sin. He brought soundness of mind and balance of emotions. He ministered to the whole person.

BORN AGAIN

Jesus said to Nicodemus, *"you must be born again,"* John 3:3, 7. This experience is needed by all not only to be properly related unto the Father through the Son, but also because a person cannot rightly perceive the things of God outside of the Kingdom.

Spiritual things are perceived by spiritual people. The Kingdom is a sacred mystery as perceived by a believer. It is a most baffling mystery to one who stands on the outside of the Kingdom of God.

It is as a member of the Kingdom a person perceives that miracles can and do happen. When entering the Kingdom by way of the New Birth, a believer beholds the reality of Jesus's power and purpose.

PHYSICAL ONLY

The healing many receive of the body does not necessarily lead to a deeper devotion unto the Lord. Nor does a physical healing necessarily lead to a life devoted to advancing the message of the Good News.

Ponder the fact that we have no biblical record of a person physically healed who became a great proclaimer of the Gospel. For instance, we hear nothing more from the Centurion whose servant was healed (Matt. 8:5-13), the man whose withered hand was restored (Matt. 12:9-14), the one leper who returned to thank Jesus for his healing (Luke 17:11-19), or even Lazarus who was restored to life after being dead four days (John 11:1-4). Nor does the Bible record a meaningful ministry by any of the five thousand miraculously fed (Matt. 14:15-21). There is no record of an attendee at the wedding feast where water became wine becoming a great witness of our Lord (John 2:10-11). Malchus, whose ear was restored by Jesus seemed to take it in stride and go on in his pagan ways (John 18:10); and those who witnessed it still took Jesus prisoner and turned Him over to the officials.

In fact, you can review the miracles of the New Testament as listed in Chapter 6 and you will discover there is no biblical record of any of those physically healed becoming great witnesses for the Lord.

The physical healing did not necessarily move a person to make a commitment to proclaim the healing power of the Lord. It led to telling others about Jesus for the moment (Matt. 9:31), but none of them left a lasting imprint on the Church. There are several references to others bringing individuals to Christ to be healed. The point I am striving to make is there is no record of any of them becoming one of the remembered disciples or writers of the Word.

Another interesting insight is there is no record of any of the 12 disciples or of the 70 other disciples receiving a physical or emotional healing prior to their being willing to follow Jesus. The apostle Paul was not raised from the bed of affliction and, because of the healing, turned to Jesus. NO! All of these great leaders experienced a "spiritual" healing which resulted in acceptance of Jesus as The Way, The Truth and The Life!

EMOTIONAL HEALINGS

There were a few who made positive steps toward proclamation of the Good News after being emotionally healed. The woman at the well went and told the entire town a prophet was in their midst, (John 4:28-30). The demon-possessed man delivered by Jesus wanted to become a disciple (Mark 5:18). Jesus simply told him to go tell others, (Mark 5:19, 20).

BAPTISM OF THE HOLY SPIRIT

The individuals having a lasting and profound effect upon the Church were those filled with the Holy Spirit.

Jesus appeared after the resurrection with the news all power had been given unto Him, (Matt. 28:18). He tells His disciples they shall receive power, (Luke 24:29; Acts 1:8).

The day of Pentecost involved the power (God dwelling within us!) being imparted unto the faithful, (Acts 2). It was after this experience the followers of our Lord became bold, fruitful, and fearless.

All the healings of body and emotions in the world could not suffice to impart what was needed on the inside for a person to fearlessly serve the Lord. The Holy Spirit of God had to bear witness with one's spirit before devotion unto the end was possible.

The first elected church leaders were filled with the Holy Spirit, (Acts 6:3). Paul was filled with the Holy Spirit, (Acts 9:17).

Peter, Paul, Phillip, and many others set the example of faithfulness. They did this not because they had been physically healed, but because they had been spiritually filled. The early church, and the church today, does not move on those "healed" of body, but on those "filled" with the Spirit!

WHY HEAL?

If the Church goes forward because of those filled with the Holy Spirit, then why proclaim healing of the body?

This is a good question, and many in the church do not seek to answer it, but neglect to proclaim that Jesus heals the whole person.

The believer seeks to heal in the Name of Jesus because of his/her concern for the whole person. Jesus wanted to meet needs in every area of a person's life. We should desire to do likewise.

Further, the Lord is willing for His blessings to fall upon all. The sun rises on the good and the evil and rain falls on the just and the unjust, (Matt. 5:44-45).

Most importantly, the released power from the Spirit-filled believer encourages others to believe Jesus is indeed the Son of God. No other spiritual leader of any religion ever healed people like Jesus did. It is the ultimate proof of His Divinity and compassion!

SOMETHING MORE

The point is, healing of the body and emotions is not the end of the matter. Individuals must be led to know Jesus Christ as their personal Saviour and to receive the fullness of the baptism of the Holy Spirit.

Most individuals do not enter into these spiritual experiences. They may be healed physically and emotionally by the grace of God, but neglect to witness for Him and to remain faithful unto His Church.

The neglect of many does not deter the devotion of a few. The Spirit-filled person goes on in faithful service. He/she does not cease to faithfully serve regardless of how the healed may respond, but realizes devotion is unto the Lord and not unto those helped.

Yes, you must be born again! Yes, you must experience the power and presence of the baptism of the Holy Spirit! You are not really whole until you have been healed spiritually. All the physical healings in the world will not be sufficient to meet your needs. You must know that God's Holy Spirit may bear witness with your spirit at all times, (Rom. 8:14-16).

Don't abandon the message of healing of body and soul, but accept the message, "you must be born again!" It is not a matter of either the body or the spirit, but a message of body and spirit. The healing you seek is for your whole being of body, soul, and spirit! Jesus is the healer of your life only if you are healed spiritually by accepting Him as your Lord and Savior, the very God!

20

FAITH AND HEALING

I am often asked, "Is faith a prerequisite to my being healed?"

I am sure this question is prompted by the many scripture references such as:

"Jesus said unto him, If thou canst believe, all things are possible to him that believeth," (Mark 9:23).

"Therefore I say unto you, What things soever ye desire, when ye pray, believe that ye receive them, and ye shall have them," (Mark 11:24).

"And the Lord said, If ye had faith as a grain of mustard seed, ye might say unto this sycamine tree, Be thou plucked up by the root, and be thou planted in the sea; and it should obey you," (Luke 17:6).

FAITH - A VITAL PART

It is important to realize faith is a vital part of the healing process. It is important you believe the Lord is able to make you whole.

It is even of greater importance for you to believe He wants you to be whole.

ACTS OF FAITH

The Lord Jesus commended acts of faith. It was to the woman who touched the hem of His garment He said, "...*thy faith hath made thee whole...*" (Matt. 9:22).

In like manner He spoke to the centurion, "...*as thou has believed, so be it done unto thee...*" (Matt. 8:13). (See also: Mark 1:41; 2:5; 10:52)

In addition to these examples of faith and healing, Jesus encourages His followers to believe God for great things. In addition to the three verses I list at the beginning of this chapter, please consider: "...*He that believeth on me, the works that I do shall he do also; and greater works than these shall he do; because I go unto my Father.*" This reference to John 14:12 certainly applies to Believers today.

It is obvious faith is an important aspect of healing for you and others.

HEALED WITHOUT FAITH

Even though faith is an essential part of our relationship with the Lord, there are many who are healed who do not in and of themselves have great faith. In fact, there are many healed who never expected to be healed. Why is this?

CORPORATE FAITH

What answers are there for those who question the saint's continued illness and the unbeliever's healing?

I feel it is important for us to appreciate corporate faith. It is not simply an individual's faith, but the faith of many people which accounts for many healings.

It is at healing services where the fruit of faith is often seen in the lives of those who seem to have little faith. However, they are in the presence of many with great faith. This corporate faith accomplishes fantastic results.

The Lord is not bound by our human frailties, pet theories, or limited insight into His ways. He is the One whose ways are above our ways, (Isaiah 55:8-11).

SCRIPTURE REFERENCE

There are several examples of individuals being healed who gave no indication of great faith on their part. Those who brought them to Jesus believed, but the healed one apparently did not. In fact, some of those healed were dead and so could not have believed on their own.

I often ask individuals, "What is the greatest miracle of the New Testament other than the Resurrection?" The reply is always, "The raising of Lazarus from the dead." Of course this is the greatest miracle, as a man dead four days was restored to life.

I then ask, "How much faith did Lazarus have?" The answer is obvious. He was dead! He had no faith!

Faith for healing is thus more than that of the individual being ministered unto. The faith of those ministering unto others is also an important factor.

Further, the love and mercy of the Lord is an unexplained, but important factor in all situations. Consider the following and seek to ascertain if these healings were really the result of the great faith of the one healed.

    The withered hand - Matt. 12:9-14

    Gergesenes demoniacs - Matt 8:28-34

    Woman infirm for 18 years - Luke 13:10-13

    Invalid by the pool - John 5:2-9

    Cripple by the Gate Beautiful - Acts 3:1-10

    Girl with the spirit of divination - Acts 16:16-18

    Father of Publius - Acts 28:7, 8

    Raising from the dead of:

        Widow's son - Luke 7:11-17

        Lazarus - John 11:38-44

        Dorcas - Acts 9:36-41

        Eutychus - Acts 20:9-12

I feel it is essential we believe the Lord heals as He wills. We are called to praise and glorify Him forever.

Yes, faith is important in the area of healing, but obedience is of greater importance.

21

THE OCCULT AND SPIRITUAL HEALING

Millions throughout the world are pursuing the occult. They are seeking an answer to the problems of our day. They are trying to fill the spiritual void God created in all of us. They appear to be seeking an easy answer.

Witchcraft and other forms of the occult, especially the New Age movement which has become very popular today, are often a part of even the highly educated person's experiences. Large corporations are using New Age and Eastern mysticism practices with their employees. Witchcraft is even penetrating the sports field.

For instance, it is reported a Kenya soccer club revealed an annual expense item of $3,600.00 for witchcraft.

It is reported that other clubs also employ witch-doctors for consultation on strategy and chances of winning. They refuse to announce names of players in advance lest they be bewitched. Before vital games they have sentries patrolling the stadium to see that no one places a charm on the ball.

A few years ago the first lady of our land sought regular guidance through astrology. It is obvious that even intelligent people will fall back on primitive, superstitious practices if they are not close to God or filled with His Holy Spirit--the Spirit of all truth and wisdom!

WITCHES

It is reported England has at least 30,000 practicing witches. We know that in the United States the influence of the occult is staggering--it's in music, TV, movies, books and even children's cartoons!

One is led to ask of our modern day, "Is this the age of enlightenment or darkness?"

OCCULT

The dictionary defines "occult" as: beyond the bounds of ordinary knowledge, secret, involving the alleged knowledge or employment of secret or mysterious agencies. Falling into this category from the Christian viewpoint would be: New Age materials, fortune-telling, magic practices, religious cults, spiritism, ouija boards, horoscopes, clairvoyance, and witchcraft.

SCRIPTURE

The scriptures do not deny the power of the occult. They do condemn the occult!

The following reference is significant. *"There shall not be found with thee any one...that useth divination* (fortune telling), *or an observer of times* (soothsayer), *or a consulter with familiar spirits* (medium), *or an enchanter* (magician), *or a witch* (sorceress), *or a charmer* (hypnotist), *or a necromancer* (medium who consults the dead). *For all that do these things are an abomination unto the Lord...*" (Deut. 18:10-12).

Do you need further admonition? If so, please consider the following Scriptures: Lev. 19:31, 20:27, 19:26; Ex. 22:18; I Sam. 28:3; II Kings 21:5-8; II Chr. 33:5-9; Isa. 2:6; Jer. 27:8-11; Zech. 10:2; Mal. 3:5; Acts 8:4-25, 16:16-24, 19:11-20, I Tim. 4:1; Rev. 21:8, 22:15.

The prophet Isaiah thunders, "*And when they say to you, consult the mediums and the wizards who chirp and mutter, should not a people consult their God? Should they consult the dead on behalf of the living?*" (Isa. 8:19).

GOD'S POWER

The occult may imitate God's power (Ex. 7:11-13; Acts 8:11), but can never impart it. The power to become sons of God is only from Jesus Christ (John 1:12, 13). You can combat the forces and false teachings of the occult through the whole armor of God (Eph. 6:10-20). Jesus Christ is the only answer and only Mediator in our day (John 14:6).

THE EARLY CHURCH

The early Church had little patience with consulters of spirits contrary to the Spirit of the Living God. Simon the sorcerer was commanded to repent for his wickedness, (Acts 8:22). The spirit of divination in the slave girl was rebuked, (Acts 16:18).

TODAY

Plain powerful, and persistent teaching of God's Word is needed today. The darkness of the occult can only be eliminated through the Light of the World, Jesus Christ.

22

INNER ILLNESS

The importance of Inner Healing is appreciated to a greater degree when you have an understanding of Inner Illness. Therefore, I would like to present some insights concerning the causes of Inner Illness.

INNER ILLNESS

The wounds deep within your inner being have been inflicted by many forces and factors. Some of them may be as follows:

1. Undue concern for your past actions or statements. You have become deeply concerned that you said or did the wrong thing. You live with almost a constant feeling you wish you had not said or done a particular thing. You find it impossible to leave your yesterdays with the Lord. You have become a prisoner of your past.

2. An incident or event may leave a deep impression long after the details are consciously forgotten. You may have witnessed a tragedy, been involved in a tragedy, or have been badly frightened by some incident or person. An example of this is the individual who had a dread fear of dogs. One day the

completely forgotten incident of having been bitten by a dog when very young crossed his mind. A healing took place which removed this fear.

Dr. Thomas A. Harris in his book, "I'm OK - You're OK," relies on the studies of W. Penfield to support the fact that we are deeply affected by events which may have been consciously forgotten.

"Perhaps the most significant discovery was that not only past events are recorded in detail but also the feelings that were associated with those events. An event and the feeling which was produced by the event are inextricably locked together in the brain so that one cannot be evoked without the other."

Penfield reported: "The subject feels again the emotion which the situation originally produced in him, and he is aware of the same interpretations, true or false, which he himself gave to the experience in the first place. Thus, evoked recollection is not the exact photographic or phonographic reproduction of past scenes or events. It is reproduction of what the patient saw and heard and felt and understood."

3. The hurts of unpleasant relationships. You may have been treated cruelly by a parent, relative, a friend, or school mates. Perhaps you discovered you were an unwanted child and looked upon as a burden by your parents. A significant percentage of people are abused emotionally, verbally, physically or even sexually as children. Perhaps someone at work may have deliberately said unkind words, or you discovered you were not really needed or wanted by the company.

4. Your own actions can wound the inner being almost beyond repair. It may be deeds of dishonesty, immorality, or spiritual disobedience which will take their toll of your inner peace and power.

5. Some real or imagined physical disorder which becomes a stumbling block to inner wholeness. The very obese, the extremely short or tall person, an ugly birthmark, pronounced nose, deformed lip, crippled arm or leg, etc., can serve as a source of inner conflict and illness.

An acquaintance of mine would spend hours looking in the mirror at his "deformed" nose. He dropped out of college and ultimately ended up being institutionalized in a mental ward. However, in reality his nose was perfectly normal in appearance. He was one of the most handsome men on campus from the viewpoint of his friends. He was a mess from his own viewpoint.

6. The emotional state of your mother prior to your birth. Strange as it may sound, psychologists now tell us we are affected emotionally even while being carried in the womb. The emotions of the mother can affect the unborn child just as drugs or alcohol may affect the unborn.

MANIFESTATIONS

The manifestation of inner illness is varied and complicated. However, some of the outward signs of inner illness are as follows:

Aimlessness	Condemnation
Anger	Confusion
Anxiety	Despair

Despondency	Laziness
Disobedience	Resentment
Doubt	Sadness
Fear	Self-indulgence
Fear of failure	Self-pity
Fear of disapproval	Self-righteousness
Guilt	Suspicion
Hate	Unbelief
Hopelessness	Unforgiving
Indifference	Unrighteousness
Inferiority	Vacillation
Jealousy	Worry

HOPE FOR HEALING

You can be delivered from the above through the Inner Healing of your Inner Illness. The following scripture presents graphically the hope we have in Christ Jesus: "*For this cause we also, since the day we heard it, do not cease to pray for you, and to desire that ye might be filled with the knowledge of his will in all wisdom and spiritual understanding; that ye might walk worthy of the Lord unto all pleasing, being fruitful in every good work, and increasing in the knowledge of God; strengthened with all might, according to his glorious power, unto all patience and longsuffering with joyfulness; Giving thanks unto the Father, which hath made us meet to be partakers of the inheritance of the saints in light; Who hath delivered us from the power of darkness, and hath translated us into the kingdom of His dear Son: In whom we have redemption through his blood, even the forgiveness of sins:*" (Col. 9-14).

II

WHOLENESS REGAINED

The Lord desires for all to come to wholeness. He has provided for this through His Son, the Lord Jesus Christ.

Jesus said, "...I am come that you might have life and that you might have it more abundant," (John 10:10).

The ministry of Jesus was one of bringing wholeness to those afflicted of body, soul, or spirit. Peter sums it up well when he says, "How God anointed Jesus of Nazareth with the Holy Ghost and with power: who went about doing good, and healing all that were oppressed of the devil; for God was with Him," (Acts 10:36).

Jesus's death on the Cross and the Resurrection reveal to us that disease and death no longer reign supreme. I John 3:8 proclaims Jesus came for the express purpose of destroying what Satan and sin had done to creation, "For this purpose the Son of God was manifested, that he might destroy the works of the devil. The result is that the . . . pick up with . . . Lord wants to impart wholeness to us."

The Lord wants to impart wholeness to us: "If ye then, being evil, know how to give good gifts unto your children, how much more shall your Father which is in heaven give good things to them that ask Him?" (Matthew 7:11.)

God, the giver of good gifts, has provided the way unto Him whereby we may enter in and receive the good gifts He has for us. This is the blessing of the Kingdom of God on earth for us today! We can once again be whole through Christ.

DOCTRINE
AND
HISTORY

23

OLD TESTAMENT MIRACLES AND HEALINGS

It is practically impossible to list all of the miracles contained in the Old Testament. There are the interpretation of dreams, the appearances of the Angel of the Lord, revelations of coming events, special victories over Israel's enemies, fire falling upon the altar, and so forth. However, I do want to list some of the most outstanding ones. You may desire to carefully consider each scripture reference. It is obvious that the power of the Lord was revealed to many individuals throughout the ages.

I. MIRACLES IN THE BOOK OF GENESIS

1. Creation - Genesis Chapter 1
2. Enoch's translation - Genesis 5:24
3. The flood - Genesis Chapters 6-8
4. Sodom and Gomorrah destroyed - Genesis 19:15-29

II. MIRACLES IN THE TIME OF MOSES AND JOSHUA

5. The burning bush - Ex. 3:1-4

6. The rod a serpent - Ex. 4:1-5
7. The leprous hand - Ex. 4:6-8
8. Nile water to blood - Ex. 4:9-12
9. Rod a serpent - Ex. 7:8-13
10. Water into blood - Ex. 7:14-24
11. Plague of frogs - Ex. 8:1-15
12. Plague of lice - Ex. 8:16-19
13. Plague of flies - Ex. 8:20-32
14. Plagues of death of cattle and of boils - Ex. 9:1-12
15. Plague of hail and fire - Ex. 9:13-35
16. Plague of locusts - Ex. 10:1-20
17. Plague of three days of darkness - Ex. 10:21-29
18. Death of first born - Ex. 11:1-10; 12:29-36
19. Pillar of cloud and fire - Ex. 13:21, 22
20. Crossing of Red Sea - Ex. 14
21. Marah water healed - Ex. 15:23-26
22. Manna given - Ex. 16:14-36; Num. 11:7-9
23. Quails given - Ex. 16:12, 13; Num. 11:18-34
24. Water from the rock - Ex. 17:1-7
25. Water from another rock - Num. 20:1-13
26. Kept 40 days on mount - Ex. 24:18
27. Kept again 40 days on mount - Ex. 34:28
28. Moses face shining - Ex. 34:29-35
29. Miriam's leprosy - Num. 12:10-15
30. Earth's opening - Num. 16:29-34
31. Fire from the Lord (Korah) - Num. 16:35
32. Fire (Nadab, Abihu) - Lev. 10:2
33. The quail and plague - Num. 11:31-35
34. The murmuring and plague - Num. 16:41-50
35. Baal of Peor and plague - Num. 25:1-9
36. Aaron's rod blossoms - Num. 17:1-11

37. Brazen serpent - Num. 21:6-9
38. Balaam's ass - Num. 22:22-33
39. God writes the commandments - Deut. 10:1-4
40. Moses mysterious burial - Deut. 34:1-8
41. Jordan divided - Josh. 3:14-17
42. Manna ceased - Josh. 5:12
43. Walls of Jericho fall - Josh. 6:1-20
44. Hailstones - Josh. 10:10, 11
45. Sun standing still - Josh. 10:12-14

III. MIRACLES IN THE TIME OF THE JUDGES

46. Dew on Gideon's fleece - Judges 6:36-40
47. Water in jawbone for Samson - Judges 15:19

IV. MIRACLES IN THE TIME OF SAMUEL

48. Dagon falls - I Sam. 5:3-5
49. God answers by thunder - I Sam. 7:10

V. MIRACLES IN THE TIME OF THE PROPHET OF JUDAH

50. Jeroboam's hand withered - I Kings 13:4
51. The altar rent - I Kings 13:1-5

VI. MIRACLES IN THE TIME OF ELIJAH AND ELISHA

52. Fed by ravens - I Kings 17:4-6
53. Barrel of meal and cruse of oil - I Kings 17:12-16
54. Widow of Zarephath's son raised - I Kings 17:17-24
55. Answering by fire on Carmel- I Kings 18:20-39

56. Forty days sustained on Horeb - I Kings 19:8
57. Fire from heaven - II Kings 1:10-15
58. Elijah divides Jordan - II Kings 2:8
59. Elijah caught up - II Kings 2:11, 12
60. Elisha divides Jordan - II Kings 2:13-15
61. Water healed - II Kings 2:19-22
62. Water given and victory over Moab -
    II Kings 3:16-20, 22, 23
63. Pot of oil - II Kings 4:1-7
64. Shunammite's son raised - II Kings 4:20-37
65. Pottage healed - II Kings 4:38-41
66. Food multiplied - II Kings 4:42-44
67. Naaman healed - II Kings 5:1-14
68. Gehazi smitten - II Kings 5:27
69. Axe-head restored - II Kings 6:5-7
70. King's words repeated - II Kings 6:8-12
71. Horses and chariots shown - II Kings 6:15-17
72. Syrians smitten with blindness and restored -
    II Kings 6:18-20
73. Syrians flee at the sound of chariots -
    II Kings 7:6, 7
74. Dead man raised - II Kings 13:20, 21

VII. MIRACLES IN THE TIME OF ISAIAH

75. Sennacherib's host destroyed - II Kings 19:35;
    II Chron. 32:21; Isa. 37:36
76. The shadow moved backwards -
    II Kings 20:9-11; II Chron. 32:24; Isa. 38:8

VIII. MIRACLES IN THE TIME OF DANIEL

77. The fiery furnace - Dan. 3:18-27
78. Handwriting on the wall - Dan. 5:5

79. The lion's den - Dan. 6:16-23

It is obvious times of miracles happened spasmodically and were never considered the normal part of the life of a believer. Jesus imparted the message healings should be a normal part of the lifestyle of the believer. He plainly said, "*And these signs shall follow them that believe...*" (Mark 16:17). The miraculous was the common place with Jesus. He expected and still expects it of His followers.

The Old Testament set the stage for the complete revelation of the New Testament.

24

NEW TESTAMENT MIRACLES AND HEALINGS

The New Testament abounds with healings and other miracles. I want to present them in a concise form and point out some interesting insights concerning the ministry of Jesus and His faithful followers.

1. Changing of water into wine - John 2:7-9
2. Healing of the nobleman's son - John 4:50
3. Healing of the Capernaum demoniac -
   Mark 1:25; Luke 4:35
4. Healing of Peter's mother-in-law - Matt. 8:15
   Mark 1:31; Luke 4:39
5. Catching a great number of fish - Luke 5:5, 6
6. Healing a leper - Matt. 8:3; Mark 1:41
7. Healing a paralytic - Matt. 9:2, 6, 7;
   Mark 2:5, 10-12; Luke 5:20, 24, 25
8. Healing a withered hand - Matt. 12:13;
   Mark 3:5; Luke 6:10
9. Healing a centurion's servant - Matt. 8:13;
   Luke 7:10
10. Raising a widow's son - Luke 7:14

11. Calming the stormy sea - Matt. 8:26; Mark 4:39; Luke 8:24
12. Healing the Gadarene demoniac - Matt. 8:32; Mark 5:8; Luke 8:33
13. Healing a woman with internal bleeding - Matt. 9:22; Mark 5:29; Luke 8:44
14. Raising Jairus' daughter - Matt. 9:25; Mark 5:41; Luke 8:54
15. Healing two blind men - Matt. 9:29
16. Healing a dumb demoniac - Matt 9:33
17. Healing of a thirty-eight-year invalid - John 5:8
18. Feeding 5,000 men and their families - Matt. 14:19; Mark 6:41; Luke 9:16; John 6:11
19. Walking on the sea - Matt. 14:25; Mark 6:48; John 6:19
20. Healing a demoniac girl - Matt. 15:28; Mark 7:29
21. Healing a deaf man with a speech impediment - Mark 7:34-35
22. Feeding 4,000 men and their families - Matt. 15:36; Mark 8:6
23. Healing a blind man - Mark 8:25
24. Healing a man born blind - John 9:7
25. Healing a demoniac boy - Matt. 17:18; Mark 9:25; Luke 9:42
26. Catching a fish with a coin in its mouth - Matt. 17:27
27. Healing a blind and dumb demoniac - Matt. 12:22; Luke 11:14
28. Healing a woman with an eighteen-year infirmity - Luke 13:10-17
29. Healing a man with dropsy - Luke 14:4
30. Healing ten lepers - Luke 17:11-19

31. Raising of Lazarus - John 11:43-44
32. Healing a blind man - Matt. 20:34; Luke 18:42
33. Healing a blind man - Mark 10:46-52
34. Destroying a fig tree - Matt. 21:19; Mark 11:14
35. Restoring (healing) a severed ear -
    Luke 22:50, 51
36. Catching a great number of fish - John 21:6

HEALED IN PUBLIC

Believers should realize there is no record of a private healing or miracle by our Lord during His earthly ministry.

He spent many hours in private prayer. It can be stated that He prayed in private, but that He healed in public. Many times today the Church wants to do it the opposite. Pastors and lay persons pray in public, and if there is any prayer for healing, it is done in secret. I know many who feel spiritual healing should not be mentioned in public, let alone practiced in public. In fact, I know people who do not even want to reveal they have been healed by the Lord. Isn't it strange how we pervert the ministry of our Lord and His desire for us to proclaim His presence and power publicly?

Below are listed the places of His healings and miracles. It is obvious they took place in public places and in the midst of the ordinary activities of people. Jesus, through His miracles, certainly fulfilled His teaching, *"Let your light so shine before men that they may see your good works, and glorify your Father which is in heaven,"* (Matt. 5:16).

I list the public places and the number from the beginning of this chapter denoting chapter and book of miracles and healings which occurred there:

    a. At a wedding (1)
    b. At a funeral (10, 14, 31)
    c. In a graveyard (12)
    d. At the synagogue (3, 8, 28)
    e. At a home (4, 7, 14, 20, 29)
    f. On the seashore (36)
    g. In a garden (35)
    h. On a mountain (18, 22)
    i. By a pool (17)
    j. In a boat (5, 11)

VARIETY

There is no set pattern as to what Jesus did when He healed. His actions and motions varied with each person. The following examples demonstrate that we cannot put our Lord in a little methodical or theological box:

1. There are eleven healings where Jesus touched the one healed (4, 6, 14, 15, 19, 21, 23, 25, 28, 33, 35).

2. There was one time He was touched by an individual (13). There is also the account of many people touching Him and being healed (Matt. 14:36).

3. Would you believe there are three times when He spat as part of His ministry of healing? (21, 23, 24).

4. There are five references to a healing taking place on the Sabbath (8, 17, 24, 28, 29). Healing on the Sabbath got Him into much trouble. It helps us

to understand the attitude of many who do not want an emphasis upon healing at a Sunday morning service. It is too disturbing to the "religious."

5. There are six references to the spirit of compassion which swept over Jesus as He healed (6, 10, 18, 22, 32, 33).

6. Jesus groaned as He was about to perform His greatest miracle (21). (Also John 11:33).

7. Jesus also wept at the raising of Lazarus (31). (Also John 11:35).

8. There are seventeen times He asked a question in relationship to the miracle:

   a. *"Woman, what are you doing to me?"* (1).
   b. *"Which is easier to say, 'Your sins are forgiven you,' or, 'Take up your bed and walk?'"* (7).
   c. *"Is it lawful to do good on the sabbath?"* (8).
   d. *"Where is your faith?"* (11).
   e. *"What is your name?"* (12).
   f. *"Who touched me?"* (13).
   g. *"Do you believe I can do this?"* (15).
   h. *"Do you want to be healed?"* (17).
   i. *"Where shall we buy bread?"* (18).
   j. *"What made you doubt?"* (19).
   k. *"How many loaves do you have?"* (22).
   l. *"Do you see anything?"* (23).
   m. *"From whom do the kings collect tribute?"* (26).
   n. *"If Satan casts out Satan, how can His Kingdom endure?"* (27).
   o. *"Where have you laid him?"* (31).
   p. *"What do you want me to do?"* (32, 33).
   q. *"Children, have you anything to eat?"* (36).

9. There are ten times He issued a command in regard to the miracle:

    a. *"Fill the jars,"* (1).

    b. *"Launch out into the deep,"* (5).

    c. *"Stretch forth your hand,"* (8).

    d. *"Rise, take up your bed and walk,"* (7, 17).

    e. *"Gather the men into groups of fifty,"* (18).

    f. *"Come,"* (19).

    g. *"Go and wash in the pool of Siloam,"* (24).

    h. *"Go cast a hook,"* (26).

    i. *"Come forth,"* (31).

    j. *"Cast the net on the right side,"* (36).

TYPES

There are several types of healings by our Master:

1. There are seven miracles which involved the rebuking of demons:

    a. Concerning convulsions (3).

    b. Concerning convulsions (25).

    c. Concerning insanity (12).

    d. Concerning muteness (16).

    e. Concerning an unknown affliction (20).

    f. Concerning blindness and muteness (27).

    g. Concerning paralysis (28).

2. There are three references to the raising of the dead:

    a. The little girl (14).

    b. The young man (10).

    c. Lazarus (31).

3. There are three miracles which really served to protect one or more of His disciples:

    a. While they were in the boat (11).

b. When Peter walked on the water (19).

c. Restoring the ear Peter cut off (35). The soldiers surely would have killed Peter for using the sword if Malchus had not been healed.

4. There are six references of miracles by our Lord to provide for needy and hungry people:

a. Wedding guests (1).

b. 5,000 men (18).

c. 4,000 men (22).

d. Four of His disciples (5).

e. Five of His disciples (36).

f. Providing tax money (26).

HUMAN REACTION

It is interesting to consider the human reaction to the healings of our Lord:

a. The lack of faith (2, 11, 19).

b. The wickedness of the heart revealed in the presence of great miracles (5, 16, 17, 27, 28). Also Luke 5:8, Matt. 9:34, John 5:18, Matt. 12:24, and Luke 14:1.

c. The ingratitude of the heart (30).

MINISTRY UNTO INDIVIDUALS

There are seventeen references to Jesus ministering unto individuals. However, these incidents were not done in private. Many people saw them:

a. Delivered of a fever (2).

b. Delivered of a fever (4).

c. Paralysis (7).

d. Paralysis (9).

e. Paralysis (17).

f . Withered hand (8).

g . Internal bleeding (13).

h. Blindness (15).

i . Blindness (23).

j . Blindness (24).

k. Blindness (32).

l . Blindness (33).

m. Deafness (21).

n. Dropsy (29).

o. Severed ear (35).

p. Leprosy (6).

q. Leprosy (30).

THE GOSPELS AND MIRACLES

It is interesting to note that only two of the same miracles are recorded in each of the four Gospels (18, 35).

The first and the last miracles Jesus did are only recorded in the Gospel of John (1, 36).

There are sixteen miracles of our Lord which are only mentioned by one of the Gospels, consider:

1. Matthew - There are twenty-two miracles recorded in the first Gospel. Matthew records three, (15, 16, 26), which are only in his Gospel.

2. Mark - There are nineteen references to miracles in Mark. Two of them are only in this Gospel, (21, 23).

3. Luke - There are nineteen miracles appearing in Luke. There are five which appear only in Luke (5, 10, 28, 29, 30).

4. John - There are nine miracles recorded in John. There are six which are told only by John (1, 2, 17, 24, 31, 36).

MULTIPLE HEALINGS

There are eleven references to multiple healings by our Lord Jesus Christ. We have no way of knowing how many thousands were healed by our Lord. We do know:

1. That not all of the individual healings which Jesus did are recorded in the Gospels. In fact, only a very small portion of what He did is recorded, (John 21:25).

2. We have no idea if tens, hundreds, or thousands could have been touched in the moments of multiple healings.

Consider the following multiple healing incidents:

Incident	Matthew	Mark	Luke
1. Crowd at Peter's door	8:16, 17	1:24, 32	4:40, 41
2. Crowds after leper healed			5:15
3. Crowd near Capernaum	12:15-21	3:7-12	5:17-26
4. Answering John's questions	11:2-6		7:18-23
5. Before feeding 5,000	14:13-14		9:11
6. At Gennesaret	14:14-36	6:53-55	
7. Before feeding 4,000	15:29-31		
8. Crowds beyond Jordan	19:1, 2		
9. Blind and lame in temple	21:14		
10. Some sick of Nazareth	13:53-58	6:1-6	
11. All kinds of disease	4:23	6:56	
12. Every sickness & disease	9:35		
13. All oppressed by the devil	Acts 10:38		

It is obvious from the above analysis of the miracles of the New Testament they were exciting and frequent. They were the natural fruit of the Kingdom being recognized and entered into by Christ and His followers.

25

THE GREATEST COMMISSION

Jesus definitely told His disciples to go forth to proclaim the Kingdom of God is at hand and to heal the sick. I call this command by Him the Greatest Commission.

The Great Commission (Matthew 28:18-20) is challenging and should be fulfilled. However, this commission is not specific in what should be preached and what should be done. It simply says, *"teach all that I have commanded you."* And what did He command His followers to do?

He commanded them to heal the sick. He also gave power unto them to do this. He would not ask us to do something that would be impossible. He knew in His Name we could heal the sick.

Seven times His followers are told to heal. How many times do we have to be told before we heed His Word?

1. The commissioning of the twelve...
   Matthew 10:1-15.
2. The commissioning of the twelve...Mark 3:13-1.
3. The commissioning of the twelve...Mark 6:7-13.

4. What believers should do...Mark 16:14-20.
5. The commissioning of the twelve...Luke 9:1-6.
6. The commissioning of the seventy...Luke 10:1-20.
7. The challenge to all believers for all time...
   John 14:12.

HIS FOLLOWERS

The first followers of the Lord Jesus Christ did as He did. They healed individuals. They believed healing of body, soul, and spirit was possible in the Name of Jesus. They lived out His power in their lives.

We have several incidents of individuals being healed by the apostles:
1. The man lame from birth...Acts 3:1-2.
2. Paul regains his sight...Acts 9:10-22; 22:11-13.
3. Aeneas the paralytic...Acts 9:32-35.
4. Raising of Dorcas from the dead...Acts 9:36-42.
5. Crippled man at Lystra...Acts 14:8-18.
6. Girl with the spirit of divination...Acts 16:16-18.
7. Eutychus restored to life...Acts 20:7-12.
8. Paul healed of the snake-bite...Acts 28:1-6.
9. Father of Publius healed...Acts 28:7, 8.

As in the life of our Lord, there are times when multiple healings took place through the Apostles:
1. Many signs and wonders...Acts 2:41.
2. Many sick healed in Jerusalem...Acts 5:12-16.
3. Stephen performs many miracles...Acts 6:8.
4. Philip heals many in Samaria...Acts 8:5-11.
5. Paul and Barnabas work signs and wonders...
   Acts 14:3.
6. Paul heals at Ephesus...Acts 19:11, 12.
7. The sick healed at Melita...Acts 28:9.

OTHER REFERENCES

There are several other New Testament references to miracles and healings. Some of them are as follows:

1. Signs and Wonders...Romans 15:18, 19;
    II Corinthians 12:12; Hebrews 2:4.
2. Healing...I Corinthians 12:9, 12:28-30;
    I Peter 2:24; Revelation 22:2.
3. Anointing...Mark 6:13; James 5:14.
4. Perfect eternal healing...Revelation 21:4.

CONCLUSION

It is my firm conviction that a careful study of the above will reveal that the lifestyle of our Lord's earthly ministry was one of healing and hope. He believed in wholeness of body, soul, and spirit. He not only taught this truth, but conveyed it through His miracles.

He certainly wants His followers to do as He has done. *"Verily, verily, I say unto you, he that believeth on me, the works that I do shall he do also, and greater works than these shall he do; because I go unto my Father,"* (John 14:12).

26

HEALING THROUGHOUT THE CENTURIES

The New Testament abounds with references to healings.

Did the power of healing cease with the death of the apostles? Was the first generation of Christians the only ones who were to witness the healing power of our Lord? Are we to believe that the healings of the Great Physician were for the Apostolic Age only?

THROUGH THE CENTURIES

Some believers may respond with a "YES" to all of the above questions. They are wrong. The church through the ages has had a healing witness. At times it has waned, but it has never disappeared!

Perhaps most Christians of any age are reluctant to fully appropriate the power of the Lord. However, there are always the bold and believing. They are souls who stand out as great examples of the power of the Lord to heal.

JUSTIN MARTYR (165 A.D.)

"For numberless demoniacs throughout the whole world and in your city, many of our Christian men, exorcising them in the Name of Jesus Christ, who was crucified under Pontius Pilate, have healed, and do heal, rendering helpless and driving the possessing devils out of the men though they could not be cured by all the other exorcists and those who used incantations and drugs."

IRENAEUS (200 A.D.)

"Those who are in truth His disciples, receiving grace from Him, do in His name perform miracles; and they truly cast out devils. Others still heal the sick by laying on their hands upon them, and they are made whole. Yes, moreover, as I have said, the dead even have been raised up, and remained among us for many years."

ORIGEN (250 A.D.)

"And some give evidence of their having received through their faith a marvelous power by the cures which they perform, invoking no other name over those who need their help than that of the God of all things, and of Jesus, along with a mention of His history. For by these means we too have seen many persons freed from grievous calamities, and from distractions of mind, and madness, and countless other ills, which could be cured neither by men or devils."

CLEMENT (275 A.D.)

"Let them (young ministers), therefore with fasting and prayer, make their intercessions, and not with the well arranged, and fitly ordered words of learning, but as men who have received the gift of healing confidently, to the glory of God."

THEODORE OF MOPUCSTE (429 A.D.)

"Many heathen amongst us are being healed by Christians from whatever sickness they have, so abundant are miracles in our midst."

MARTIN LUTHER (1483-1546)

"The tax collector in Torgau and the councilor in Belgern have written me to ask that I offer some good advice for Mr. John Korner, afflicted husband. I know of no worldly help to give. If the physicians are at a loss to find a remedy, you may be sure that it is not a case of ordinary melancholy. It must rather be an affliction that comes from the devil, and this must be counteracted by the power of Christ and with the prayer of faith. This is what we do, and that we have been accustomed to do, for a cabinet maker here was similarly afflicted with madness and we cured him by prayer in Christ's Name."

ZINSENDORF (1700-1760)

"To believe against hope is the root of the gift of miracles and I owe this testimony to our beloved church, that Apostolic powers are there manifested. We have undeniable proofs thereof which could not humanly have been discovered, in the healing of maladies in themselves incurable, such as cancers, consumptions, when the patient was in the agencies of death, all by means of prayer, or of a single word."

TODAY

We live in an age which is again seeing the power of the Lord through the ministry of healing. The Great Physician invites each believer to accept His invitation to wholeness. He also wants us to impart it to others!

27

CHRIST IS HEALER

Our Lord Jesus Christ is referred to in scripture in at least 128 different ways as follows:

1. Adam - I Cor. 15:45
2. Advocate - I John 2:1
3. Almighty - Rev. 1:8
4. Alpha - Rev. 1:8, 11; 22:13
5. Amen - Rev. 3:14
6. Apostle of our Profession - Heb. 3:1
7. Arm of the Lord - Isa. 51:9; 53:1
8. Author of our Faith - Heb. 12:2
9. Author of Eternal Salvation - Heb. 5:9
10. Beginning of the creation of God - Rev. 3:14
11. Beloved son - Matt. 12:18; Mt. 3:17
12. Bishop of Souls - I Peter 2:25
13. Blessed Potentate - I Tim. 6:15
14. Branch - Isa. 4:2
15. Bread of Life - John 6:35
16. Captain of Salvation - Heb. 2:10
17. Chief Shepherd - I Peter 5:4
18. Christ Jesus - Heb. 3:1; I Tim. 2:5
19. Christ of God - Luke 9:20
20. Commander - Isa. 55:4
21. Consolation of Israel - Luke 2:25
22. Cornerstone - Psalm 118:22
23. Counsellor - Isa. 9:6
24. Creator - John 1:3
25. Dayspring - Luke 1:78

26. Deliverer - Romans 11:26
27. Desire of all Nations - Hag. 2:7
28. Door - John 10:7
29. Elect of God - Isa. 42:1
30. Everlasting Father - Isa. 9:6
31. Faithful Witness - Rev. 1:5
32. Finisher of our Faith - Heb. 12:2
33. First and Last - Rev. 1:17
34. First Begotten - Rev. 1:5; 3:14
35. Forerunner - Heb. 6:20
36. Glorious Lord - Isa. 33:21
37. Glory of the Lord - Isa. 40:5
38. God - Isa. 40:3; John 20:28
39. God Blessed - Romans 9:5
40. Good Shepherd - John 10:11
41. Governor - Matt. 2:6
42. Great High Priest - Heb. 3:1; 4:14
43. Head of the Church - Eph. 1:21
44. Heir of all things - Heb. 1:2
45. High Priest - Heb. 3:1; 6:20
46. Holy Child - Acts 4:27
47. Holy One - Acts 3:14; Isa. 55:5
48. Holy One of God - Mark 1:24
49. Holy One of Israel - Isa. 41:14
50. Horn of Salvation - Luke 1:69
51. I Am - John 8:58
52. Image of God - II Cor. 4:4
53. Immanuel - Isa. 7:14
54. Jehovah - Isa. 26:4 73
55. Jesus - Matt. 1:21
56. Jesus Christ - Rev. 1:5, 9; Mt. 1:1
57. Jesus of Nazareth - Matt. 21:11; John 1:45;
    Luke 24:19
58. Judge - Isa. 33:22
59. Judge of Israel - Micah 5:1
60. Just One - Acts 7:52
61. King - Zech. 9:9; Isa. 33:22
62. King of the Ages - I Tim. 1:17
63. King of the Jews - Matt. 2:2; 27:37

64. King of Kings - I Tim. 6:15; Rev. 19:15
65. King of Saints - Rev. 15:3
66. Lawgiver - Isa. 33:22
67. Lamb - Rev. 5:12; 13:8; 15:3
68. Lamb of God - John 1:29
69. Leader - Isa. 55:4
70. Life - John 11:25; 14:6
71. Light of the World - John 8:12
72. Lilly of the Valleys - Song of Solomon 2:1
73. Lion of the Tribe of Judah - Rev. 5:5
74. Lord - Rev. 15:4
75. Lord God Almighty - Rev. 15:3
76. Lord of All - Acts 10:36
77. Lord of Glory - I Cor. 2:8
78. Lord of Lords - I Tim. 6:15; Rev. 19:16
79. Lord our Righteousness - Jer. 23:6
80. Man of Sorrows - Isa. 53:3
81. Mediator - I Tim. 2:5
82. Messenger of the Covenant - Mal. 3:1
83. Messiah - Dan. 9:25; John 1:41
84. Mighty God - Isa. 9:6
85. Mighty One of Jacob - Isa. 60:16
86. Morning Star - Rev. 22:16
87. Nazarene - Matt. 2:23
88. Offspring of David - Rev. 22:16
89. Omega - Rev. 1:8, 11; 22:13
90. Only Begotten Son - John 1:18
91. Only Potentate - I Tim. 6:15
92. Our Passover - I Cor. 5:7
93. Prince - Dan. 9:25
94. Prince of Kings - Rev. 1:5
95. Prince of Life - Acts 3:15
96. Prince of Peace - Isa. 9:6
97. Prophet - Luke 24:19
98. Purifier - Mal. 3:3
99. Redeemer - Job 19:25; Isa. 60:16
100. Refiner - Mal. 3:3
101. Resurrection - John 11:25
102. Rock - I Cor. 10:4

103. Root of David - Rev. 5: 5; 22:16
104. Rose of Sharon - Song of Solomon 2:1
105. Saviour - Luke 2:11; Isa. 60:16
106. Servant - Mt. 12:18; Isa. 42:1
107. Seed of Woman - Gen. 3:15
108. Shepherd of Souls - I Pet. 2:25
109. Shiloh - Gen. 49:10
110. Son of Abraham - Mt. 1:1
111. Son of David - Matt. 1:1
112. Son of Joseph - John 1:41
113. Son of God - Matt. 2:15; John 1:49; Mark 1:1
114. Son of Man - Matt. 8:20; John 1:51; Rev. 1:13;
      Mark 14:62
115. Son of Righteousness - Mal. 4:2
116. Son of the Blessed - Mark 14:61
117. Son of the Highest - Luke 1:32
118. The Christ - John 1:20, 41; I Cor. 5:7
119. The Righteous - I John 2:1
120. The Son - Mt. 28:19
121. True Light - John 1:9
122. True Vine - John 1:14
123. True Witness - Rev. 3:14
124. Truth - John 1:14, 14:6
125. The Way - John 14:6
126. Witness - Isa. 55:4
127. Word - John 1:1
128. Word of God - Rev. 19:13

How can we best sum up the 128 names for Jesus?
It is my feeling Paul Tillich did it beautifully in his
book, the New Being. He wrote as follows:

HOW PAINT JESUS?

"How do we paint Jesus the Christ? The stories
of the gospel of Matthew contribute to the answer;
they add color, an expression, a trait of great intensity. They paint Him as the Healer; it is astonishing
that His color, this vivid expression of His nature, this

powerful trait of His character, has more and more been lost in our time.

"The grayish colors of a moral teacher, the tense expression of a social reformer, the soft traits of a suffering servant have prevailed, at least amongst our painters and theologians and life-of-Jesus novelists; perhaps not so much in the hearts of the people who need somebody to heal them.

"The gospels, certainly, are not responsible for this disappearance of power in the picture of Jesus. They abound in stories of healing; but we are responsible ministers, laymen, theologians, who forgot that "saviour" means "healer." He Who makes whole and sane what is broken and insane, in body and mind.

"The woman who encountered Him was made whole. The demoniac who met Him was liberated from his mental cleavage. Those who are disrupted, split, disintegrated, are healed by Him. And because this is so, because this power has appeared on earth, the Kingdom of God has come upon us. This is the answer Jesus gives to the Pharisees when they discuss His power of healing the mentally possessed; this is the answer He gives to the Baptist to overcome his doubts; this is the order He gives to His disciples when He sends them to the towns of Israel. "And as ye go, preach, saying, 'the Kingdom of God is at hand.' Heal the sick, raise the dead, cleanse the lepers, cast out demons."

"That is what they shall do and for this He gives them authority and power; for in Him the Kingdom of God has appeared, and its nature is salvation, healing of that which is ill, making whole what is broken.

"Are we still able to experience this power? I do not speak of theological inhibitions about the acceptance of such a picture of Christ. They do not weigh very heavily. Of course, we were worried about miracle-stories for many decades. Today we know what the New Testament always knew--that miracles are signs pointing to the Presence of a divine power in nature and history. And that they are in no way negations of natural laws.

"Of course, we were and we are worried about the abuse of religious healing for commercial and other selfish purposes or about its distortion into magic and superstition. But abuses occur when the right use is lacking and superstitions arise when faith has become weak. All these are not serious problems; good theology and good practice can solve them."

Paul Tillich has said it so very well. Jesus Christ, whatever Name is used to speak of Him, is our Healer. The word "Healer" sums up Jesus and His ministry more adequately than any other word in our language.

Someday He will completely heal the world's relationship with our Father God, when He comes again!

28

MARTIN LUTHER AND HEALING

Did the Reformers believe in the Lord's healing power? Have the devout men of God through the ages believed in the power of the Lord to heal? Is healing a new fad and one which will fade in the years ahead?

These and many other questions come to the sincere seeker after the truth of healing in the church.

It is reported Martin Luther wrote the following letter to Pastor Severin Schulze on June 1, 1545.

It certainly reveals Luther's belief in the power of prayer, and also in his belief of the Lord's ability and desire to heal.

I have put in bold the references to prayer. I feel this will accent Luther's practice of Christian concern through prayer.

Venerable Sir and Pastor,

The tax collector in Torgau and the councilor in Belgern have written me to ask that I offer some good advice and help for Mr. John Korner, afflicted husband. I know of no worldly help to

give. If the physicians are at a loss to find a
remedy, you may be sure that it is not a case of
ordinary melancholy. It must rather be an affliction that comes from the devil, and this must be
counteracted by the power of Christ and with
prayer of faith. This is what we do, and that we
have been accustomed to do, for a cabinet maker
here was similarly afflicted with madness and we
cured him by **prayer** in Christ's name.

Accordingly you should proceed as follows:
Go to him with a deacon and two or three good
men. Confident that you, as Pastor of the place,
are clothed with the authority of the ministerial
office, lay your hands upon him and say,

"Peace be with you, dear brother, from God
our Father and from our Lord Jesus Christ."

Thereupon repeat the Creed and the **Lord's
Prayer** over him in a clear voice, and close with
these words:

"O God, Almighty Father, who has told us
through Thy Son, verily, verily, I say unto you,
whatsoever ye shall ask the Father in my Name,
He will give it to you; who has commanded and
encouraged us to **pray** in His Name 'Ask and you
shall receive;' and who in like manner has said,
'Call upon me in the day of trouble; I will deliver
thee, and thou shalt glorify me;' we unworthy
sinners, relying on these words and commands
pray for the mercy with such faith as we can
muster.

"Graciously deign to free this man from all
evil, and put to nought the work that Satan has

done in him, to the honor of thy Name and the strengthening of the faith of believers; through the same Jesus Christ Thy Son, our Lord, who liveth and reigneth with thee, world without end, Amen."

Then, when you depart, lay hands upon the man again and say,

"These signs shall follow them that believe; they shall lay hands on the sick and they shall recover."

Do this three times, once on each of three successive days. Meanwhile let **prayers** be said from the chancel of the church, publicly until God hears them.

Insofar as we are able, we shall at the same time unite our faithful **prayers** and petitions to the Lord with yours.

Farewell, other counsel than this I do not have.

I remain,
Martin Luther

29

JOHN WESLEY AND SPIRITUAL HEALING

Many of the great Christians through the centuries have believed in the Lord's healing power. This was an important part of the ministry of John Wesley.

He firmly believed the Lord desired to send His healing. He had confidence in the power of the Lord to heal. Consider the following incidents reported by Wesley.

SPOTTED FEVER

"...I visited several of the sick. Most of them were ill of the spotted fever, which, they informed me, had been extremely mortal, few persons recovering from it. But God had said, 'Hitherto shalt thou come.' I believe that there was not one with whom we were, but recovered."

THE CONFINED

Wesley's JOURNAL discloses, "...I was desired to visit one who had been eminently pious, but had now been confined to her bed for several months, and was utterly unable to raise herself up. She desired us to pray that the chain might be broken. A few of us prayed in faith. Presently she rose up, dressed herself, came downstairs, and I believe had not any further complaint." In a letter to Alexander Knox he wrote, "...He wants to give you and my dear Mrs. Knox both inward and outward health. And why not now? Surely all things are ready: believe, and receive the blessing...Look up, and wait for happy days."

SORE THROAT

Consider what happened to Wesley when he was 86 years old. He found himself so hoarse he could neither sing nor preach. A large congregation had assembled to hear the gospel message. Wesley reports, "I trusted in God, and began to speak. The more I spoke, the more my voice was strengthened, so that in a few minutes I think all could hear; and many, I believe, took knowledge that what they heard was not the word of man, but of God."

Wesley's confidence in the Lord seemed to constantly abound. One woman was in great pain. After Wesley prayed for her she received such relief that immediately she arose and went about her work. Previously to his becoming a very famous clergyman, Thomas Merrick was healed from a critical illness. He was near to the door of death when Wesley and some other believers prayed for him.

LAYING-ON-HANDS

Wesley firmly believed distance did not limit the power of prayer. However, at the same time he believed and practiced the ministry of laying-on-hands for the ill. This he considered an apostolic injunction to be followed by the believers of his day.

RIGHT WITH GOD

Insistence upon right relations to the Lord was central to Wesley's ministry. He felt God's plan was to heal the spirit and body together. Thus he insisted upon the individual getting "right" with God, and trusting for healing. The Lord has "good things" in store for His believers. This conviction made it possible for Wesley to minister to the practical needs of people of his day.

CHRISTIAN PIETY

Wesley tried to get individuals to live a life of deep Christian piety. He knew violent passions were dangerous to health. The soul which remained calm in the Lord would more likely remain strong in body.

He says, "And by the unspeakable joy and perfect calm, serenity, and tranquility it gives the mind, it becomes the most powerful of all the means of health and long life." Wesley saw acceptance of and belief in the love of God as preventive medicine.

30

PRESBYTERIANS AND HEALING

The Task Force of the Presbyterian General Assembly dealing with Health Costs/Policies proposed this question, "What would it mean for the Presbyterian Church to place concern for health and healing, in all wholeness, at the center of faith and life?"

This is one of the most penetrating questions a denomination could ever ask. The Task Force agreed a positive response to this question would "produce profound changes in Presbyterian worship, program, and lifestyle among members as well as in our corporate existence. Such changes could well, in and of themselves, affect the society."

The above is from the policy statement adopted by the 200th General Assembly in 1989 entitled, LIFE ABUNDANT: Values, Choices and Health Care; the Responsibility and Role of the Presbyterian Church USA.

The following are some significant insights from this policy statement:

ABUNDANT LIFE

"God's intention of health--shalom--for the earth and its people, and Jesus' promise of abundant life--health, healing and restoration to wholeness of body, mind and spirit--are central dimensions of the faith we profess and the vocation to which we are called as Christians." (page 1)

CARING CONCERN

"The health of a society is measured in a very important way by the quality of its concern and care for the health of its people." (page 1)

FOCUS

"We understand health to focus upon the person and community within a total environment." (page 8)

TODAY'S CHALLENGE

"The contemporary challenge to the Presbyterian Church in regard to health, then, is to affirm and serve the values of justice, compassion, and service at the heart of our Reformed biblical faith. The role of the church is to be a center of responsibility and motivation for the promotion of health, an advocate for compassionate justice in health in the political economy, and a model which leads by example." (page 11)

JESUS HEALED

"Health and healing were central in the work of Jesus and the early church. The Gospel of Mark early and amply demonstrated Jesus' powerful concern for the total wellbeing of those he encountered. Lepers and 'mad men,' outcasts and Samaritans, women and children were restored to health and effective life. The same Greek word, SODZO, is translated as 'to save,' 'to heal,' and 'to make whole.' Jesus' effect on those he touched has been described by Lutheran theologian, Krister Stendahl, as a 'pushing back the frontier of all destructive and distorting forces,' a 'mending of creation.' The calling of the twelve disciples (Mark 6:7), the expectations of healing powers from Peter and John (Acts 3:1), Paul's list of gifts (I Corinthians 12), and the letter of James (5:13)--all show the central role which healing held in the early church." (page 11)

HEALING THE BROKEN

"In Jesus, life is seen as complete, whole. Brokenness may exist. However, the healing of that which is broken, the restoration to life in fullness, is clearly a part of what it means to be in Christ." (page 12)

CENTRAL DIMENSIONS

"Health and healing are central dimensions of the faith we profess...Our understanding of ourselves and God is mirrored by the way we do or do not seek health and wholeness for ourselves, our communities, and the world." (page 15)

CALLED TO HEAL

"Because it is the body of Christ, the church is called to be a community of health and healing at every level and at every location, seeking to manifest, sustain, and protect health in its fullness in its own life and within the wider human community." (page 15)

I believe our denomination could never have arrived at the above conclusions without the cumulative effect of efforts such as The Relation of Christian Faith to Health. This is a comprehensive report adopted by the General Assembly of the Presbyterian Church USA in 1960.

This report was prepared by a group of prominent Presbyterians which included a number of physicians. Through the years clergy and lay persons have received instruction and encouragement for the healing ministry from this report. Consider the following comments from the report:

CONQUERING EVIL

"The redemption which God in Jesus Christ brings to the world through His church is sufficient for the ultimate conquest of every evil. Among the evils from which God in Christ is able to redeem man are the myriad forms of physical and mental illness. It is plainly the understanding of the New Testament that health in body, mind and spirit is the ultimate will of God. The conquest of various diseases and infirmities is one of the chief evidences given in the New Testament for believing that God in Christ is overcoming the power of evil. The Church of Jesus Christ has a ministry to the sick which cannot be compartmentalized or limited."

THE CHURCH AND SUFFERING

"Nothing is more indicative of the Church's fidelity to Christ than her care of the sick and the handicapped. The Church has something to offer sufferers which the world cannot give. The Church must reach out to those in need with what she has, namely, with the Gospel of Jesus Christ who came that men might have life...and have it more abundant." (John 10:10)

COOPERATION NEEDED

"The Church's ministry to the sick is not a substitute for medical care. The callings of Christian nurses and other members of the physical and mental team are of Christ. The time has come for all vocational groups involved in the healing process to understand and cooperate with one another in a work that includes them all."

CHRIST'S MINISTRY

"The earthly ministry of Jesus Christ set the pattern for the Christian Church and it is to Him that we must look for guidance and instruction in the healing aspect of our ministry today.

"It is important that the Church make a fresh study of biblical teaching regarding the relation of Christian faith and health. Such a study will show that the healing of physical and mental illnesses was indeed a part of our Lord's work and is intended to be a part of His disciples' work in every generation."

PREVENTIVE AND CURATIVE

"The Church's ministry to the sick is both preventive and curative. Health is not an end in itself, but a means of serving God. We are interested in health because we want to serve God to the best of our ability."

WHY JESUS HEALED

"Jesus healed out of mercy in the knowledge that it is God's will to deliver men from all kinds of evil, including physical and mental illness.

"He prayed and worked for the removal of suffering. He regarded the healings which took place as so many signs of God's power breaking in upon the kingdom of evil. Healings were regarded as certain signs of God's nearness, portents of the age to come when all mourning and crying and pain would be done away." (Revelation 21:4)

CHRIST'S COMMISSION

"During His earthly ministry our Lord sent out His disciples to preach, teach, and heal...Christ directed His Church to heal and...gave them power to do so."

HEALING IS OF GOD

"All healing is Divine. God is the author of the natural world and all its creatures, including man. It is by His power that the universe and man are sustained. Natural law is God's law. Some of the mechanisms of healing are understood; but as it has been so often pointed out, the doctor dresses the wound, but the Lord heals. All healing is of God, whether it occurs through what we call natural law or according to laws we do not know. Many laws remain undiscovered."

ILLNESS IS AN EVIL

"Illness is an evil. Jesus Christ regarded illness as something to be overcome. He coped with illness, and he conquered it. It was His teaching that God wills healing. For the Christian, whether physician or layperson, the compassionate and effective ministry of Christ to the sick is an inspiration and a challenge to overcome this evil with good."

BRING YOUR NEED

"Within the Christian understanding of fellowship with God there is room for lifting physical and mental needs to God in prayer. Jesus taught us to do this.

"We must recognize the limits and the possibilities of not only the established therapies, but of new ones such as the discipline of prayer.

"This is a time for exploration and experimentation in the religious dimension of healing. God has many therapies, and it is contrary to the spirit of science as well as to the faith of Christianity to absolutize any therapeutic method."

SPIRITUAL NEEDS

"Great and grave as the dangers in 'faith healing' are, there is the equally great danger of limiting the power of God to work in the Church because of timidity and fear. Non-medical ministries to the sick have a vital place because the sick have spiritual needs."

TYPES OF MINISTRIES

"We recommend that Pastors consider the possibilities inherent in this report for the extension of their pastoral ministries to the sick by means of public worship, Christian Education, small groups and the possible use of services related to the physical and mental needs of members of the congregation."

HELP BY THE SESSION

"We recommend that Session help the Pastor to develop an adequate program of shepherding the congregation and that they assist the Pastor in initiating and maintaining an effective program in this area."

THE BOOK OF ACTS

"The Book of Acts contains a number of general statements to the effect that the Church continued to heal after the death and resurrection of Christ.

"For example:

'And more than ever believers were added to the Lord, multitudes both of men and women, so that they even carried out the sick into the streets, and laid them on beds and pallets, that as Peter came by at least his shadow might fall on some of them. The people also gathered from towns around Jerusalem, bringing the

sick and those afflicted with unclean spirits, and they were all healed,'" (Acts 5:14-16).

You may also desire to consider: Acts 3:1-10; 9:17-19; 9:36-42; 16:16-18; 28:3-6; 28:7, 8.

NEW DIRECTORY FOR WORSHIP

All of the above and much more truly has been part of the foundation upon which the Presbyterian Church USA Directory For Worship has been built. A greatly revised Directory For Worship was adopted and made a part of the Constitution of the Presbyterian Church USA in 1989. The most significant part of the Directory as far as healing is concerned is Section W-3.5400. It appears as follows in the Directory:

"SERVICES FOR HEALING"

"Healing was an integral part of the ministry of Jesus, which the church has been called to continue as one dimension of its concern for the wholeness of people. Through services for wholeness, the church enacts in worship its ministry as a healing community.

"Services for wholeness are to be authorized by the session, and shall be under the direction of the pastor. Such services may be observed as regularly scheduled services of worship, as occasional services, or as part of the Service for the Lord's Day. (W-3.3506) These services should be open to all and not restricted to those desiring healing for themselves or for others of special concern to them. The services should be held in a place readily accessible to those who may be seeking healing.

"The vital element of worship in the service of wholeness is prayer since this is essentially a time of waiting in faith upon God. Thanksgiving for God's promise of wholeness, intercessions, and supplications should be offered. Adequate time for silent prayer should be provided, as well as occasions for prayer spoken and sung. Enacted prayer in the form of the laying on of hands and anointing with oil is appropriate, (James 5:14). The enactment of prayers involves the presiding minister of the Word and Sacrament together with representatives of the believing community.

"These prayers are a response to the Word read and proclaimed. Particular focus should be on announcing the gospel's promise of wholeness through Christ. The sealing of this promise in the Lord's Supper may be celebrated, and should follow the prayers and the laying on of hands. Occasion for offering one's life and gifts for ministry may be provided, as well as opportunities for reconciliation and renewed commitment to the service of Jesus Christ in the world.

"When a service for wholeness includes anointing and the laying on of hands, these enacted prayers should be introduced carefully in order to avoid misinterpretation and misunderstanding. Healing is to be understood not as the result of the holiness, earnestness, or skill of those enacting the prayers, or of the faith of the ones seeking healing, but as a gift of God through the power of the Holy Spirit."

OTHER REFERENCES

There are several other references in the 1989 Directory For Worship concerning healing. In fact, the concept of healing in the name of Jesus permeates the spirit of the Directory. Healing is not seen as an isolated experience, but as part and parcel of the community of believers as it worships and serves the Living God.

W-1.3032 says, "...he (Jesus) blessed and healed people, reconciled and bound them into community, and exhibited the grace, power, and presence of the Kingdom of God."

W-2.1005 is a section which deals with Enacted Prayers and includes the following, "...to anoint and to lay on hands in intercession and supplication, commissioning and ordination."

W-3.3506 says,"...Prayers of supplication are offered for...those who are sick, grieving, lonely, and anxious, that they be comforted and healed."

W-4.2007 stresses that an appropriate action of worship is "...anointing."

W-6.3008 is the section which considers "Care in Broken Relationships." It states, "The church provides pastoral care which calls people to healing and seeks to support those caught up in the hurts, hostilities, and conflicts of daily living which lead to broken relationships in families and households, in the school and the workplace, in neighborhoods and communities, and in the church."

W-6.3009 states, "The call to healing in pastoral care involves the recognition in each one's life of the

reality of sin, which is the source of all human brokenness. The believing community announces the
good news of God whose love gives people grace...to
trust the power of God to bring healing and peace."

W-6.3011 states, "...Prayer enacted by the laying
on of hands and anointing calls upon God to heal,
empower, and sustain."

A VALID MINISTRY

It is obvious from the above that the Presbyterian
USA denomination speaks forthrightly to all of its
members and all others concerning healing as being
a valid ministry within every local congregation.

It is my firm conviction each local congregation
should seek to fulfill what the Head of the Church,
Jesus Christ, proclaimed, namely...

The Kingdom of God is at hand!

His followers should heal the sick!

I feel the Presbyterian denomination has adequately paved the way for every congregation to
fulfill a valid ministry of healing.

If Presbyterians are to fulfill the directive of the
Master and the suggestions of the General Assembly, every local church must put forth concerted
effort to proclaim and to achieve wholeness of body,
soul, and spirit.

This ministry of wholeness will include such things
as regular healing services, anointing the sick with
oil, the laying-on-of-hands with prayer, as well as all
the other facets of a congregation's ministry to its
people.

A PERSONAL NOTE

I conducted my first public service of healing May 6, 1959. I have continued to conduct regular services of healing. It was on August 1, 1966 that I began my pastorate at Westminster Presbyterian Church in Canton, Ohio. We started healing services January 4, 1967 at Westminster and have held them every Wednesday since that time.

I would be the first to acknowledge I do not have the last word on the "why," "how," and "when" of healing services and a ministry of healing.

However, I have been privileged to have traversed our nation directing healing conferences, seminars, retreats, and other events related to a healing ministry. I have been able by mail to reach over 250,000 churches of our land to encourage them to fulfill the Lord's commission to His disciples to "...proclaim the Kingdom of God is at hand and to heal the sick."

In addition, we have held many healing conferences at Westminster to help pastors and lay persons to begin and/or maintain a vital ministry of healing.

I am grateful my denomination has so pointedly and powerfully presented the validity and vitality of a ministry of healing. I certainly want to continue to do my part to help build on the firm foundation of careful research, scholarly reports, and biblical insights provided by the Presbyterian denomination.

MEDICINE

31

MEDICINE AND HEALING

"Man operates--God heals," is a well-known statement in medical circles. Indeed, God is the Healer. Man, in whatever capacity, is only an instrument of his healing.

FALSE CONCEPTS

There are many false concepts concerning healing. I want to mention two prevalent ones:

1. "If I had enough faith I would never be ill or need to see a physician."

2. "Prayer is only psychological and has no place as far as physical disease is concerned."

Both of the above are extreme and false statements.

MEDICAL HELP

The proper services of the physician and the proper use of medicine are as Christian as prayer meetings and Bible Study. Often sincere and devout Christians have a sense of guilt if they seek the ministry of a physician. "If only I had more faith, I would be immediately healed," is the nagging guilt they feel.

I feel this is wrong. God does indeed heal through physicians and medical science. Medical insights and belief in the Healing Christ are not contradictory. In fact, many of the most ardent believers of the validity of Spiritual Healing are physicians, nurses, and others in the allied professions of healing.

In like manner, ministers and teachers of Spiritual Healing do not hesitate to seek the services of physicians. They realize that when a person seeks the services of a physician, this does not deny the presence and power of the healing Christ.

WHAT IS THE ANSWER?

In a nutshell the message of God's healing is that an individual has not done all that can be done until:

1. You have prayed.
2. You have prayed with other believers.
3. You have been prayed for by others.
4. You have sought the best professional help available.

ABUSE, THE PROBLEM

Abuse, not use, is the problem regarding miraculous methods of healing. It is not a matter of pills vs. prayer. It is the improper use of any of the above which is wrong.

Some by their own volition or through the encouragement of others have thrown away their pills and/or stopped seeing their physician. Many have suffered immeasurably from such foolishness.

However, the other side of the coin is that millions are looking only to the physicians and pills as the answer to their illnesses. They neglect the spiritual.

GUIDELINES

A few sensible guidelines concerning medicine and Spiritual Healing are worthy of your consideration:

1. Appreciate that the Lord is the Healer regardless of whether it is accomplished in the natural, or the supernatural.

2. Realize that the field of medicine will never have the complete answer to problems of illness.

3. Acknowledge that healing involves spiritual as well as physical aspects.

4. Don't lean on the wonders of medicine as a crutch for your problems. There are no "magic" pills for any and all illnesses.

5. Realize that the healing of the spirit is the most important goal. Even Jesus told His enthused followers, "...*rejoice not, that the spirits are subject unto you, but rather rejoice, because your names are written in heaven,*" (Luke 10:20). There are many mysterious and unexplainable physical healings. However, the greatest and most mysterious of all healings are of the spirit.

6. Give thanks and praise unto the Lord for His healings regardless of the methods He may use.

7. Pray for all who are in any way involved in the ministry of healing. This should include pastors, lay persons, physicians, nurses, psychiatrists, researchers, administrators, laundry help, etc.

8. Faithfully participate in Healing services and believe Jesus is willing and able to meet your every need. He is most willing that you come unto Him. You acknowledge publicly your willingness to come through participation in these services.

32

WHY AN EYE SURGEON BELIEVES IN SPIRITUAL HEALING

Dr. Clair B. King served many years as an eye surgeon and highly respected physician. He was a very close personal friend of mine. I asked his permission to publish his beliefs about Spiritual Healing several years ago.

The following are some of the reasons he gave for his becoming an enthusiastic ambassador for the message of Spiritual Healing:

A SPIRITUAL BEING

Man is made up of body, soul, and spirit. The three are intricately interwoven. It is wrong to think that when man is physically ill he should seek only medical help. All illnesses have their spiritual component.

SKEPTICAL AT FIRST

I must admit that at first I was very skeptical of Spiritual Healing. I feel most doctors feel as I felt. However, the more I studied about it, the more I was convinced.

The study of the Bible and other books concerning healing helped me to accept its message. I arrived at the conclusion that Spiritual Healing has a major role to play in the healing process.

MORE THAN PSYCHOSOMATIC

Physicians are discovering there may be a lack of complete healing until the soul is also considered in the search for health. Psychosomatic medicine recognizes the power of disorders of the mind such as anxiety, stress, strain, etc.

These may cause diseases of the body such as ulcers, high blood pressure, heart diseases and many other afflictions. However, the wholeness Christ imparts to the body, mind, and soul is not the same as psychosomatic medicine.

WEAKNESS OF MEDICINE

The physician is not trained to treat spiritual ills such as hate, jealousy, pride, envy, resentment, and guilt. Yet, these spiritual ills have a dominating influence over both soul and body.

Christ is the answer in the cure of them.

THE GREAT PHYSICIAN

I believe the ministries of the Church are wonderful channels of God's healing. They enable the power of the Living Christ to bring healing.

The ill should receive the ministries of the Church, not as a last resort, but concurrently with medical treatment.

SALVATION IS WHOLENESS

Jesus came to bring us salvation. This includes wholeness of body, soul, and spirit.

*God is on the side of good health in all three of these areas. He is actively working toward your good health and mine. Jesus said, "**Ask, and it shall be given you; seek, and ye shall find; knock, and it shall be opened unto you,**" (Matt. 7:7).*

God does not force good health on anyone any more than He forces us to be sinless.

ALL HEALING OF GOD

All healing is of God. He uses the physician, the surgeon, the psychiatrist, the nurse, pharmacist, technician, etc.

However, He alone is the Source of healing. He can also cure disease without help from any of us. After all, He made us and not we ourselves.

Our little finite minds will never understand His infinite power. In fact, with Him there are no incurable diseases or unsolvable problems. There are too many cases of healings through prayer to simply explain such happenings as coincidence or mis-diagnosis. The Lord is in the healing business!

33

THE WEAKNESS OF MEDICINE

It was my privilege to hear Dr. C.B. King, M.D. present the message, "The Weakness of Medicine," at a meeting of the International Order of St. Luke the Physician. His unabridged message is as follows:

I love medicine.

In my discussion this evening I have no intention of disparaging medicine. I am quite cognizant of the great medical progress over the past fifty years and I am proud to be a member of the medical profession.

When I was a child I dreamed of becoming a doctor. I just wanted to help people who were in trouble.

After some years of study and struggle I was graduated from the University of Pennsylvania with a medical degree. After graduation I served eighteen months internship in the Presbyterian Hospital in Philadelphia and then started on my life's work.

For thirty-six years I practiced medicine without knowing that the Church had a healing ministry. That the Church is involved in healing was certainly never mentioned in medical school nor was it ever mentioned from the pulpit, and I was a regular attender. The healing miracles were confined to New Testament times. I took no stock in the healings claimed by the Christian Scientists or the so-called Faith Healers. For me the practice of medicine and the ministry of the Church had nothing in common; they were separated as far as the East is from the West. For me medicine was complete, independent, self-sufficient, and the Church had nothing to offer except prayers for the forgiveness of sins, comfort, and the last rites.

In 1958 I was led into the healing ministry of the Church. As I became more and more involved in the Church's healing ministry I began to recognize certain weaknesses in the practice of medicine. I began to see that medicine is indeed incomplete without the healing touch of our Lord and Savior, the Great Physician, Jesus Christ.

*We read: "**When Jesus saw him lie, and knew that he had been now a long time in that case, he saith unto him, 'Wilt thou be made whole?'**" (John 5:6).*

CHRIST TO THE WHOLE PERSON

The ministry of the Early Apostolic Church was to the whole person. In those days the priest and the physician were often the same man. There was faith but not science in medicine until the time of Hippocrates. For some 300 years the Church ministered to the whole man.

At this time, due to lack of faith and other causes, the healing ministry of the Church gradually died out. The Church became involved with the soul only and Science became involved with the body and the mind. Thus a wide gulf was formed between medicine and the

Church and a weakness developed in the ministry of both the Church and Medicine in that neither considered man as a whole person--body, mind and spirit. In spite of the great scientific advancements that medicine has made in the past 50 years, this weakness persists. I wish to point out this weakness in medicine and wherein lies the remedy.

THE WEAKNESS OF MEDICINE

1. Medicine is weak when it fails to consider disease of the spirit as an underlying cause of disease of soul and body.

2. Medicine is weak when it fails to include the Healing Ministry of the Church alongside scientific skills in the treatment of disease.

3. Medicine is weak when it fails to recognize man as a spiritual being.

4. Medicine is weak when it fails to communicate through prayer with the source of all power and healing--Jesus Christ.

5. Medicine is weak because it is on a horizontal plane. It is humanistic and materialistic.

6. Medicine is weak when it fails to recognize the presence of the Lord Jesus Christ to praise Him and to thank Him.

In recent years medical men are recognizing more and more that disease has in many cases a definitely moral and spiritual, as well as a physical basis. Dr. Rynearson, of the Mayo Clinic, has said, "70% of my patients turn out to be people who have no need of pills, prescriptions or surgery. There is nothing really wrong with them but they are my most dissatisfied patients, *more so than those who have cancer or heart trouble. What they have is functional disease--temporary shortness of breath, rapid heart beat, pain in the chest or stomach, headache and a dozen other complaints for which examinations and laboratory tests can find no physical cause. These are not all people with imaginary disease but individuals with real pain. The pains are due to sore muscles, indigestion, fatigue, or a variety of other causes which can't be helped by medicine or surgery. They leave the physician checkmated because he can't solve their problems with a prescription or treatment of any kind." Yes, physicians today are failing in many cases just as in the time of St. Luke, who recorded, "**And a woman having an issue of blood twelve years, which had spent all her living upon physicians, neither could be healed of any, came behind him and touched the border of his garment, and immediately her issue of blood stanched,**" (Luke 8:43, 44).*

Since becoming involved in the Healing Ministry of the Church, I have become more aware of this weakness in the practice of medicine: that, if we as physicians are truly intent on working to the best interests of our patients, we must consider the soul, the spirit of man as well as his body and mind. We must treat the whole person. We must do this of our own accord in our daily practice of medicine and/or work in close cooperation with the Church. We must believe and consider basic in our treatment of human ills that strong religious beliefs protect people from tension and anxieties which might damage or destroy them if they had no such beliefs; that the Church gives hope and purpose for life which is necessary for human existence. Medicine and the Church must join hands, learn to know and respect the other and believe in each other's part in the total health of man.

At this point the idea of the Church as a Healing Church is just beginning to make inroads into the thought and belief of the Church itself. Very few Seminaries teach the Healing Ministry of the Church. There is a great unbelief among the Christian Clergy as well as among the laity. In many places the Christian physician would have great difficulty in finding a clergy person who believes and knows how to cooperate with him in the Healing Ministry. As I go from place to place introducing the Healing Ministry of the Church I find that medical doctors are more likely to go along with me in accepting the Healing Ministry of the Church than the Clergymen. And so, a great work needs to be done here in the 20th Century Church itself.

I was fortunate because soon after I became involved in the Healing Ministry of the Church, I could say to one of my patients: "Now, I think the real cause of your trouble is spiritual, not medical. There is a church downtown where Spiritual Healing Services are held on Thursday evenings at 7:30. I suggest that you take your first opportunity to attend." And, at times, I would see one of my patients there. But, this happened all too rarely. If I would refer them to another specialist in medicine they would go without question, but they lacked background in knowledge, experience and belief in the Healing Ministry of the Church and so did not follow through with my recommendations. And so, I decided to share with them the good news of the Healing Ministry of the Church and at times pray for them, then and there. This is, of course, extracurricular--beyond the call of duty for a doctor. Nevertheless, some appreciated it.

Now I wish to cite a few cases illustrating the weakness of medicine and how medicine can be helped by cooperating with the Church.

GUILT

Guilt saps the vitality - undermines health.

Guilt destroys one's usefulness in the Kingdom of God.

Medicine has no cure for guilt, but the Church has.

*In James 5:15-16, we read, "**And if he have committed sins, they shall be forgiven him. Confess your faults one to another, and pray for one another, that ye might be healed.**" And in Psalm 51:17, we read, "**A broken and a contrite heart, O God, thou wilt not despise.**" And in Psalm 103:11-12, we read, "**For as the heaven is high above the earth, so great is his mercy toward them that fear him. As far as the east is from the west, so far hath he removed our transgressions from us.**" Yes, God is willing and ready to forgive but the healing of guilt is not simple. One trouble is that we are often unwilling to forgive ourselves. Another trouble is that at times no amends can be made. Another trouble is that often the person has this guilt so deeply embedded within his subconscious that he is not aware of it.*

A patient came into my office last month who was conscious of her guilt and she confessed it to me. For 20 years she had felt this burden of guilt. Due to a misjudgment she felt guilt for causing the loss of useful vision in one of her son's eyes. This feeling of guilt had affected her health and it showed in her face. As a medical doctor I had nothing to offer, but as a Christian I did have something to offer. I reminded her of how the Lord had forgiven King David and how He is more willing to forgive than we are to receive His forgiveness. I told her that through her confession she was already forgiven and that she should reflect the joy that Jesus Christ intended us to have. I have a feeling that she was helped because as she left she said, "I feel as though I had been to church."

Now, I wish to cite another example of guilt beyond the reach of medicine--a guilt undefined, more subtle, often unrecognized. On August 9, 1969, I picked up our local Canton Repository and read this item: Cambridge, Massachusetts--An eminent gynecologist is convinced that guilt plays an important role in convincing many women that oral contraceptives cause minor side effects. "Why should women taking estrogen to relieve painful menstruation so rarely complain of side effects?" asks Dr. Robert Kistner rhetorically. The assistant professor at Harvard Medical School says patients taking estrogen for diseases related to the lining of the womb are remarkedly free from side effects. "I think that many women who are on the oral contraceptives who do have side effects have these side effects because their subconscious minds tell them they're doing something wrong in avoiding pregnancy," the gynecologist says. "If they take the same pill for painful menstruation they feel they are not doing anything wrong and so they feel fine. We've used estrogen for 25 years for painful menstruation and, amazingly enough, we didn't have any of these complaints."

This is just one case of a subtle, unrecognized guilt --causing disease. I am sure you can think of other cases and I know I can. Unresolved guilt can and does cause disease and medicine can do nothing about it. The real cure of guilt is in the realm of the Healing Ministry of the Church through confession and assurance of pardon.

WORRY, ANXIETY AND SORROW

All of these undermine health and medicine has no remedy. Last month Mabel came into my office for an eye examination. She looked thin, tired, anxious and worried. During the office visit the reason for her anxiety came out. Her mother, now in her 80's, was in failing health.

She was unable to carry on her duties keeping house for an unmarried son on the farm. And so Mabel had to go down to the farm some 35 miles away twice a week to help out with the work. The extra work and the anxiety with it was undermining Mabel's health. As a physician I could do nothing, but as a Christian I was led to speak. First, I asked Mabel if her mother knew the Lord and had accepted Him as her Lord and Saviour. The answer was "Yes." Then I asked her if she had ever read the Bible--familiar passages--to her mother and prayed with her. The answer to both questions was "No." Then I suggested that she do both these things and told her how to go about doing them. Then, I said, "Do you know that these times you will share the Lord Jesus Christ with your mother are going to be times of joy and after your mother has gone you will look back on them as among the most precious mo-

*ments of your life." Then she said, "I think you are right.
I am going to do as you say." As she left my office she
thanked me and there was a different look on her face.
Good medicine? Yes. But medicine for the soul as well
as for the body. And I knew that this was in answer to
our early morning prayer at the office that the Lord
would point out some persons who needed spiritual
help and that He would give us the words and the
courage to say them. God does answer prayer.*

FEAR

As time went on, other cases impressed me.

*I found that fear may be a cause of death and that
doctors can do little or nothing about it. One day we
were preparing a man in the operating room for a
routine operation under local anesthesia. Suddenly he
went into profound shock from fear and it was only
with prompt and strong measures that we were able to
save him. If he had died, I would have had to put down
on his death certificate as the cause of death--FEAR.
Prayer in the room or ward of the patient previous to
operation helps to prevent fear of operations and surgeons welcome this ministry of the Church. I have
found that audible prayer in the operating room before
operations is also helpful in bringing the patient to a
calm acceptance of the operation. If the mind and the
heart of the patient is one with the Lord Jesus Christ
there is no room for fear. Scripture teaches us that
"perfect love casteth out fear." Medicine has nothing to
offer for the cure of fear--another weakness of medicine.*

MIGRAINE--RESULT OF RESENTMENT

Another case which impressed me was a case of migraine--severe disabling attacks of migraine--which developed in an office some time ago. A personality clash had developed between two office girls. Resentment was deep--much more so than we realized. Time came when the older girl was removed from the office through death. After this the other girl who had suffered with migraine noticed that the attacks became farther and farther apart and less and less severe until they finally disappeared altogether. We had done everything medically for the migraine attacks but we were helpless from a medical standpoint to cure the resentment. Doctors have no pill to cure resentment which is a form of hate. The cure of hate lies within the Healing Ministry of the Church.

MEDICINE GIVES NO PURPOSE FOR LIVING--NO HOPE

I am reminded of a man who died from lack of hope; lack of purpose for living. Soon after I became interested and involved in the Healing Ministry of the church a man whom I knew very well met a tragic and unnecessary death. Bob had been in failing health for some time and then he was sent into the hospital for a routine gall-bladder operation. The operation was uneventful but four to five days later the wound broke open and it was necessary for Bob to return to the operating room for resuturing the wound. This depressed him very much, more so than the incident called for--more than we realized at the time. A few days after the second operation Bob climbed out of the window and jumped to his death three stories below. It was a great shock to everyone. Everything possible had been done for him from a medical standpoint but almost nothing had been done in the way of spiritual healing. The Church (and the Church included myself) had failed to give Bob hope and purpose for living. We had failed to pray for him and with him. We had failed to tell him that God loved him and had a purpose for him to live; that God had a Plan for the rest of his life here on Earth. We had failed to share with him the healing words of the Living Christ--His great promises. And so, Bob died a spiritual death. This death brought home to me the realization of the weakness of medicine--a profession through which healing could be brought to mind and body but not to the spirit. As I dwelt on this I realized that some of my patients had lived who in my opinion should have died while others died who should have lived. I came to a realization that there was an unfathomable something in the heart of man above and beyond the scope of medicine and that this something was important when it came to life or death. I learned that man is a trinity and must be treated as such. Somehow or other, man must be given the Balm of Gilead, the healing love of the Lord Jesus Christ if he is to be made whole.

It is not in the realm of medicine to give purpose for living. WHY you should keep on living. And herein lies one of the weaknesses of medicine.

RESENTMENT

Medicine has nothing to offer as a cure for resentment.

Resentment is a form of hate and is a subtle cause of arthritis.

One of my favorite books is "Arthritis, Medicine and Spiritual Laws," by Dr. Loring T. Swain (Chilton Company).

In this book Dr. Swain tells of many cases of arthritis caused by resentment. During the past year I spoke to a large Sunday School class in a nearby city. In my talk I spoke of this book and of resentment as a cause of arthritis. There was a man in the audience who had a severe wry neck as a result of an automobile accident. He had gone everywhere for relief, but to no avail. Being a religious man he asked the Lord in his prayers that night to point out any man against whom he had resentment. The Lord told him that he had great resentment against his boss. And so, the next day this man went to his boss, confessed his hate and asked for his forgiveness. And, do you know, his pain in the neck was healed.

I saw this man sometime later and he told me that sometimes his pain returns and that he knows now the cause--it is due to some return of his former resentment.

*Jesus Christ summed up all the laws of the prophets in two sentences--"**Love the Lord thy God with all thy heart, and with all thy soul, and with all thy mind. This is the first and great commandment. And the second is like unto it. Thou shalt love thy neighbor as thyself,**" (**Matt. 23:37**). This man had been to many doctors and* *was not healed. He was healed through confession and forgiveness. His healing was beyond the sphere of medicine. This again shows the weakness of medicine in the healing of disease brought about because of spiritual ills.*

VALUE OF COOPERATION OF MEDICINE AND THE CHURCH

Since man is a trinity, there must be close cooperation between medicine and the Church if the Whole man is to be healed. I was called to see a patient friend of mine. She was in very poor health, having just recently returned from the hospital. She was worried and distressed about her only good eye and suffered much pain. Her mother had had glaucoma and she feared that she had it also. Examination of her eye showed nothing more serious than a mild conjunctivitis. She was greatly relieved of her fear and distress by the assurance that there was nothing seriously wrong with her eye. I felt that this patient needed something more than the ointment for her eye. And so I asked her husband to stand at one side of the bed and hold her left hand while I stood on the other side and held her right hand and then I prayed for the healing touch of the Lord Jesus Christ. She thanked me and seemed very grateful. Then I suggested that she call the pastor of a church nearby--one whom I knew to be a believer in the Healing Ministry of the Church--and ask him to come and anoint her with oil and pray for her healing. Then she told me that she was a member of this church and that she would be happy to follow my suggestion. The pastor complied with her request and came weekly to anoint her with oil and pray for her healing. And this is the way it should be, my friends, the physician and the pastor, each ministering to the patient in his own way, cooperating for the best interests of the whole person.

A poem appeared in SHARING Magazine, written by Rev. W. Barrett, entitled, "Your Patient, My Parishioner." He wrote it from the viewpoint of a pastor. I have rewritten it from the viewpoint of a physician and entitled it,

YOUR PARISHIONER, MY PATIENT

Across the patient's bed, we face each other.
You in your black coat, with a prayerbook in
*   your hand;*
I, in my white coat, a stethoscope in my hand.
At the beginning we were one, since the beginning
we have always been together, unavoidably
*   related.*
And when you were true to your ordination vows
and I was true to the oath of medicine,
The center of interest has been, is and must
*   always be*
in the man on the bed, your parishioner,
my patient, God's creation.
And if we work in unity together,
the patient will come to see, to know,
to love the Father God,
Who through us, in us, by us and in spite of us,
remains the Ultimate One,
"Who healeth all our diseases
And forgiveth our iniquities."

GOD'S
LOVE
AND
POWER

34

INNER HEALING THROUGH GOD'S LOVE

The great need of our day is for Inner Healing. This I can state in the presence of much physical distress on every hand.

However, regardless of how devastating a physical affliction may be, it still is not as dreadful as the hell of inner turmoil and conflict.

Betty Tapscott in her excellent book, Inner Healing, writes, "Inner healing is the healing of the inner man: the mind, the emotions, the painful memories, the dreams. It is the process through prayer whereby we are set free from feelings of resentment, self-pity, depression, guilt, fear, sorrow, hatred, inferiority, condemnation, or worthlessness, etc."

I am intrigued with the way the Apostle Paul presented inward victory. *"When you came to Christ he set you free from your evil desires, not by a bodily operation of circumcision but by a spiritual operation, the baptism of your souls. For in baptism you see how your old, evil nature died with him and was buried with him; and then you came up out of death with him into a new life because you trusted the Word of the mighty*

God who raised Christ from the dead. You were dead in sins, and your sinful desires were not yet cut away. Then he gave you a share in the very life of Christ, for he forgave all your sins, and blotted out the charges proved against you, the list of commandments which you had not obeyed. He took this list of sins and destroyed it by nailing it to Christ's cross. In this way God took away Satan's power to accuse you of sin and God openly displayed to the whole world Christ's triumph at the cross where your sins were all taken away," (Col. 2:11-15 LB).

BACK TO BASICS

Where do you start with Inner Healing? How does one begin the pilgrimage of spiritual surgery which will bring the Inner Healing so desired and needed?

I believe it comes most frequently with a return to the basic concept of the Lord's love for each individual. One's basic relationship to Jesus is the key to ultimate Inner Healing. Herein lies the solution to sin, sickness, and the feelings of unworthiness.

A person came to me out of deep desperation. He had received counseling from six psychiatrists and several clergy over a period of two decades. He would at times receive temporary relief. However, his nagging inner problems and turmoil continued. He was still living a tormented and defeated life. He had come to me hoping for some help.

It was during the first counseling period that I felt led to discuss with him the basic problem of his relationship to God through our Lord Jesus Christ.

In my opinion, he would never be delivered of inner turmoil until he had come to grips with his relationship with the Lord. I presented the dynamic but simple message of God's love for him and he seemed to change immediately. He realized his sins were forgiven. He was a new creature in Christ Jesus!

I will never forget one of his statements after the reality of the Lord's presence and forgiveness got through to him. He said, "Why didn't someone explain this to me years ago?" The Good News met his most urgent need and then further Inner Healing took place. Today he is even better.

GOD LOVES YOU

What was the good news which I presented to him? It was simply, "God loves you." He was like many I know who try desperately to love God. However, they cannot accept the fact God loves them. In their own way they are trying to love God and yet feel estranged from the Lord. Many times this is because they have not met Jesus as their personal Savior and perfect sacrifice for them before God. This creates the situation of love going only one way, and this is devastating.

Some of the most tragic situations I have encountered are those where love goes only one way. I see it with couples when one spouse desperately loves and the other has lost or never had love for their mate. Or with the teenager who feels her parents do not love her, even though in reality they love her very much. The result in the teenager's life is chaos.

Or another example of the frustrations of unre-turned love is the high school girl madly in love with the star football player who does not even notice her. Here again love is going only one way and the results are terrifying. Love, to be vital and dynamic, must be a two-way street.

The secret of life is not our frantic efforts to love God, but our humble acceptance of the fact that He loves us. It is reported that the famous Karl Barth was asked, "What is the greatest truth you have learned from your years of study of Scripture and theology? His answer, "Jesus loves me this I know, for the Bible tells me so."

ACCEPT GOD'S LOVE

The first step to your Inner Healing is to accept God's love for you. He loves you far more than you could ever love Him. Respond to His love. Jesus Christ's real love leads to your real life.

35

INNER HEALING OF THE MEMORIES

You may ask, "Why the emphasis upon healing of the memories when there is a discussion on Inner Healing? Was not all of this cared for when I came to Jesus and received Him as my Lord and Saviour?"

Yes, it was cared for by Him. However, many do not realize this. They do not appropriate His healing to every aspect of their lives. Many continue to carry burdens and to suffer emotionally, spiritually, and physically in ways from which they can be delivered.

Just because you are a believer is no reason to automatically expect you will know and understand all spiritual laws. You may own a farm, but this does not necessarily mean you are an excellent farmer. In like manner, you may be a child of the King, but this is not a valid reason to assume you understand everything about His Kingdom. Thus, the healing of the memories is a vast new frontier for most believers.

JESUS IN THE NOW

Any consideration of healing of the memories necessitates the important truth Jesus is in the NOW. He is and always has been. A simple and yet profound truth is that, for Jesus, tomorrow will never be and yesterday never was. It is always this moment for Jesus.

"Before Abraham was, I am," (John 8:58).

"Jesus Christ the same yesterday, and today, and forever," (Heb. 13:8).

INNER HURTS

Many of you carry inner hurts which have long since been forgotten as far as the incident is concerned. But the consequences remain. Many of the hurts are small ones but their accumulative effect is devastating to your emotional and spiritual life.

Some hurts are enormous and leave an immediate and powerful impact which you may never fully forget. Yet, you yearn to be relieved of them. Whatever the magnitude or quantity, the net result is an aching heart and frustrated life. You yearn to have the inner drag removed and your spirit set free.

TRUTH NEEDED

One of the truths you need to really understand and accept is that Jesus is the same yesterday, today, and forever. Most of the inner conflict concerning memories is conquered when this truth is grasped. It is no more difficult for Jesus to heal the past than for Him to heal a present affliction. This truth, once grasped, removes the negative power of the past and the haunting fear of the future. He can forgive your sins as well as heal your body, (Matt. 9:1-8).

Jesus can heal any aspect of your memories. He was there when the event occurred. The past is always NOW for Him. There is no time to the timeless Jesus. His forgiveness, cleansing, and healing power are manifest in every second of your life. He is always there.

May you use your God-given gift of memory to go back through your life and let Jesus heal in all areas. Your mind can prayerfully recall the events of today, yesterday, last week, last month, last year, the past many years, your early twenties, teenage years, Jr. High, elementary grades, kindergarten, pre-school, and the moments of your first conscious recollections. You can even ask for the Lord's healing to come to the moments of your birth and into all the events surrounding your entrance into the world. He was even with you when you were in your mother's womb. In other words, all of your life can be engulfed in the healing love of our Lord!

FOR YOU

The healing of the memories is for you. Probably everyone reading this chapter has some area of memory which needs the healing touch of the Lord. Isn't it good news to know He can and will heal your memories? He is in the NOW of your life--be it yesterday or 80 years ago--that the event took place.

I encourage you to permit Jesus to enter into every area of your past. He will frequently reveal areas of need you had long forgotten and often times there is a need for you to forgive someone or seek forgiveness for yourself. He will bring an awareness which will issue forth into a wonderful healing.

FREE AT LAST

You have permitted Christ to sweep back through your memories. You have asked for His healing in every situation you have forgiven and have been forgiven. Now, do not become a garbage collector. Do not gather up all your hurts from whence you have been delivered. You have given your burdens to Him and He is most willing to keep them. He does not want you to have them any more.

"Cast all your care upon him; for he careth for you," (I Pet. 5:7). Please consider the following verses: II Cor. 3:17; John 8:36.

36

SOME STEPS TO INNER HEALING

We live in a very fast-moving and mobile age. A classic example of the mobility of our society and the frantic search for thrills is an event which happened during the Bicentennial year of our nation.

The Concord plane loaded in Texas and flew to Paris for celebration of New Year's Eve. The New Year was greeted in Paris. The plane took off and the passengers celebrated over the Atlantic. Because the plane can travel over 1,300 miles per hour, they were able to celebrate again in Washington, D.C., still on New Year's Eve!

As exciting as multiple celebrations of the New Year may be, it won't help one of those privileged people spiritually. A few rich people were able to make this historic journey. However, people of all ages and status in life need to make the Journey to inner wholeness.

IMMOBILIZED

Isn't it a shame that in this mobile day so many are bound and immobile? They are immobilized by the forces of evil and even Satan himself.

Inner healing eludes many even though they so desperately desire it.

YOUR INHERITANCE

Every believer has an inheritance which includes freedom in the Lord, (John 8:36; II Cor. 3:17).

You need not remain a prisoner of your past nor of your future. Jesus is in the NOW of your life. Your inner turmoil can be healed through Him.

Howard Hughes, who was one of America's richest men, illustrates so vividly the way many of us live spiritually. TIME magazine said this about the multibillionaire:

"...a tortured, troubled man who wallowed in self-neglect, lapsed into periods of near-lunacy, lived without comfort or joy in prison-like conditions and ultimately died for lack of a medical device that his own foundation had helped to develop."

Many believers live as helplessly in the spirit. They do not appropriate the power available for the inner healing which is desired. They miss the eternal truths expressed by Paul when he wrote,

"But my God shall supply all your need according to his riches in glory by Christ Jesus," (Phil. 4:19).

STEPS TO INNER HEALING

There are some suggested steps which are very helpful when it comes to receiving inner healing. I list below a few of them:

1. Look only to the Lord for your wholeness-- There can be no real release for you and yours through false gods or the occult. The Lord is your Healer.

"Regard not them that have familiar spirits, neither seek after wizards, to be defiled by them; I am the Lord your God," (Lev. 19:31; Deut. 18:9-14).

2. Trust in Jesus Christ only as the giver of freedom, peace and purpose--the basic need of each person is fellowship with the Lord. This can be achieved through Christ and sets the stage for a wholeness within and without. The Scriptures point the way of confession which brings deliverance.

"That if thou shalt confess with thy mouth the Lord Jesus, and shalt believe in thine heart that God hath raised him from the dead, thou shalt be saved," (Rom. 10:9).

"If we confess our sins, he is faithful and just to forgive us our sins, and to cleanse us from all unrighteousness," (I John 1:9).

3. Forgive any and all--God has chosen to limit Himself in some areas. One such area is forgiveness. He says we cannot really be forgiven until we are willing to forgive. Resentfulness is the root of much illness. The inner turmoil of inner resentment will frequently manifest itself in emotional and physical disorders. Plato ages ago is reported to have said,

"All diseases of the body proceed from the mind or soul."

An unknown author penned the following profound insights: "Saints are men who permit God's forgiveness to come into them so fully that not only are their sins washed out, but also their very selves, their egos, and the root of their self-will...I forgive to the level that I have been forgiven, and if that level is moderate (because...I wanted only to lose my vices and not myself) I can forgive only people who have offended moderately, and my forgiveness helps them only moderately."

The only aspect of the model prayer which was amplified by our Lord dealt with forgiveness, (Matt. 6:14, 15). Forgive and live!

37

A PRAYER FOR INNER HEALING

There is no magic formula for Inner Healing. However, there are some steps which have helped thousands. One of these steps is to pray a sincere prayer for Inner Healing.

This prayer for Inner Healing is not a perfect prayer. You may desire to revise it to fit your own needs and life situations. Some of the aspects covered in the prayer will not be applicable to you. However, I suggest you pray the prayer and let the Spirit of the Living Christ permeate every facet of your being.

PREPARATION FOR PRAYER

There are some steps which will help prepare you for this prayer. I would encourage you, first of all, to quiet yourself before the Lord. Endeavor to the best of your ability to quiet your mind and try to shut out every thought and focus all on Jesus.

Then seek to quiet your heart or emotions. You can do this for at least a few moments regardless of the distractions in your life or the frustrations you may be facing.

Now move to the quieting of your body from the top of your head to the bottom of your feet.

Now after you have quieted your entire being, keep in mind that the Holy Spirit is going to enter every thought, every emotion, and every cell and fiber of your body. You are open to God Who helps and heals. You rebuke all the forces of unrighteousness and illness.

As you pray, I hope you will appropriate into your present and past life the forgiveness, power and strength of the Lord Jesus.

Many find it most helpful to pray this prayer out loud:

THE PRAYER

Lord Jesus, I pray that at this very moment I will realize you are receiving me just as I am. You know my every thought of each second of my present and past life.

You know every hurt I have experienced and fear I carry, and every painful memory which haunts me.

FUTURE

You are completely aware of the areas of guilt that leave me defeated. Now Lord Jesus, I want to give to you my future. A future which I often dread and fear because of the pressures and problems of the past as well as the uncertainty of what lies ahead. I ask that you reach into my mind right now in such a way as to take away the fear of the future. Help me to walk into that future fully aware of your power, presence and love.

Enable me to leave the future in your hands, and with confidence I now commit my life to you anew and at greater depth. I know that the peace you give this moment is the same peace I can have in the future. It is your peace. The world did not give it. The world cannot take it away from me. Yes, Lord, I believe as never before that my future is in Your hands. I thank you, Lord Jesus, for healing me abundantly. I invite you to come into the areas which weigh heaviest on my heart and mind. Heal my anxiety, enter into the very center of all my present problems, bring wholeness in the midst of my illness, and permeate the lives of those I love with your glory and power. I believe you are in the NOW of my life and are bringing just what I need to face each moment and each situation.

PAST

And now Lord Jesus, I invite you to heal my memories of the past. The immediate, as well as the distant past I bring to you. I pray you will heal my yesterday, my past week, month, and year. In areas where I have failed--please forgive. The troubled areas which cling to my mind and heart I submit to you and ask that you please cleanse.

I want you to walk through the conscious memory of my working years. Bring your healing to the many hurts, frustrations, and failures of people and positions.

I open to you the years when I left home to establish my own home. During this period heal the scars which developed through relationships with parents, friends, and with spouse. Where there have been resentments, may they be replaced and removed by your Spirit. Where frustrations have left their ugly scars, I turn them all over to you.

I bring my teenage years to you, Lord Jesus. It was a time when I rapidly moved through the trauma of new emotions. There were new fears and alot of painful memories. Many of the incidents as a teenager left me humiliated and with feelings of guilt. I give these years to you and thank you for the healing you bring to them.

My junior high years come to my mind Lord Jesus. I pray you will move back through them and help me.

Please enter my elementary grade years as I started to go to school. I had so many new things to face and new facts to learn. There were new faces and many new adjustments.

Lord, I invite you into my preschool years even though I can't consciously remember much about them. Let your healing come and set me free from those things of this period of my life which would hinder fullness of life now.

Jesus, I know you were present at the moment of my birth. Present during the moments of the trauma of my breaking into this strange and terrifying world. May I feel and know your peace surrounding my birth. Please move through the months I was in my mother's womb. May all those moments be bathed in your love and tender care. I want you to be in every emotion of my days from conception to now. I am grateful you have walked with me back through my life. Thank you for your Inner Healing. Amen!

38

THE BIBLE AND HEALING

Many believers do not appreciate the power of the Holy Scriptures. They fail to appreciate that the Bible contains the most needed messages of our day.

If I were to give you a quart of diamonds, they would not be as valuable and practical as a proper understanding of the Word. Diamonds cannot suffice for obtaining and maintaining the spiritual, physical, and emotional health you desire. Many almost literally die grasping for "diamonds" when what they really need is to understand the truth of the Holy Bible.

"He is eating better, and we are encouraged. His appetite is returning." These are common statements when one who is ill begins to recover. The desire for food is an indication that health is returning.

In like manner, I feel the great hunger for God's word today is a sign of returning health to many churches. The desire to study the Word at depth is greater today than probably in the entire history of the world. In every nation there are thousands hungering for an understanding of the Bible. New translations of the Book have sales in the millions. Bible study groups are increasing daily. It is a new day for God's people, with former communist countries open to God's word like never before.

How important is the Word? What can we find in the Word to help us for each day we face? The writer of Proverbs tells us that health shall spring forth from the Word when it is rightly received and believed.

"My son, attend to my words: incline thine ear unto my sayings. Let them not depart from thine eyes; keep them in the midst of thine heart. For they are life unto those that find them, and health to all their flesh," (Prov. 4:20-22).

These words speak to us today!

The Bible does not have to remain a closed Book. The Lord wants you to read and to understand it. A careful study of the Word reveals the Lord's deep desire for your wholeness. You discover that the Lord Jesus was revealed for all of your diseases as well as for all of your sins. This is a message to be received joyfully and to be understood by every believer.

"...Himself took our infirmities, and bare our sickness," (Matt. 8:17).

"Who his own self bare our sins in his own body on the tree, that we, being dead to sins, should live unto righteousness: by whose stripes ye were healed," (I Pet. 2:24).

"Beloved, I wish above all things that thou mayest prosper and be in health, even as thy soul prospereth," (III John v. 2).

If you were to discover a cure for just one disease you would be heralded as a great scientist. It is a mystery to me that the Word is neglected so much when it presents a message of healing and hope for all diseases. The Old and New Testaments both present the Lord as your healer.

"Who forgiveth all thine iniquities; who healeth all thy diseases," (Ps. 103:3).

"And Jesus went about all Galilee, teaching in their synagogues, and preaching the Gospel of the kingdom, and healing all manner of sickness and all manner of disease among the people," (Matt. 4:23).

Our Lord told us the message of healing and miracles will continue until the end of the age. *"...he that believeth on me, ...greater works...shall he do,"* (John 14:12).

The Bible is not a book of magic, but a book of miracles. It does not present false hope, only a sure, blessed, and glorious hope! (Titus 2:13, 14).

39

CHRIST'S MINISTRY

The Good News of the Christian faith is that Jesus Christ has come to be the Savior of the world. He has revealed to us the Father's love. He was willing to give His own life for us while we were yet sinners.

How did the Lord and others of His day see this expression of His power and love? How did He tangibly express His desire for salvation (wholeness) for individuals of His day and for you and me today?

You will be encouraged as you consider the emphasis our Lord put upon wholeness of body, soul, and spirit. Please prayerfully consider the following concerning our Lord's ministry:

CHRIST'S OWN APPRAISAL

There are several occasions when Christ refers to His own ministry. He could have said anything He desired. It is interesting to me how many times His summary of His own efforts stressed healing.

1. He chose a passage of healing and hope to explain His ministry to those present at the synagogue:

"The Spirit of the Lord is upon me for the Lord hath anointed me to preach good tidings unto the meek; he hath sent me to bind up the broken hearted, to proclaim liberty to the captives, and the opening of the prison to them that are bound; To proclaim the acceptable year of the Lord, and the day of vengeance of our God; to comfort all that mourn..." (Luke 4:16-24).

2. The Lord's response to the disciples of John included the centrality of healing in His ministry. He did not send John a deep theological or philosophical answer:

"Now when John had heard in the prison the works of Christ, he sent two of his disciples, and said unto him, Art thou he that should come or do we look for another? Jesus answered and said to them, 'Go and show John again those things which ye do hear and see: The blind receive their sight, and the lame walk, the lepers are cleansed, and the deaf hear, the dead are raised up, and the poor have the gospel preached to them...'" (Matt. 11:2-6).

3. Jesus' response to the Pharisees who were concerned Herod was going to kill Him was one of love and power. He wanted Herod to know His ministry included healing the body, soul, and spirit of those who came to Him:

"And he said unto them, Go ye, and tell that fox, 'Behold, I cast out devils, and I do cures today and tomorrow, and the third day I shall be perfected,'" (Luke 13:32).

4. Jesus pointed out the difference between His ministry and that of John the Baptist. He showed the working of miracles to be that difference. Miracles

to Him were the distinguishing facet of His earthly ministry. The witness to His ministry was not that He preached love and John preached repentance. No! The difference was what He did through His miracles:

"But I have greater witness than that of John: for the works which the Father hath given me to finish, the same works that I do, bear witness of me, that the Father hath sent me," (John 5:36).

5. What Jesus told His disciples He must do stressed miracles. They were what determined if He were truly fulfilling the will of the Lord in His life:

"Jesus answered, Neither hath this man sinned, nor his parents: but that the works of God should be made manifest in him. I must work the works of him that sent me, while it is day: the night cometh, when no man can work," (John 9:3,4).

6. Jesus could have mentioned a number of things which should lead individuals to believe, such as His message of love, His ability to use parables, His willingness to die for others, etc. You will notice He used the working of miracles as the thing which should lead to belief in His being in the Father and the Father in Him:

"If I do not the works of my Father, believe me not. But if I do, though ye believe not me, believe the works: that ye may know, and believe, that the Father is in me, and I in him," (John 10:37, 38).

CHRIST'S ASSIGNMENT

The above speaks of Christ's appraisal of His ministry. Now we consider the assignments He gave to His followers. Isn't it interesting He did not in-struct them to form committees or to be expert organizers. He did not even assign them to develop creeds or structures of worship. The following scrip-ture references clearly show what he wanted His followers to do:

1. He chose to give the assignment unto His 12 disciples of proclaiming the Kingdom of God is at hand and of healing the sick:

"And when he called unto him his twelve disciples, he gave them power against unclean spirits, to cast them out and to heal all manner of sickness and all manner of disease. And as ye go, preach, saying, 'The kingdom of heaven is at hand.' Heal the sick, cleanse the lepers, raise the dead, cast out devils: freely ye have received, freely give," (Matt. 10:1, 7, 8).

This assignment to the twelve is also reported in the following references: Mark 3:13-15; Luke 9:1, 2.

2. The Lord's assignment to the 70 disciples was for them to proclaim wholeness:

"And heal the sick that are therein and say unto them, 'The kingdom of God is come nigh unto you'...And the seventy returned again with joy, saying, 'Lord, even the devils are subject unto us through thy name,'" (Luke 10:9, 17).

3. The Lord let His followers know what would be the sign of their being in Him. He told them to lay hands on the sick and to behold His power being released:

"These signs shall follow them that believe; ... they shall lay hands on the sick, and they shall recover," (Mark 16:17, 18).

4. The Great Commission given unto His followers for every age certainly included proclaiming the message of healing. He states believers should teach all they have been commanded. Certainly they were commanded to heal the sick:

"Teaching them to observe all things whatsoever I have commanded you: and, lo, I am with you alway, even unto the end of the world," (Matt. 28:20).

5. The Lord's prediction concerning His future followers was one of great power and wholeness:

"Verily, verily, I say unto you, He that believeth on me, the works that I do shall he do also; and greater works than these shall he do; because I go unto my Father," (John 14:12).

OTHER'S APPRAISAL

The above presents how the Lord appraised His earthly ministry. Also, what he expected and continues to expect from His followers. Here is what others saw as the outstanding characteristic of His ministry:

1. Herod was not bothered by what Jesus said, but by what He did. He was shaken by the healings of our Lord:

"And said unto his servants, 'This is John the Baptist; he is risen from the dead; and therefore mighty works do shew forth themselves in him, '" Matt. 14:2.

2. Nicodemus was intrigued by Christ because of the power he witnessed issuing forth from our Lord. He did not come to the Lord because of Christ's sermons or administration ability. He came because He knew no one could do the miracles Christ did, except He be from God:

"The same came to Jesus by night, and said unto Him, Rabbi, we know thou art a teacher come from God; for no man can do these miracles that thou doest, except God be with him," (John 3:2).

3. The miracles of Christ are what led John's disciples to appraise His ministry as powerful. This is the facet of the ministry which they conveyed to John and which really caught John's attention:

"Now when John had heard in the prison the works of Christ, he sent two of his disciples, And said unto him, 'Art thou he that should come, or do we look for another?'" (Matt. 11:2, 3).

4. Peter's summary of our Lord's ministry was that it was a ministry of healing:

"How God anointed Jesus of Nazareth with the Holy Ghost and with power: who went about doing good, and healing all that were oppressed of the devil; for God was with him," (Acts 10:38).

5. The two on their way to Emmaus felt the Lord's mighty works were known by all. They saw the works as the outstanding characteristic of the ministry of our Lord:

"And he said unto them, 'What things?' And they said unto him, 'Concerning Jesus of Nazareth, who was a prophet mighty in deed and word before God and all the people, '" (Luke 24:19).

6. The members of the early church witnessed the healing power of the Lord. It was this type of ministry which they desired and requested of the Lord. They wanted the power to flow through them to His glory:

"And now, Lord, behold their threatenings: and grant unto thy servants, that with all boldness they may

speak thy word. By stretching forth thine hand to heal; and that signs and wonders may be done by the name of thy holy child Jesus," (Acts 4:19, 10).

CONCLUSION

If His appraisal of His own ministry included healings, if He assigned His followers to proclaim wholeness, and if others were attracted to and appraised His ministry from the viewpoint of miracles, should not Christ's ministry of healing be our ministry today?

40

SURVIVING STRESS

Excessive stress and the devastating results of it are on every hand today. Many books have been written and many seminars held to help individuals cope with stress.

I present the following suggestions to help believers cope with excessive stress.

ALWAYS WITH YOU

The world is going to be with you always. Stress is going to be a part of this world. It is not going to change simply because you worry and fret. It will never be a perfect world until Jesus returns. Most things are not going to change as you want, nor will all people change as you might desire. Imperfect as the world may be, it is the best one you will live in this side of eternity! You must learn to live with the stress and tensions of our day.

PURPOSEFUL LIVING

The key to conquering tension is to discover your purpose for living. All else is pretty much in vain if purpose is absent.

Commitment to Jesus Christ will add depth and desire to all areas of your life. He is the One who gives the abundant life!

TALK THERAPY

It is true that "confession is good for the soul." It is also good for the body. You will discover verbalizing what is troubling you will bring great relief from emotional turmoil.

It will also bring new insight into your problems. It will often help you to become aware of solutions you would otherwise have missed. An honest, heart-to-heart talk with someone in whom you have confidence is excellent therapy.

ESCAPE

Problems are never solved by escapism. However, to get away from a situation for awhile is often a good thing. Tensions at home, office, school need balanced with time away from them. This enables you to catch your emotional breath. You see yourself and your situation from a different perspective.

PHYSICAL ACTIVITY

It is surprising how different your situation will appear after a game of tennis, a long walk, some hours in the garden, or after scrubbing down walls!

It is better pent-up emotions be released through physical activity than through excessive response of your glands.

Dr. Frank Katch of Queens College in New York reports concerning women in his classes who are running up to a half hour a day. "...their stamina is up, their weight is down and their pride of accomplishment is terrific."

PLAN YOUR WORK

What do you do when the magnitude of your responsibilities staggers you? A positive response would be to list the tasks which you must accomplish. Place priorities upon each and seek to accomplish them one by one in order of priority. Keep your list and goals within reason. Superman exists only in the comic book. You are limited in strength, knowledge, talent and time. Accept your limitations and set "possible" goals for yourself.

LIVE AND LET LIVE

Honestly appraise your own abilities and at the same time be charitable toward others. Many keep themselves in constant turmoil because they expect too much of others.

May you resist the temptation of trying to make others over to suit yourself. Seek to live to the glory of God and to the fullest. Give others the opportunity to do likewise. The overly critical person will become an overly tense person.

WILLING TO BE LOVED

It is intriguing to me that many seek desperately to be loving, but are unwilling to be loved. Even their good works and kind words serve as instruments to keep others at arm's length. You will discover relief from many tensions if you are willing to receive the love and warmth of others.

RE-CREATION

Everyone needs to be re-created from time to time. Recreation comes into proper perspective when it is viewed as re-creation. Two individuals were given the assignment of lifting a few ounces with their index finger. One did it constantly and was finally unable to go on. The other rested after every three lifts. He could have gone on for years. Even Jesus took time to pause from the grind of life (Mark 1:35, 6:46; Luke 5:15, 16, 6:12, 9:18).

41

DEFEATING DEPRESSION

I am appalled at the number of Christians who are living in an almost constant state of depression. It seems depression is reaching epidemic proportions even among believers.

The suggestions I offer for defeating depression may sound simple, but I sincerely believe they are worthy of your careful consideration.

DEPRESSION

The definition of depression is "the act of depressing, or the state of being depressed; low spirits or vitality; dejection, melancholy."

The depressed individual feels unhappy, useless, without purpose in life, and almost to the place of wondering if they can go on with life.

INWARD

Depression comes from within and not from without. No amount of water can sink a ship until it gets on the inside. The smallest vessel ever made could sail the Atlantic ocean if water did not get on the inside. However, the largest ship ever built will sink in a placid river if water gets on the inside.

In like manner, no circumstance in life can really defeat and depress until you permit it to overwhelm you within.

John Ford put it very well when he wrote, "Melancholy is not, as you conceive, indisposition of body, but the mind's disease."

COMMIT

You must come to see that the problem of depression which you have within must be dealt with by the only One who can really reach within the deepest recesses of your heart.

I would pray you will turn to Jesus in full reliance upon His desire and power to save, sustain, and to satisfy.

You may say, "I have already committed my life to the Lord." If you are deeply depressed, I would urge you to review your life and heart. Seek to determine if your commitment is of the heart, or principally of the intellect.

"Trust in the Lord with all thine heart; and lean not unto thine own understanding," Prov. 3:5. See also: Isa. 26:3; Mark 9:23; John 14:27.

Above all else you will want to see Jesus. Leonardo da Vinci had finished painting "The Last Supper." He invited all his students to see it. They gasped a chorus of "Ohs" and "Ahs." The students then began to look at the exquisite lace table cloth on the Lord's table which was the product of their master's genius. They all spoke to him about it. Leonardo reached for his brush, dipped it in his paints, and with one full stroke wiped out the lacework. He then turned to his students and said, "You fools, look at the Master's face!"

GOD'S PLAN

Believe me when I say the Lord desires wholeness and joy for you. Jesus gives abundant life!

"I am come that you might have life," John 10:10. Force your mind into sunshine thoughts. Do this especially when your mind starts the "instant replays" of old fears and depressive thoughts. Glen Clark wrote so beautifully of God's Plan. It is as follows:

God has a plan for me. It is hidden within me, just as the oak is hidden within the acorn, or the rose within the bud. As I yield myself more fully to God, His Plan expresses itself more perfectly through me. I can tell when I am in tune with it, for then my mind and heart are filled with a deep inner peace. This peace fills me with a sense of security, with joy, and a desire to take steps that are a part of the Plan.

God's plan for me is a perfect part of a larger Plan. It is designed for the good of all and not for me alone. It is a many-sided Plan and reaches out through all the people I meet. All the events and people who come into my life are instruments for the unfolding of this Plan.

God has chosen those people He wants me to know, to love and to serve. We are continually being drawn to one another in ways that are not coincidental. I pray that I may become a better instrument to love and to serve, that I may become more worthy to receive the love and service of others.

I ask the Father within me for only those things which He wants me to have. I know that these benefits will come to me at the right time and in the right way. This inner knowing frees my mind and heart from all fear, greed, jealousy, anger, and resentment. It gives me courage and faith to do those things which I feel are mine to do.

I no longer look with envy at what others are receiving, nor do I compare myself with them. Therefore, I do not cut myself off from God, the Giver of all good things.

God's gifts to me can be many times greater than I am now receiving. I pray that I may increase my capacity to give and to receive for I can give only as I receive, and receive only as I give.

I believe that when I cannot do those things I desire to do, it is because God has closed one door only to leave ajar a better and larger door. If I do not see that door just ahead, it is because I have not seen, heard, or obeyed God's guidance.

It is then that God uses the trouble or seeming failure which may result to help me face myself, and see the new opportunity before me.

The real purpose of my life is to find God within my own mind and heart, and to help my fellow men. I thank my Father for each experience which helps me to surrender myself to His will. For only as I lose myself in the consciousness of His Great Presence can His Plan for my life be fulfilled.

I would suggest that you read and reread the above Plan. It so beautifully presents insights which will help you grasp the Lord's love and care for you.

Your depression can be defeated. I pray you may believe...with all your heart, mind, and soul. It is the Lord who is your Helper. Turn to Him. Amen!

42

FEAR

There is no doubt that depression has reached an epidemic proportion in our nation. Granted, it is normal to sometimes feel blue and even at moments to be depressed.

However, extreme depression has hit thousands. They find themselves unable to really cope with all the realities of life. Often they do not sleep well, or they feel tired and worn out all the time. Many are bored with life, and perhaps even suffer a loss of desire for food and even sex.

Fear is usually a prominent part of the dreaded state of depression. There are some tangible steps you can take to face and to overcome your fears.

LIST YOUR FEARS

An exercise of immense value to many, and which may be to you, is to write down a list of everything which depresses you. You should be brutally honest and leave none out. You may want to share your list with a friend, or you may choose never to share it. One thing you will discover is your depression will probably boil down to some area of fear in your life.

You may desire to pray right now for the Lord to reveal unto whom you should talk concerning your fears. Your list will serve a very practical purpose as you share it with the one the Lord leads into your life for this purpose.

WORK ON YOUR FEARS

Begin to work on deleting your fears from your mind and life. You may want to begin with some lesser ones, but do not unduly delay dealing with your worst fear or fears. Claim the promise, *"God hath not given us the spirit of fear, but of power, and of love, and of a sound mind,"* II Tim. 1:7.

Speak this scripture over and over, and rebuke the devourer with it. After all, the word of God is our "sword" to fight the devil. It is the whole armour we need to put on to face each moment of each day, (Eph. 6:12-18).

FEARS TO JESUS

Jesus is the only one who can really handle your fears. He wants you to give them to Him. Picture your fears as a bag of garbage. You tightly seal the bag and cast it at the feet of Jesus. You may want to audibly pray as you tell Him how you feel about your fears.

Do not become a garbage collector who takes back the garbage which was left with the Lord. *"Cast your every care on the Lord,"* I Pet. 5:7.

Giving your fears to Jesus means you are trying to realistically confront them. The Lord is your defender. He can and will help you throw off the shackles of fear in your life.

It is not what you fear which creates the problem. It is the intensity of that fear.

An individual came to our healing service who was plagued with a fear of dogs. This fear kept him depressed and defeated. It was through the ministry of laying-on-of-hands with prayer he was able to give the fear to Christ.

The fear was confronted, defeated, and abandoned. This believer now realizes the Lord can enter every area of life. Victory was achieved to the glory of the Lord and to his good.

BEHOLD THE GOOD

The creation story stresses that the Lord beheld what He had made and declared it was good, (Gen. 1:12,15,18,21,31).

If this is true of creation, how much more is it true of the new creation. *"Therefore if any man be in Christ, he is a new creature; old things are passed away; behold, all things are become new,"* II Cor. 5:17.

The Lord's children should develop the habit of seeing something fine and good in all things. You may have to force your mind and emotions to behold the good and you may have to deliberately look for something good in your situation. However, believe me, there is something good, yea, many things good, in your life--right now. Your thought patterns must be changed from the sick and ugly to the well and wholeness concept--God's desire for you!

Your accomplishments in this area will be well worth your time and effort.

Positive thoughts of God and His beauty in His creation brings a joy which will help defeat depression.

It is reported that a friend asked Haydn why his church music was almost always of an animating, cheerful, and even festive quality. This great composer replied,

"I cannot make it otherwise, I write according to the thoughts I feel. When I think upon God my heart is so full of joy that notes dance and leap, as it were, from my pen, and since God has given me a cheerful heart, it will be easily forgiven me that I serve Him with a cheerful spirit."

GIVE THANKS

Depression accents the negative and leads you to magnify the ugly events of your day. May you develop the habit of observing and thinking upon the non-ugly events of each day. These may be such simple things as a pleasant clerk, a smile, a sunny day. Give thanks unto the Lord in all things as you overcome fear in all areas.

43

LOW SELF-ESTEEM

How you look at yourself will determine to a large degree how you view life in general. You cannot rise higher toward others than you are toward yourself.

I feel it is no coincidence there are many scripture references to loving one's neighbor as him/herself. This is an important part of a wholesome and victorious life. (Leviticus 19:18; Matt. 19:19, 22:39; Mk. 12:31-33; Lu. 10:27; Rom. 13:9; Gal. 5:14; James 2:8).

The above scripture very well could have said, "You shall love yourself as your neighbor." The dark depths of depression have low esteem lurking in the shadows. You can't really love others until you love yourself.

A recent survey revealed approximately 15% of Americans aged 18-74 suffer symptoms of serious depression.

Depression now rivals schizophrenia--a mental illness known as "split personality"--as the nation's number one mental health problem.

The cause of depression is complex and varies with each person. It may be because of chemical changes in the body, reaction to outside events,

unconscious effects of behavior and personal relationships, or a combination of any or all of these
things.

I want to consider an honest look at yourself as a
tangible step toward defeating depression.

A good, honest, inward look at yourself is important. Are you really in a state of depression or are
you simply having a few days of the "blues?" The
normal reaction to many experiences in life is a
feeling of depression. This may come from experiences of disappointments, loss, stress, tragedy, or
from physical or mental exhaustion.

It is sometimes difficult to distinguish between the
normal times of temporary depression and the more
serious occasions when help will be needed to overcome a depressive state.

The National Association of Mental Health sug-
gests 10 "danger signals" of a possible serious state of
depression.

You will want to carefully consider the following:

1. A general and lasting feeling of hopelessness
and despair.

2. Inability to concentrate, making reading, writing and conversation difficult. Thinking and activity
are slowed because the mind is absorbed by inner
anguish.

3. Changes in physical activities like eating, sleep-
ing and sex. Frequent physical complaints with no
evidence of physical illness.

4. A loss of self-esteem which brings on continual
questioning of personal worth.

5. Withdrawal from others, not by choice but from immense fear of rejection by others.

6. Threats or attempts to commit suicide, which is seen as a way out of a hostile environment and a belief that life is worthless. About one in 200 of deeply depressed persons do commit suicide.

7. Hypersensitivity to words and actions of others and general irritability.

8. Misdirected anger and difficulty in handling most feelings. Self-directed anger because of perceived worthlessness may produce general anger directed at others.

9. Almost always assuming you are wrong, or responsible for the unhappiness of others.

10. Extreme dependency on others. Feelings of helplessness and then anger at the helplessness.

It is evident from the above that depression is widespread. Your self-esteem is important to combat this problem.

I hope you will search your own life to ascertain the depth of any depressive feelings you may have. May I say we have not honestly faced our situation until we have done more than simply analyze. You need to take the positive step of believing the Lord Jesus when He said, "*I am come that you might have...the abundant life,*" John 10:10.

We are not called to always look inward, but to look outward and upward to our Redeemer!

44

PRAYER PARTNER

One of the most important facts of the life of each Christian is that he/she has the Holy Spirit as a Prayer Partner!

It is wonderful to know you are not alone in your struggle with depression. You have a 24-hour-a-day Prayer Partner. He is the Holy Spirit (Romans 8:26).

The defeat of depression must be a team effort and He is the Captain of the team. Begin each day seeking the Holy Spirit's guidance and take one step at a time. Permit yourself to be molded by His gentle leading (John 16:13). Thank Him for the healing which will take place in your life today (I Thess. 5:18).

So many feel they must do everything alone. They evidently are unaware of the presence and power of the Lord. Or perhaps they are neglectful of His presence and desires for their life.

Many believers are like the little boy who tried to move a heavy stone. He could not do it. His father was observing through the window how he pushed, pulled, and even pried with a big board to move the stone. It was all to no avail.

The child came into the house and the father remarked about his being unable to move the stone. He asked if he had tried everything. The boy replied that he had. The father's response was, "But you didn't ask me to help." The child's face brightened and together they went out and easily moved the stone. This is a beautiful lesson for the believer because we so often fail to really ask our Prayer Partner to help.

FOLLOW HIS GUIDANCE

Once you begin to rely upon the Holy Spirit, then follow the guidance He gives to you. It may be to mentally and emotionally pour His love and blessing upon those whom you feel have hurt or misused you. It may be simply to ask someone to forgive you for having borne resentment toward them. It may be placing your nerves in His calm power and presence.

PHYSICAL ACTIVITY

Along with the old saying, "confession is good for the soul," can be added the statement, "physical exercise is good for the soul and body." Exercise will help relieve tension and make you stronger to resist periods of depression. Tests have shown that after 15 minutes of exercise the electrical activity in muscles declined 20% and continued declining for an hour. A tranquilizing drug, used on the same person, produced very little difference in electrical activity in the muscles. Your exercise period will be enhanced even more if you think of the wonder of the universe, of your body, and of nature around you, if you walk or jog outside.

CONCLUSION

In conclusion, may I emphasize that no one has all the answers to defeating depression. However, I hope the tangible steps I have outlined will prove of help.

I pray you will get beyond constantly taking your own Emotional Quotient (E.Q.). Many are constantly asking themselves if they are happy or depressed. This habit is very destructive. When these negative evaluations enter your mind seek to develop the desire and ability to mentally or verbally say "stop." This is the wholesome maturity for which you have been seeking. You are on the right track when you put a stop to unwholesome thinking.

There are far too many who want to receive before they believe. May you begin now to dwell upon the wonderful change that is taking place within you, even if it is not evident at the moment. The walk of faith is to believe and then to receive.

May you plant the seeds of health by disciplining yourself to display a cheerful spirit. You are only punishing yourself when you remain constantly displaying your depression through actions and looks. May I rephrase an old axiom, "Laugh and the world laughs with you, be depressed and you are depressed alone."

Self-pity is corrosive and saps your vitality as sure as corrosion stops the flow of power on the battery terminals. Seek to be filled with the Holy Spirit of

God, Who can guide you into all wisdom and truth
(John 14:26)!

45

GOD'S HEALTH CARE PLAN - COMPASSION

The Lord has a health care plan for you. It is based on His very nature of compassion. This foundation truth must be grasped prior to considering the facets of His health care plan as revealed in Galatians 5:22, 23. When His compassionate nature is perceived His health care plan can be received.

I meet many people who are deeply distressed and they wonder if God really cares. It is from them I hear statements such as:

"I pray and pray but nothing happens and it is as if God doesn't even hear me."

"I find myself so depressed and I wonder if the Lord loves me and I sometimes find myself thinking terrible things even about God."

"I don't believe God wants me to be well."

"I just feel so lost."

If one of the above fits you today, then I have Good News for you. God does care for you. He wants you to know He cares. He does have a wonderful health care program for you!

GOD DOES CARE

We hear a lot about a health care program for all of our nation. I feel a more urgent message needed by millions is Jesus Christ has a health care program.

God's program includes wholeness of body, soul, and spirit. He is not simply a powerful Creator who left struggling humanity with no help or hope. He is a loving Father who cares for your health and mine.

A BASIC INGREDIENT

Basic to His health care program is His compassion and mercy. The Word plainly teaches God does care. Compassion is indeed part of the bed-rock of God's health care plan.

"The Lord is gracious, and full of compassion; slow to anger and of great mercy, The Lord is good to all: and His tender mercies are over all His works," Ps. 145:8, 9.

If the Lord cares, which He definitely does, then He is not only able to heal, but he is willing to heal. The Bible imparts more than details of a God of power. It reveals our God of Love. Power infers He is able to do great things, and this is true. Love and mercy revealed through His Word teach us He is willing to do great things. There is a great difference between being able to do something and being willing to do it. God is able and willing, as well as willing and able.

Many do not doubt the Lord's power to heal, but often these same individuals will doubt His desire to heal. Is it not as bad to doubt willingness as it is to doubt ability?

You may doubt my ability to do good for you. However, I would be bothered if you doubted my desire to do good for you. I can understand someone saying to me, "I know you would help me if you could." It would be terrible if they would say, "I know you could help me if you would."

You must bring honor to the Lord by not only believing in His ability, but also believing in His availability. You and I must believe that He is able to heal, and that He is most willing to heal. His health care program is for you.

The heavenly Father's health care program was beautifully accepted and fulfilled in the life of our Lord Jesus. His earthly ministry was one of great compassion. He revealed a Father of mercy and compassion.

"And there came a leper...and Jesus, moved with compassion,....said, I will; be thou clean..." Mark 1:40-45.

"...and Jesus...saw a great multitude, and He was moved with compassion toward them, and He healed their sick," Matt. 14:13, 14.

"And as they departed from Jericho...two blind men...cried out...have mercy...Jesus had compassion...their eyes received their sight..." Matt. 20:20-34.

God's health care program begins with His very nature. You can no more hold back His mercy than can the flood waters be kept from the crevices of buildings and lands. He is the "...*Father of mercies...*" II Cor. 1:3.

46

GOD'S HEALTH CARE PLAN - LOVE

Now that we have established compassion as a basic part of the nature of our heavenly Father we can move on to the facets of His health care plan. Paul reveals the plan as follows:

"But the fruit of the Spirit is love, joy, peace, long-suffering, gentleness, goodness, faith, meekness, temperance: against such there is no law," Gal. 5:22, 23.

Your wholeness of body, soul, and spirit is determined to a large extent upon your understanding and application of God's health care plan as presented in Galatians.

LOVE

Love is one of the vital facets of His health care plan. He desires your wholeness, but expects love to be an avenue to receive and to maintain it. It is the foundation of all that is meaningful and as Swedenborg has said, "Love in its essence is spiritual fire."

DOES GOD LOVE?

You may ask, "Now really, does God love? Does God love me?" I would answer, "Do birds fly? Do fish swim? Does the sun rise each day? Do thirsty plants revive with water?"

May you grasp the truth--the love of God is as natural as the many natural things we daily take for granted. Sure, it is impossible to give complete answers to all the suffering in the world. It is also impossible to account for all the goodness and beauty in the world without acknowledging a God of love.

"...*God is love*..." I John 4:8, 16.

"*If ye then, being evil, know how to give good gifts unto your children, how much more shall your Father which is in heaven give good things to them that ask Him?*" Matt. 7:11.

"*Greater love hath no man than this, that a man lay down his life for his friends,*" John 15:13.

WHEN DOES GOD LOVE?

I feel the problem with many is they suspect God's love is spasmodic and conditional. They feel if they are "good" and/or "lucky" the Lord may occasionally pamper them with a dose of His love.

It's as if He dispenses His love from a love "dropper"--a precious little drop at a time and very infrequently.

Nothing could be further from the truth. The Lord's love is with you always. He desires wholeness for you because of His love. There is nothing which can come between you and His love.

"*...nothing shall be able to separate us from the love of God which is in Christ Jesus our Lord,*" Romans 8:39.

"*...while we were yet sinners, Christ died for us,*" Romans 5:8.

The assurance of His abiding love is of great comfort in all ways and during all of our days.

HOW DOES GOD LOVE?

The complete answer as to how God loves is hidden in the mysteries of the universe. However, we know His very nature is love.

There is no way to exhaust His love. It is literally true as Bailey has said, "Love spends his all, and still hath store." The following words beautifully speak of the Lord's inexhaustible love for you at all times.

Could we with ink the ocean fill,
And were the skies of parchment made,
Were every stalk on earth a quill,
And every man a scribe by trade.
To write the love, of God above,
Would drain the ocean dry.
Nor could the scroll, contain the whole,
Though stretched from sky to sky.

God's love is often revealed through others. He sends His healing on the wings of friends and loved ones.

"What stopped you from taking your own life?" This question I asked a school teacher who said she had planned to do so a few days before. Her answer, "Because of one of my students."

She went on to explain the day she intended to take her life one of her pupils had come up and kissed her on the cheek. It was a spontaneous expression of love. The little girl uttered no words, but only kissed her teacher.

Depressed, dejected, and lonely, there loomed before her eyes and heart the kiss of this little girl. It sustained her in her most desperate moment.

There are many through whom God shows His love to us each day. You are called to receive this love as well as to seek to impart love. His health care plan is carefully balanced. It is a balance of giving and receiving--receiving and giving. Both aspects must be present.

Love not only reaches in, but it reaches out as well. Markham put it succinctly when he wrote:

He drew a circle that shut me out--
Heretic, rebel, a thing to flout.
But love and I had the wit to win;
We drew a circle that took him in.

47

GOD'S HEALTH CARE PLAN - JOY

Joy is defined as, "to be glad; rejoice; a lively emotion of happiness; gladness."

Ardis Whitman speaks of joy as, "Awe and a sense of mystery are part of it; so are the feelings of humility and gratitude. Suddenly we are keenly aware of every living thing--every leaf, every flower, every cloud, the mayfly hovering over the pond, the crow cawing in the treetops."

There are many references to joy.

"A merry heart maketh a cheerful countenance; but by sorrow of the heart the spirit is broken," Prov. 15:13.

"...he that is of a merry heart hath a continual feast," Prov. 15:15.

"A merry heart doeth good like medicine; but a broken spirit drieth the bones," Prov. 17:22.

It is obvious from these verses disposition influences one's health condition. Also, we know one's health condition influences disposition. You feel worse when you are disgruntled and sorrowful of heart. You feel better when you are full of joy. Joy does serve as a wonderful medicine.

WHERE DO YOU FIND JOY?

Joy cannot be contrived or falsely assumed. It is found in the very essence of life itself. The Giver of life and the One who is the Life is the Lord Himself. It is in His presence and because of His presence we are able to have true joy.

"*Thou wilt shew me the path of life: in thy presence is fullness of joy; at thy right hand there are pleasures for evermore,*" Ps. 16:11.

Jesus was specific in saying joy was His gift to all who believe in Him. "*These things have I spoken unto you, that my joy might remain in you, and that your joy might be full,*" John 15:11. "*And ye now therefore have sorrow; but I will see you again, and your heart shall rejoice, and your joy no man taketh from you,*" John 16:22.

DISCOVER JOY

Someone has said, "The religion that makes a man look sick certainly won't cure the world." Some believers act as if the world is the victor instead of the One whom they worship.

God's health care program certainly includes joy. There are some steps which will help you on your pilgrimage to and with joy.

1. Realize your position in the Lord. He has granted you the honor of being His child. He cares for you more than for all the material world, (I Peter 5:7).

2. Develop the desire and ability to praise the Lord in all things and at all times. This does not mean

you piously act as if all things were as the Lord wants them to be. This is not true. However, praise does acknowledge you believe the Lord is with you. He will see you through the darkest night and the deepest problems. (See Ps. 46:1; Isa. 41:10; Mt. 28:20)

The Dead Sea Scrolls revealed great truth concerning praise as found in their "Manual for Discipline."

"As long as I live it shall be a rule engraved on my tongue to bring praise like fruit for an offering and my lips as a sacrificial gift.

"I will make skillful music with lyre and harp to serve God's glory, and the flute of my lips I raise in praise of His rule of righteousness. Both morning and evening I shall enter into the Covenant of God; and at the end of both I shall recite His commandments, and so long as they continue to exist, there will be my frontier and my journey's end.

"Therefore I will bless His name in all I do, before I move hand or foot, whenever I go out or come in, when I sit down and when I rise, even when lying on my couch, I will chant His praise. My lips shall praise Him as I sit at the table which is set for all, and before I lift my hand to partake of any nourishment from the delicious fruits of the earth. When fear and terror come, and there is only anguish and distress, I will still bless and thank Him for His wondrous deeds, and meditate upon His power, and lean upon His mercies all day long... So when trouble comes or salvation, I praise Him just the same." (See Phil 4:4).

48

GOD'S HEALTH CARE PLAN - PEACE

God has designed His health care program to help you remain healthy. If you do become ill, His program will hasten recovery.

An important facet of His program is peace. He desires it for you. It is something the unbelieving and rebellious person does not have. *"There is no peace saith the Lord, unto the wicked,"* Isa. 48:22.

WHAT IS PEACE?

The dictionary defines personal peace as, "a state of quiet or tranquility; freedom from disturbance or agitation; calm; repose; freedom from mental agitation or anxiety; spiritual contentment." There is little doubt everyone wants this peace.

IMPORTANCE

Peace is so important to your wholeness. There can be no really whole life without it. Matthew Henry said, "Peace is such a precious jewel that I would give anything for it but truth." Jesus felt peace was so important that practically the last thing He said to

His disciples was they would receive His peace. "*My peace I leave with you, my peace I give unto you: not as the world giveth...*" John 16:33. Peace was the only estate He left them. He had no earthly possessions, but He had the most important possession. He wanted them to have it, too.

Many Scriptures speak of the importance of peace:

"*...seek peace, and pursue it,*" Ps. 34:14.

"*...let peace rule in your hearts,*" Col 3:15.

OBSTACLES

There are many obstacles to personal peace. Many people never overcome these obstacles. They seek peace more and more and find it less and less.

The biggest obstacle is the inner person. The real obstacles are not outward circumstances, but inward feelings. An ancient writer summarized obstacles to peace, "Five great enemies to peace inhabit with us: vice, avarice, wicked ambition, envy, anger, and pride. If these enemies were to be banished, we should infallibly enjoy perpetual peace."

Thus the disturber of peace and the preventer of peace is the spirit which permeates the inner person. Every spirit which is contrary to the Holy Spirit of the Lord will rob you of peace. Every action which is contrary to the moral and spiritual laws of God contributes toward your continuing lack of peace.

GIVER OF PEACE

Peace is so desirable that practically everyone is searching for it. But what or who brings peace? Many are seeking it through artificial means. They are traveling under the illusion they will be given peace through drugs, or sex, or the occult, or religious cults, or humanistic meditation or a combination of these. The ultimate end of such efforts is not peace, but more problems.

There are no peace pills available. Peace is a gift of the Lord. The Giver of the only peace which ultimately satisfies is Jesus. He says, *"My peace I give unto you."* (See Eph. 2:14; Col. 1:20; Isa. 53:5.)

STEPS TO PEACE

The road to peace leads directly to Jesus. The road to peace has the Lord as your traveling companion.

The following steps will get you started on the road of peace and will keep you on this road.

1. Sincerely believe the Lord loves you and commit yourself to Him. Eliphaz spoke eternal truth when he said, *"Acquaint now thyself with him, and be at peace..."* Job 22:21. Paul was even more specific with, *"For Christ is our peace..."* Eph. 2:14. Someone has said, "There is but one way to tranquility of mind and happiness, and that is to account no external things thine own, but to commit all to God."

2. Search the Scriptures and obey their teachings. The Psalmist declares, *"Great peace have they which love thy law: and nothing shall offend them,"* Ps. 119: 165.

Reading, seeking to understand and to obey God's Word is a giant stride toward peace. I like Smiley Blanton's (Director of the American Foundation of Religion and Psychiatry) reply to the question of his reading the Bible.

"I not only read it, I study it. It's the greatest textbook on human behavior ever put together. If people would just absorb its message, a lot of us psychiatrists could close our offices and go fishing."

3. Realize peace is a Person and not a place or a position. I suggest you picture yourself at the most beautiful and perfect spot you can imagine. Now, let the Lord Jesus enter into your life. Quiet your body, mind, and spirit. Absorb the peace of His presence. He will impart His peace during these moments. This peace can be yours every moment. Claim His peace today! (I Cor. 1:3).

49

GOD'S HEALTH CARE PLAN - PATIENCE

Patience is certainly a part of God's health care plan. It is included in His prescription for a full and healthy life.

The fruit of the Spirit as mentioned in Gal. 5:22 helps you to live a healthier lifestyle of wholeness. The Lord is not simply interested in healing you after you have become ill. His biggest concern is keeping you healthy at all times.

A skilled medical person told me physicians are taught primarily to treat diseases. They are not taught how to direct people to help them live and maintain a healthy life. Their practice and efforts are primarily directed toward crises instead of preventive measures.

The greatest need in your life and mine is how to keep from becoming ill. Patience developed to its fullest will help a great deal.

WHAT IS PATIENCE?

The dictionary defines patience as, "the exercise of sustained endurance and perseverance; the forbearance toward the faults or infirmities of others; tranquil waiting or expectation; ability to await events without perturbation. Patience is keeping kindliness of heart under vexatious conduct; long-suffering is continued patience. Patience may also have an active force denoting uncomplaining steadiness in doing. Synonyms are: calmness, composure, endurance, forbearance, fortitude, leniency, long-suffering, resignation, submission, and sufferance."

FRUITS OF IMPATIENCE

Impatience spawns many problems. It leads to flared tempers, unproductive short-cuts to solve problems, and uneasiness and unhappiness with life. It will lead to your doubting the Lord. You will want things you are not receiving. Often your desired timing is not the Lord's timing and the result is a frustrated life for you.

A friend of Dr. Phillips Brooks observed him pacing the floor like a caged animal. "What's the trouble?" he asked. Dr. Brooks replied, "Trouble, I'll tell you the trouble. I'm in a hurry and God isn't." Isn't this often your problem? You want to have all the answers by sundown. However, the Lord's timetable is often different than yours. He will answer in His own time and in His own way.

There are many examples of impatience in the Bible. Consider: Moses when Israel murmured (Num. 20:10); Naaman at Elisha's suggestion (II Kings 5:11, 12); Jonah at the short-lived gourd (Jonah 4:8, 9); Disciples with the Syrophoenician woman (Matt. 15:23); James and John at the Samaritans (Luke 9:54); Martha with Mary (Luke 10:40); and Abram and Sarai which led to the birth of Ishmael (Gen. 16:1-6).

WAIT ON THE LORD

The life of patience and perseverance is one that waits upon the Lord. We are to wait upon the Lord. Many expect the Lord to wait upon them. The Psalmist wrote, *"Wait on the Lord, be of good courage, and he shall strengthen thine heart: wait I say, on the Lord,"* Ps. 31:24.

There is no way we can set the Lord's pace. We are to fit into His plans and thereby find the power and peace which can be ours.

STEPS TO PATIENCE

There are some tangible steps which can help you to develop and maintain patience:

1. Recall and remember how patient the Lord has been and continues to be with you. Thank God for this truth, *"The Lord is merciful and gracious, slow to anger, and plenteous in mercy...For he knoweth our frame; he remembereth that we are dust,"* Ps. 103:8, 14.

2. Realize you are not called to be the judge or the one who imparts the punishment. The Bible tells us God judges and delivers the punishment. *"Dearly beloved, avenge not yourselves, but rather give place unto wrath; for it is written, 'Vengeance is mine, I will repay,' saith the Lord,"* Rom. 12:19. (See Pro. 20:22).

3. Be willing to suffer for the Lord and for righteousness sake. You may be irritated by the actions and/or inaction of others. However, it is to the Lord

you must constantly look. *"For what glory is it, if, when ye be buffeted for your faults, ye shall take it patiently? But if, when ye do well, and suffer for it, ye take it patiently, this is acceptable with God. For even hereunto were ye called; because Christ also suffered for us, leaving us an example..."* I Pet. 2:20, 21.

4. Last but not least realize as you develop patience the Lord becomes more real to you and strengthens your inward being. He enables you to face all circumstances. You are then healthier and truly a participant in the Lord's health care plan. *"They that wait upon the Lord shall renew their strength..."* Isa. 40:31.

50

GOD'S HEALTH CARE PLAN - KINDNESS

Partaking of the fruit of the Spirit certainly enables an individual to be healthier. One of the most precious aspects of the fruit of the Spirit is kindness.

Kindness is the gentle, tender, good deed which reaches out to others, while at the same time reaching deep within yourself. The Apostle Paul sums it up, *"Be kindly affectioned one to another with brotherly love; in honour preferring one another,"* Rom. 12:10.

Kindness is not easily defined, but is easily felt and experienced. It encompasses more than can be readily verbalized. It is an act in the best interest of the one for whom it is done. It blesses the blessed and the blesser.

EACH DAY

You should seek to do at least one act of kindness each day. Kindness is a tangible step to overcoming the human tendency of selfishness. It is very much a part of God's health care plan. The selfish life is a sick life. The selfish soul is a stifled soul.

I suggest each participant in my 30-Day Prayer Pilgrimage do a planned and deliberate kind deed each day. Would you believe, this is the hardest part to do? Individuals find it almost impossible to really plan to be kind.

Bailey has said, "Both man and womankind belie their nature when they are not kind." Acts of kindness accent the higher nature of man. They release the power of the Lord in and through you.

Years ago an experiment was conducted concerning energy efficiency and the condition of the pavement. The electric trolley was tested on several different types of pavement. It was learned 20% more power was needed to run at twelve miles an hour over a poor asphalt pavement than over a good one. It took 40% to 60% more power with a pavement in various stages of deterioration.

Isn't this illustrative of our lives? Our meanness, injustices, and selfishness can make it very difficult for ourselves and others. On the other hand, kindness can smooth out the road of life for others and ourselves. The wear and tear on an individual is a great deal less when kindness is the dominant aspect of life.

A STRAIGHT LINE

You should not expect a direct return of kindness from the one to whom you are kind. So often it just doesn't work that way. My wife's Grandma Bell always said, "Acts of kindness travel in a straight line." You pass on to another an act of kindness in response to the many you have received from others.

A young man returned from visiting a shut-in and expressed his good feeling. The shut-in will never be able to return his call. But through other means, I'm sure kindness will come to this young man.

A postman friend of mine beamed as he told how good it felt to tramp through the snow to secure a letter being mailed by an elderly man. Simple acts of kindness, yes; but what a difference they make in the life of the one conveying them and the ones to whom they are conveyed.

UNKINDNESS CANNOT DEFEAT

Please do not let an unkind act toward you defeat your reaching out in kindness. Nurturing a resentment or an unkindness can only lead to distress and disease.

God's health care plan calls for you to be kind in the face of any and all unkindness. Dr. Dan Poling was complaining about the hypocrites and spiritual leaders in his congregation. His good friend, Dr. Cadman, gave sage advice, "I know, I know, but if you want to help them and save yourself, you'll have to learn to love them, my boy."

An ounce of kindness is worth a ton of admonition. God's health care plan requires we maintain a life of devotion to Him which is generously sprinkled with kindness.

RECEIVE KINDNESS

One of the most difficult things for many of us is to graciously receive a kindness. We often feel so unworthy. May you never say no to a kindness with either words or actions. Simply receive the kindness as from the Lord, regardless of whom He uses. Thoreau said, "It is something to be able to paint a particular picture, ...make a few objects beautiful; ...but it is far more glorious...to affect the quality of the day--that is the highest of arts." (See Eph 4:32.)

Kindness puts quality into your life. It is a vital facet of God's divine health care plan.

CONCLUSION

I feel the following poem by John Boyle O'Reilly serves as a worthy way to close this chapter concerning kindness.

"What is good?"
I asked in musing mood.
Order, said the law court;
Knowledge, said the school;
Truth, said the wise man;
Pleasure, said the fool;
Love, said the maiden;
Beauty, said the page;
Freedom, said the dreamer;
Home, said the sage;
Fame, said the soldier;
Equity, the seer;
Spoke my heart full sadly:
"The answer is not here."
There within my bosom
Softly this I heard:
"Each heart holds the secret;
Kindness is the word."

51

GOD'S HEALTH CARE PLAN - GOODNESS

William Penn said, "I expect to pass through life but once. If therefore, there be any kindness I can show, or any good I can do to any fellow-being, let me do it now, and not defer nor neglect it, as I shall not pass this way again."

He placed an emphasis upon goodness which is true to Scripture and the principles of good health. Goodness is indeed part and parcel of God's health care plan. The ultimate end of neglecting goodness is alienation from the Lord, others, and oneself. Walt Whitman certainly put the proper emphasis upon goodness when he wrote, "Roaming in thought over the universe, I saw the little that is good steadily hastening towards immortality, and the vast that is evil I saw hastening to merge itself and become lost and dead."

OUR GOODNESS

Most of us possess what I call an "Archie Bunker" type of goodness. That is, a bit of goodness and mercy among a lot of bigotry, prejudice and injustice.

Montaign put it succinctly, "There is no one so good, who, were he to submit all his thoughts and actions to the law, would not deserve hanging ten times in his life."

God's health care plan calls for your life to be aimed at consistent goodness. The direction you walk affects the health of your body, soul, and spirit.

WHAT IS GOOD?

The dictionary definition of good is, "having or characterized by admirable moral or spiritual qualities; especially, governed by dutiful regard for the moral and divine law, conformed to the law of right; righteous; virtuous, religious: opposed to bad, evil, vicious, wicked."

I was amazed to discover the dictionary listed 75 synonyms for the word good. In fact, it finally gave up listing synonyms and summarized with, "Good may at some time be a synonym of almost any adjective in the language implying advantage, benefit, utility, worth, etc."

THE BIBLE AND GOODNESS

The Apostle Paul lists goodness as a characteristic of the fruit of the spirit (Gal. 5:22). Dr. William Barclay says the word used for goodness in this verse is not found in secular Greek. It has a unique Biblical significance. He defines the Greek word translated goodness as, "virtue equipped at every point." It is a quality of life which can rebuke, correct, and discipline. It often presents problems for some as it runs counter to their concepts or conduct. For instance,

Jesus sought to do good by cleansing the temple, but incurred the wrath of some in so doing.

Paul speaks of the brethren being filled with goodness (Rom. 15:14). He also says goodness is a quality of the fruit of the spirit (Eph. 5:9); and desired in the believer's life (II Thess. 1:11). Also consider: Gal. 6:10; Phil. 4:8; and I Thess. 5:15, 21.

BE GOOD FOR GOODNESS SAKE

There can be no fullness of the fruit of the spirit without goodness. Goodness is the measure of success far more than acquisition of things. A speaker was heralding the attractiveness of the advances of technology. He pointed out how it had brought so many better things to many people. One of the old timers sobered the thinking of all when he remarked, "To be better off is not to be better." Bishop Horne drives this point home with his insights, "In the heraldry of heaven goodness precedes greatness, and so on earth it is more powerful. The lowly and lovely may often do more good in their limited sphere than the gifted."

Make goodness a vital part of your health plans for goodness sake. "...*For he that...will see good days...let him...do good,*" I Pet. 3:10, 11.

52

GOD'S HEALTH CARE PLAN - FAITHFULNESS

Faithfulness is a stirring word. It almost shouts its message of devotion, firmness, loyalty, truth, trustworthiness, and unwavering style of life. It is the respected way of living in the world and the required way in our relationships with God. The clarion call of scripture is to faithfulness. *"Be faithful unto death, and I will give you the crown of life,"* Rev. 2:10.

It is one thing to begin to follow the Lord and another to finish the race. Many start with great enthusiasm which quickly wanes and, in some, completely dies. There is nothing more heartbreaking than to counsel an individual in distress because of unfaithfulness to a spouse, business partner, neighbor, or family member. Their loyalty to the ways of the Lord has been compromised through their relationship with others. Jesus gave a call to faithfulness. *"No man having put his hand to the plough, and looking back, is fit for the kingdom of God,"* Luke 9:62.

UNFAITHFULNESS

The health the Lord desires for you can be impaired and destroyed by acts of unfaithfulness toward the Lord and/or those around you. It can lead to mental and emotional illnesses which can ultimately affect you physically. The final fruit of unfaithfulness is not the sweet and nourishing fruit anticipated. Ultimately, bitter fruit is harvested from unfaithfulness.

What leads to unfaithfulness? What causes a person to get eyes off the real goal and to gaze upon lesser goals? Why does one step from the path of openness and light into the realm of unfaithfulness and darkness? Jesus gave three reasons for unfaithfulness and they can be applied to practically any area of life. He presents them through the parable of the sower (Luke 8:1-15):

1. The devil--The evil one immediately takes away the word of truth from the heart so you will not believe. Your desire for faithfulness is immediately ignored or suppressed.

2. Temptation--There are those who are determined to be faithful, but only continue this way for a short time. They yield to the temptation to take the easy way and choose short-term benefits:

(Frequently the temptations of the flesh are too much for them. It is intriguing to read in the book, "Daughter of Destiny," that even some of Kathryn Kuhlman's co-workers succumbed to the passions of immorality and the love of money. Even Kathryn, as a young woman, could not resist the lure of her passions and married a divorced man. This act put her ministry in mothballs for nearly ten years and remained a blight on her efforts to the day of her death. The path of unfaithfulness is inviting. The end of the path is disappointment, heartache, and often mental, emotional, or physical illness.)

3. Life's attractions--There are many who have been unable to resist the cares, riches, and pleasures of this life. Many a great and promising ministry has been devastated through unfaithfulness caused by a creeping love of riches, glory, and honor which crowds out loyalty, devotion, and submission to the Lord Jesus Christ. Unfaithfulness is not new to our day. Demas forsook Paul as did all others (II Tim. 4:10, 16).

YOU CAN BE FAITHFUL

It is possible to remain faithful to the Lord and to others. Faithfulness is a part of God's health care plan. Try these steps:

1. Take a long look at your life and your present situation. What is most wholesome is not always what is expedient.

2. Keep close to and open to other believers. The members of Alcoholics Anonymous are instructed to talk to another member when the moments of temptation come to return to the bottle. This is good advice for any area of temptation. Sharing with another person that you are going through moments of great temptation will often help you receive the strength to remain faithful.

3. Keep your eyes upon Jesus. He is your salvation and strength! Unfaithfulness results when you look elsewhere for your joy or pleasure. I recall a cartoon which dramatically presented the fundamentals of faithfulness. Pictured was a blazing sun in the heavens, a daffodil growing near a basement window, and a dim electric light bulb which could be seen through the dirty window. The daffodil was bent toward the dim light bulb and away from the glorious sun. The caption underneath was one word, "infidelity." (See I Cor. 10:13.)

Faithfulness faithfully and fully pursued is a great contributor to health. It is part and parcel of God's health care plan.

53

GOD'S HEALTH CARE PLAN - GENTLENESS

"You are going to have to calm down, and learn to control your anger and keep relaxed." These are the words his physician spoke to a friend of mine who was recovering from a third heart attack. His turbulent spirit had and would continue to affect his heart. A more gentle spirit would determine not only the quality but the quantity of his years.

YOUR GENTLENESS

Your gentleness of spirit is certainly part of the Lord's plan for your overall health. The gentle spirit helps us to live a more abundant and healthful life.

The gentle individual is one who is mild of disposition and gracious in spirit. It is the spirit to which believers are called. "*And the servant of the Lord must not strive; but be gentle unto all...*" II Tim. 2:24. "*To speak evil of no man, to be no brawlers, but gentle, showing all meekness unto all men,*" Tit. 3:2.

POWER OF GENTLENESS

Paul could be blunt and to the point. However, he still sought to minister in a spirit of gentleness. The gentle spirit affected not only the health of the individual but the health of the church. Paul knew the power of gentleness. It was a great persuader in his eyes. *"Now I, Paul, myself beseech you by the meekness and gentleness of Christ..."* II Cor. 10:1. *"But, we were gentle among you even as a nurse cherisheth her children,"* I Th. 2:7.

The fable concerning the north wind and the sun illustrates the power of gentleness. They had a contest to see which could most quickly get a man to remove his coat. The north wind made the first attempt and blew fiercely. The harder he blew the tighter the man drew his coat around him.

The sun took his turn and focused his gentle warmth upon the man. It was not long until the coat was loosened, then completely unbuttoned, and soon removed. The sun had accomplished by gentleness what the north wind could never do through harshness. The gentle spirit is ultimately the most powerful in our own lives and the lives of others.

PURSUE GENTLENESS

The following are some of the reasons you should seek to develop the spirit of gentleness:

1. The Lord Jesus reached out to others in a spirit of gentleness. *"Come unto me...for I am meek and lowly in heart..."* Matt. 11:28-30.

2. One of the qualities of wisdom which the Lord wants you to possess is gentleness. Consider: *"But the wisdom that is from above is first pure, then peaceable, gentle, and easy to be entreated..."* James 3:17.

3. The mature and confident spirit is a gentle spirit. Fenelon has said, "It is only imperfection that complains of what is imperfect. "The more perfect we are, the more gentle and quiet we become toward the defect in others."

Gentleness begets gentleness. Your health and the well being of others will be enhanced if you develop and maintain a spirit of gentleness.

How beautifully the following speaks to us.

"Go placidly amid the noise and haste, and remember what peace there may be in silence. As far as possible without surrender be on good terms with all persons. Speak your truth quietly and clearly; and listen to others, even the dull and ignorant; they too have their story.

"Avoid loud and aggressive persons, they are vexations to the spirit. If you compare yourself with others, you may become vain and bitter; for always there will be greater and lesser persons than yourself. Enjoy your achievements as well as your plans.

"Keep interested in your own career, however humble; it is a real possession in the changing fortunes of time. Exercise caution in your business affairs; for the world is full of trickery. But let this not blind you to what virtue there is; many persons strive for high ideals, and everywhere life is full of heroism.

"Be yourself. Especially, do not feign affection. Neither be cynical about love; for in the face of all aridity and disenchantment it is perennial as the grass.

"Take kindly the counsel of the years, gracefully surrendering the things of youth. Nurture strength of spirit to shield you in sudden misfortunes. But do not distress yourself with imaginings. Many fears are born of fatigue and loneliness. Beyond a wholesome discipline be gentle with yourself. You are a child of the universe, no less than the trees and the stars; you have a right to be here. And whether or not it is clear to you, no doubt the universe is unfolding as it should.

"Therefore be at peace with God, whatever you conceive Him to be, and whatever your labors and aspirations, in the noisy confusion of life keep peace with your soul.

"With all its sham, drudgery and broken dreams, it is still a beautiful world. Be careful. Strive to be happy."

I pray the gentle spirit will be yours now and always.

54

GOD'S HEALTH CARE PLAN - SELF-CONTROL

While taking his daily walk an ancient king was startled by the sudden appearance of an old bearded man. The surprised king blurted out, "And who are you?" The aged man's answer, "I am a king," was even more startling than his sudden appearance. "A king! Over what country do you reign?" asked the amazed and amused monarch.

"Over myself. I rule myself because I control myself. I am my own subject to command," was the old man's humble but wise and honest answer.

CALL TO SELF-CONTROL

Self-control is part of the fruit of the spirit which issues forth in better health for all who practice it. It is part of God's health care plan (Gal. 5:22). It is part of the life which is lived to the fullest. "*He that is slow to anger is better than the mighty; and he that ruleth his spirit than he that taketh a city,*" Pro. 16:32. (See Rom. 6:12, 13; II Pet. 1:5, 6.)

LACKING

Much of my time is consumed counseling those who have not been able to practice self-control. Also, frequently I see those who have been hurt by the uncontrolled actions of others.

The fruit of the lack of self-control is ultimately chaos. Lack of self-control manifests itself in strife, drunkenness, overweight, sexual immorality, dependence upon drugs, indifference to the feelings and needs of others, and an extremely selfish view of life, etc. All of the above and their consequences lead to a life of defeat, remorse, frustration, depression, desperation, and spiritual bankruptcy.

CONTRIBUTES TO WHOLENESS

Self-control helps you to live the life which produces and maintains the wholeness the Lord desires for you. You, as a believer, practice self-control not because of the law which forbids; but because of God's love which frees.

Any worthwhile achievement requires self-control and discipline. The achiever is one who is willing to pay the price. Paul puts it well, "*And every man that striveth for the mastery is temperate in all things...*" I Cor. 9:25.

Each believer should seek to practice self-control in all areas even more than does the athlete. "*...now they do it to obtain a corruptible crown; but we an incorruptible,*" I Cor. 9:25.

This does not mean you must forsake life, but that you subdue the passions of life. There is a world of

difference between legitimate pleasures being enjoyed and sensual passions being unbridled.

Aristippus said, "The conqueror of pleasure is not
the man who never uses pleasure. He is the man who
uses pleasure as a rider guides a horse or a steersman
directs a ship and so directs them wherever he
wishes."

PRACTICE SELF-CONTROL

It is much easier for me to present the problems
resulting from lack of self-control than it is to give
guidance for you to practice self-control. However,
the following practical steps may be helpful:

1. Center your life upon Jesus. Make His goals
your goals. He lived His life with eternal values in
mind. You are called to do likewise (Phil. 2:5). It is
so easy to have your attention diverted to lesser goals
and desires. The winner of the race of life is the one
who looks to Jesus (Heb. 12:1-3).

2. Think upon the things which uplift and enhance. I often say that evil thoughts permitted to stay
will cause our actions soon to stray (Phil. 4:8).

3. Realize self-control is determined to a large
extent by how well you control your tongue. Observe
what James says, "*And the tongue is a fire, a world of
iniquity; ...full of deadly poison,*" James 3:6-8.

If self-control of the tongue were practiced many
of the ills of the world would be removed and controlled and even healed.

*"The boneless tongue, so small, so weak
can crush and kill," declares the Greek.
"The tongue destroys a greater horde,"*

The Turks assert, "than does the sword."
The Persian proverb wisely saith;
"A lengthy tongue, an early death."
Or sometimes takes this form instead:
"The tongue can speak a word whose speed,"
Says the Chinese, "outstrips the steed."
While Arab sages this impart!
"The tongue's great storehouse is the heart."
From Hebrew writ this saying sprung:
"Tho' feet should slip, ne'er let the tongue."
The Sacred writers crown the whole:
"Who keeps his tongue doth keep his soul."

CONCLUSION

A wise person of by-gone ages said life had four great principles. Self-control is one of them. His four great principles are:

"Wisdom, the principle of doing things aright; Justice, the principle of doing things equally in public and in private; Fortitude, the principle of not fleeing danger, but meeting it; and Temperance (self-control), the principle of subduing desires and living moderately."

IS
HEALING
FOR
TODAY?

55

HOW DOES GOD HEAL TODAY?

"Have you ever seen a miracle?" What is your answer? What is your immediate response?

I often ask this question when I am teaching a group concerning healing. Most of the people in the groups respond they have never seen a real miracle.

This negative response reveals to me that they have two basic misconceptions concerning miracles.

MANY SOURCES

First, it shows they do not appreciate the fact the Lord uses many sources to bring about His miracle of healing.

Second, it illustrates that they do not comprehend every healing is a miracle regardless of the method used.

I cannot emphasize enough the eternal truth that the Lord is in the healing business. He uses all kinds of methods. However, the healing is always from Him.

1. DIET

There is abundant evidence diet affects health. There are many diseases especially in third world countries which can be healed through proper diet. Even in advanced nations diet can affect nerves, cells, and spirit.

A properly balanced diet will mean much to your wholeness of body, soul, and spirit.

2. SURGERY

God heals through surgeons. Medical history is replete with cases where individuals have received restored health as a result of an operation. For instance, today the now common open-heart surgery has brought renewed health to thousands.

3. PHYSICIANS

God heals through physicians. God has laid up in nature various remedies which medical science has or is in the process of discovering. However, medicines are to be used wisely and never over-used or abused.

4. MENTAL PROCESSES

God can heal through mental processes. An individual can dwell mentally upon sickness to the point that he or she will become ill. On the other hand, he or she can think health, and discover that this aids the healing process. Many times the process of healing has been aided by constructive mental, emotional, and spiritual attitudes.

5. CLIMATE

God can heal through climate. Although this can be overstressed--for the real climate of health or ill health is within a person--nevertheless some climates are more conducive to health than others.

For instance, individuals plagued with respiratory problems often find the dry climate areas to be much more healthful than high humidity areas. Further, very few could survive the harshness of the climate of the north or south pole.

6. DELIVERANCE

The Lord heals through an individual's deliverance from underlying fears, loneliness, self-centeredness, purposelessness, resentments, guilts, etc. which produce and prolong illness.

7. SPIRIT OF GOD

The Lord heals through direct operation of the Holy Spirit upon the body. There are physical healings beyond the explanation of science. In fact, there is no nerve or tissue of your body which is beyond the healing touch of the Lord.

The Lord's arm is not shortened in this scientific and technological age. He is Lord of your whole being--body, soul, and spirit.

8. RESURRECTION

The Lord heals through the final cure--the resurrection of the body. Some diseases must await the final and complete cure in the resurrection of the body.

In the meantime He supplies sufficient grace for you. Grace not only to bear your suffering, but to use it to His glory until the final release.

CONCLUSION

The Living God does work in and through all of the above. If you realize this you can truly say that you have seen many, many miracles. Thank the Lord for them!

56

THE LORD'S PROVISION FOR WHOLENESS

Dr. R.A. Torrey in his book, "Divine Healing," says:

"Just as one gets the firstfruits of his spiritual salvation in the life that now is, so we get the first-fruits of our physical salvation in the life that now is...The Gospel of Christ has salvation for the body as well as for the soul...The atoning death of Jesus Christ secured for us not only physical healing, but also the resurrecting and perfecting and glorifying of our bodies."

The beloved disciple John wrote, *"Beloved, I wish above all things that thou mayest prosper and be in health, even as thy soul prospereth,"* III John v. 2.

The Lord does desire wholeness for you. He has made ample provision for you to receive and to maintain this wholeness. He can and will meet your physical and spiritual needs.

The Old Testament presents redemptive names for God. Even the meaning of the names reveals the Lord's desire for your wholeness, and can be used during your prayer time.

JEHOVAH-JIREH

JEHOVAH-JIREH--"*The Lord will provide,*" Gen. 22:14 RSV. The Lord was capable and willing to provide the offering in that day. He is still providing all that you need.

We know Christ is the perfect offering for each and every person. He is our fullness and our wholeness.

JEHOVAH-RAPHA

JEHOVAH-RAPHA-- "*I am the Lord that healeth thee,*" Ex. 15:26. *The privilege of wholeness is provided for you in Christ's atonement. Even the prophet Isaiah pointedly presents the reality of your wholeness in and through the atonement of Christ, (Isa. 53:4, 5).*

Matthew believed the prophet was speaking of what our Lord accomplished, (Matt. 8:17).

The writer of Hebrews clinches it when he says, "*Jesus Christ is the same yesterday, and today, and forever,*" Heb. 13:8. Christ had, has now, and always will have the power to heal. He heals you.

JEHOVAH-NISSI

JEHOVAH-NISSI--"*The Lord is our Banner,*" Ex. 17:15 RSV. The Lord is our leader. He ever sets the pace. You can believe He heals to the utmost.

"Our Banner" implies He goes before you in all matters and situations of life. You are called to believe and to receive from Him. He goes before you in all things and all days.

JEHOVAH-SHALOM

JEHOVAH-SHALOM--*"The Lord is Peace,"* Judg. 6:23, 24 RSV. Your life need not be ruined by restlessness and despair. The Lord has provided for your peace.

The wholeness millions are seeking is peace. This peace is from the Lord. This peace has truly been given through Jesus Christ our Great Physician.

Speaking of peace the prophet said, "...*the chastisement of our peace was upon him...*" Isa. 53:5. Jesus said, "...*my peace I give unto you...*" John 14:27. St. Paul said, "...*peace of God...through Christ Jesus...*" Phil. 4:7.

JEHOVAH-TSIDKENU

JEHOVAH-TSIDKENU--*"The Lord Our Righteousness,"* Jer. 23:6. Many exist with lives of defeat because of guilt. They fail to realize the Lord has provided wholeness for them in this area.

The promise of the Lord is His righteousness imputed and imparted to you, (Gen. 15:6; Acts 13:39; Rom. 5:1).

JEHOVAH-SHAMMA

JEHOVAH-SHAMMA--*"The Lord is there,"* Ezek. 48:35. There is never a moment of any given day, but what the Lord is there to help. This promise is abundantly fulfilled in Christ's words, "...*I am with you always...*" Matt. 28:20.

All that is revealed in the Names of God have been fulfilled in the redemptive act of Christ. He is your all. Believe Him for your wholeness!

57

HEALED FOR SOMEONE

The account of the healing of Peter's mother-in-law is recorded in Matt. 8:14-15; Mark 1:29-31; Luke 4:38-39.

Jesus had visited the synagogue prior to this incident. He went from teaching about God to living out the power of God in His life.

Peter's family must have been one which was very close and very committed to the Lord. This was not a temporary thing, but lasted until the end.

Tradition tells us Peter had to watch his wife tortured to death. It is said that even while being tortured, she rejoiced in the Lord. Peter was inspired by her example and as she breathed her last he called out to his faithful companion, "Remember thou the Lord."

It was natural that Peter invite Jesus to his home. It was just as natural that Jesus ministered unto this devoted family.

FOR SOMEONE

Many, when they are healed, feel they are saved for something. They miss the point that they are healed for someone. Our wholeness is to be used for others and to the glory of God.

Peter's mother-in-law rose from the sick bed to minister to others. She rejoiced in her healing, but more importantly, she used her strength to minister unto others.

I would hope that all involved in the ministry of healing would remember that individuals are healed for Someone. That Someone is Jesus. He, in turn, wants the one healed to minister to others in His name.

I have seen many people healed who then live a life contrary to the ways of the Lord. They almost live as if they were healed for continuing a selfish and rebellious life. Unless their heart is on the Lord, the healed person will soon forget Who healed and why.

The writing of Oscar Wilde reveals so vividly that we must realize we are healed for Someone and not something. Otherwise a healing leads to or prolongs a life of continued disobedience and insignificance. Consider this vivid picture which he describes:

Christ came from a white plain to a purple city, and, as He passed through the first street, He heard voices overhead. He saw a young man lying drunk upon a window sill. "Why do you waste your soul in drunkenness?" The young man replied, "Lord, I was a leper and you healed me. What else can I do?"

A little farther through the town He saw a young man following a harlot. "Why do you dissolve your soul in debauchery?" The curt answer was, "Lord, I was blind and you healed me, what else can I do?"

In the middle of the city He saw an old man sitting on the ground and weeping. He asked, "Why do you weep?" The old man responded, "Lord, I was dead and you raised me unto life. What else can I do but weep?"

The three persons had missed the whole point of their marvelous healing. It was as if they were blaming the Lord instead of praising Him. They were continuing to center upon themselves instead of seeing they were healed for Christ and others. They had their heart on something instead of on Someone.

HOW WILL YOU SERVE?

Why do you want to be healed? What will you do if you are healed? Where is your heart now and where will it be after your healing?

I hope you will answer that you want to be healed for Someone. You want to do God's will. What can guide you in the doing of His will?

After you are healed, do the task(s) at hand. Do the things and minister to people in a way which uses the talents God has given you. Peter's mother-in-law rose from her sick bed and did what she could do best. She helped prepare the meal.

I often have individuals tell me they want to really serve the Lord. They want to do something great. They hope God will part the heavens and shout a message to them. They fail to see they will serve best by doing what they have the talent to do. They miss the point that they serve best when they do the task which is at hand.

A friend of mine in his prayers cried out, "Oh God, I want to hit a home run for you." The Lord replied, "My child, just get on first."

However, he kept crying out again and again, "I want to hit a home run for you." The Lord kept saying, "Just get on first. A walk, an error, a Texas Leaguer, an infield hit is all I expect from you."

My friend, like many believers, did not want to faithfully and consistently do the little things at hand, but the "biggy" for God. So once more he cried out in anguish, "Oh God, I want to hit a home run for you."

The Spirit really got through when deep within he heard the response, "My child, can't you understand? Just get on first. I'M UP NEXT!"

We are called to do the little things in service unto others. It is the Lord who will bring us home to victory. We cannot go it alone. We truly and always need HIM and others.

After you are healed let the wonder of His miracle power be seen through your service to others in His name.

Many are willing to tell of their miracle through a verbal testimony. This has its place, but the greatest testimony is service. Paul was delivered from the bite of the deadly serpent. He did not give his time to traveling and speaking of this miracle. No! He simply continued to serve the Lord. He had a task to do and he did it. He realized he was healed for Someone and not for something.

58

HOW CAN IT NOT BE?

I am often asked, "Why do you put so much emphasis upon healing?" "Why are you so committed to the healing ministry?"

My response is that I am not committed to the healing ministry. I am not committed to any ministry. I am committed to a person, Jesus Christ.

THE GREAT COMMISSION

Jesus gave to His Church the Great Commission:
"Go ye therefore, and teach all nations baptizing them in the name of the Father, and of the Son, and of the Holy Ghost," Matt. 28:19.

The question I raise is "What shall His Church teach?

What should be the heart of this message?

Why didn't Jesus specify at the end of His ministry what His followers were to teach? I feel it is because He had already thoroughly instructed them as to what they should teach and preach.

THE GREATEST COMMISSION

I teach what is found in what I call, "The Greatest Commission," which is given in Matt. 10:7, 8 and Luke 10:9:

THE TWELVE

Matthew 10: 7, 8 describes Jesus commissioning His twelve disciples. There is no doubt as to what He would have them to do. The message of healing is definitely part of what should be taught by His loyal followers. Jesus did not hedge in this area at all. (See Mark 3:13-15; Luke 9:1, 2.)

THE SEVENTY

Luke 10:9 records our Lord's words to seventy of His disciples:

"And heal the sick that are therein, and say unto them, the kingdom of God is come nigh unto you."

Here again Jesus is very specific as to what His followers should be teaching and doing. There is no doubt, but what the Good News His followers were proclaiming included healing of the body, soul and spirit.

OBEDIENT

Thus, the Greatest Commission tells us exactly what we are to proclaim. It has specified what we are to teach. The content and emphasis of the commission is not omitted, hidden, or obscured. It is simply to take the message of wholeness to the world. The world needs this Good News. In a clear and concise manner, Jesus commissioned His followers to offer these gifts to the world.

The message of healing is not an adjunct to the message of Good News. It is the message of Good News! Wholeness is salvation and salvation is wholeness. It is healing of the body, soul, and spirit which is to be heralded by the obedient followers of the Lord. It is the message the world needs to hear, must hear, and can hear through the ones completely obedient to the commission of the Master.

THE KINGDOM OF GOD

Jesus certainly felt preaching and teaching the kingdom of God was a must for Him:

"I must preach the kingdom of God to other cities also, for therefore I am sent," Luke 4:43, Mark 1:38.

To this day we can proclaim that the kingdom of God is at hand. What better news can we proclaim?

The kingdom is not confined to the days of the Patriarchs or to the Apostolic age. The kingdom is now! It is within you! (Luke 17:21)

Jesus realized the fullness of the kingdom lay in the future. In His model prayer He instructed us to pray, *"Thy kingdom come,"* Matt. 6:10. But even as it is coming, it is here.

THE REAL QUESTION

The real question is not why do you proclaim healing. I feel the more basic question is, "How can you proclaim the Good News and omit the message of healing?" The message of wholeness has never been rescinded. Who then is distorting the message of the Gospel? I feel it is the one who neglects to bring the Good News of wholeness.

Five times in the Gospels the Greatest Commission of healing the sick is given by the Lord. Yes, five times we are specifically told what to teach and what to proclaim (Matt. 10:7-8; Mark 3:13-15, 6:7-13; Luke 9:1-2, 10:9).

How many times do we have to be told before we are willing to do it? Again may I say, the crucial question is not, "Why do you stress a ministry of healing?" to those who do, but rather, "Why don't you accent the ministry of healing?" to those who don't.

59

HEAVY RESPONSIBILITY

Jesus never tolerated a "take it or leave it" attitude on the part of those who heard His disciples proclaim the message of healing and hope. He placed heavy responsibility upon all who heard this message.

Please carefully and prayerfully consider the following words of our Lord Jesus,

To the twelve disciples:

"And whosoever shall not receive you...it shall be more tolerable for the land of Sodom and Gomorrah in the day of judgment, than for that city," Matt. 10:14, 15.

To the seventy disciples:

"But into whatsoever city ye enter, and they receive you not, ...I say unto you, that it shall be more tolerable in that day for Sodom, than for that city," Luke 10:8, 12.

Frequently believers interpret the above verses in the light of eternal salvation. Jesus was not talking about eternal life in these chapters. He was talking about the more abundant life in this world. I know He told the seventy to rejoice that their names are written in heaven. This is wonderful. However, He first said unto them,

"Behold, I give unto you power to tread on serpents and scorpions, and over all the power of the enemy: and nothing shall by any means hurt you," (Luke 10:19).

The gift of eternal life is not a substitute for power in the life of a believer in this life. It is not an excuse to neglect the message of healing and hope.

Jesus spoke of harsh judgment being brought upon those who refuse the message of healing proclaimed by His disciples.

If you have been hesitant about the message of healing for our day you should carefully study Matthew chapter 10 and Luke chapter 10. They do not leave any loopholes for evasion of the message that Christ is the Great Physician.

TRUTHS

You should keep the following truths in mind:

1. You as a believer are expected to believe Jesus and receive and exercise His power in your life.

2. Those to whom you bring the message of healing will be held accountable for how they respond to this message.

3. The church proclaiming the message of healing should not be the exception, but should be the rule.

4. You are called to enlist others to help take out the message of healing to a sick and dying world (Luke 10:2).

5. There is an urgency to the Lord's message of wholeness. A ho-hum attitude will not be tolerated by Him. He expects obedience now and always. He is Lord, Jesus is LORD!

60

YOUR LIFE SPEAKS

Have you ever heard the expression, "Your actions speak so loud I cannot hear a word you say?"

There is much truth in this statement. It is your life which speaks the loudest concerning your basic concepts and commitment. It is your lifestyle which reveals what you really believe.

It would be difficult to believe the words of a person proclaiming their devotion to the sacredness of life if they made their livelihood from child pornography.

It appears to be hypocrisy when a person speaks of the importance of the church and their love for it and they never attend nor support it in any way. Their actions speak much louder than their words.

It is difficult to hear mothers say they love their children and yet forsake them as they seek life with another mate or to live as a single. Actions speak louder than any number of words.

In like manner, what Jesus did is more important than what He said. His words are of utmost importance, but His deeds are even more important. He points this out,

"But I have greater witness than that of John: for the works which the Father hath given me to finish, the same works that I do, bear witness of me, that the Father hath sent me," John 5:36.

In a sense, John the Baptist had only words. He certainly did not have the "works" of the Lord Jesus. He did not do miracles and healings as did Jesus.

There are many who are most willing to accept the teachings of Jesus. He taught the wonderful truths of the kingdom of God in the Sermon on the Mount (Matt. 5, 6, 7). I do not deny the depth and challenge of His teachings. They are important and essential. However, His lifestyle speaks louder than His words.

It is obvious from the gospels His lifestyle was one of bringing wholeness to those unto whom He ministered. He brought to all a message of healing and of hope.

Prior to the Sermon on the Mount we have an account of the lifestyle of our Lord Jesus:

"And Jesus went about all Galilee, teaching...preaching...and healing all manner of sickness and all manner of disease among the people. And His fame went throughout all Syria: ...there followed Him great multitudes of people..." Matt. 4:23-25.

Following the Sermon on the Mount we have many incidents which depict the lifestyle of our Lord. They all bare witness of His desire and ability to bring wholeness unto those whom He met.

"...great multitudes followed Him...there came a leper...And Jesus put forth his hand, and touched him, saying, I will; be thou clean," Matt. 8:1-4.

There follows an account of miracle after miracle. I would suggest you read at this time Matthew 8:1 through Matthew 12:30.

It is indeed a mystery to me why so many are willing to accept His teaching but refuse His lifestyle. I do not infer we should neglect His teachings, but is not the lifestyle more important? Should we not seek to do what He did, as well as to study what He said? Jesus put a lot of emphasis upon His lifestyle,

"If I do not the works of my Father, believe me not. But if I do, though ye believe me not, believe the works:..." John 10:37, 38.

61

THE HEALING COMMUNITY

The Lord has ordained that healing be a part of His body, the Church, as He flows through the community of believers. It is so important for you to realize you are not alone. Others are also a vital part of your pilgrimage to wholeness.

Many individuals believe they cannot be healed or that they cannot have a meaningful healing ministry because of their lack of faith. Your faith is important. I do not want to minimize this fact. However, your individual faith is not the determining factor as far as your healing is concerned. Your effective ministry of healing is not dependent only upon your personal faith.

HEALING IS COMMUNITY

Healing is community. Healing is not something which takes place apart from others. The body of believers is the instrument of healing as the power of the Lord flows in and through the body. Our Lord Jesus has chosen to work through a body of believers and not to deposit His power in an individual.

True, there are some outstanding examples of individuals with great faith, great spiritual acumen, and great spiritual power. However, just as there may be one super player on a football team, it still takes 10 other players to win the game. Thus, in the area of healing there may be some more prominent than others, but there are none who can go it alone.

THEIR FAITH

Jesus powerfully teaches healing is community when He healed the paralytic. The incident is recorded in Matthew 9:1-8; Mark 2:1-12; Luke 5:17-26. The community of believers concept is evident when the gospels say, *"when Jesus saw their faith,"* He said *'Your sins are forgiven.'"* A few moments later He said, *"Take up your bed and walk."*

To whom does the word, "their" refer? We do not know. The only thing we know is that it means more than one person. It is plural. I do not know which of the five had faith. Did the four friends talk the sick man into coming to Jesus? Did the sick man and one or two of his friends persuade the others to carry him to Jesus? Did all five of them believe healing would come if they could get the sick man to Jesus? The answer is not given to these questions. The only thing we know for sure is that Jesus was impressed by the faith of more than one person. He honored the faith of a community of believers.

YOU DON'T GO IT ALONE

Isn't it refreshing and exciting to know your healing and the healing ministry is not completely dependent upon you? There are others whose faith is blended with yours to make possible the victories in Jesus. Corporate faith is stronger than individual faith, just as a rope is many times stronger than any one of the strands of the rope.

I meet so many people who feel they must go it alone. They fail to appreciate the fact that the Lord has provided others who also believe. They remind me of the famous organist who had come to town to present a Bach concert. The auditorium was packed and after a colorful and glowing introduction the organist announced, "I am going to play Bach like you never heard Bach played before."

He enthusiastically addressed himself to the keyboard. There was not a single sound. He tried again, but with no success. Flustered beyond words he frantically motioned to the gentleman pumping the billows to apply himself. The man just stood there looking up at the famous organist. After what seemed an eternity, a loud whisper revealed the truth of community. The man at the billows whispered, "Tell them WE are going to play Bach like you have never heard Bach played before."

We do not have the billows pumped by an individual today for the organ recital. However, can you imagine what would have happened at a Virgil Fox concert if the workers at the electric plant refused to do their job? We live, work, believe in community. We must never forget this truth.

HOW MUCH FAITH DO I NEED?

It is difficult to measure faith. Thank God we are not called to be measurers or evaluators of faith. We are called to be examples of faith. We are called to live by faith and not to develop a faith calculator to determine how much we have. Even a little faith, blended with others can accomplish a great deal.

The keeper of the lighthouse lighted a small candle and started up the stairs. The candle timidly said to him, "Why do you do this? I am so small that my light can never be seen by ships in peril." The master replied, "No, but you will lighten my way to the top of the stairs." In addition, when he had ascended the stairs he used the small candle to light the huge beacon light which could be seen for miles. A little had accomplished much.

Remember, a large bank does not have millions of dollars because of one huge account. They have millions and millions of dollars because of thousands and thousands of small accounts.

BLEND YOUR FAITH WITH OTHERS

You will be amazed at what will happen in your life and the life of your church, if you get your eyes off of worrying about your faith and trust the Lord, along with others.

He will honor the corporate faith. When your faith is weak, someone else's will be strong. When others may have weak faith, yours will be strong. The community of believers is the way of the Lord as He imparts His wholeness.

A legend tells of a person granted a tour of the universe. He beheld a long table loaded with delicious food. However, the people seated at the table looked frail and alarmingly hungry. He then noticed the utensils with which they were required to eat were so long they could not get any food to their mouths. This banquet room was designated, "Hell."

Soon he saw a similar banquet table spread with the bounties of mother earth. Those seated at the table were happy, looked well-nourished, and were enjoying the meal. It was evident that the utensils were the same length. It was then he noticed each was feeding a friend across the table. What could not be done if you sought to feed yourself, could easily be accomplished for all if you fed another person. This banquet room was designated, "Heaven."

May you reach out to others with your faith and let others reach out to you with theirs. Blend your faith with others and accept God's plan for wholeness and acknowledge it is the community of believers from whence cometh the power of the Lord.

CONCLUSION

In conclusion, may I call to your attention the fact that Jesus chose a community of twelve. He taught that where two or three are gathered"--that is, community. The early church said, "if any be sick, let him call for the elders." It was more than one elder. The healing ministry is not a hermit ministry. It is not confined to one. It is all of us together. It is all of us in and through Jesus Christ the Great Physician. Amen.

FASTING

62

THE IMPORTANCE OF FASTING

Fasting and prayer are so closely linked that they both should be a part of the disciplined life of every believer.

In his book, "God's Chosen Fast," Arthur Wallis has well stated:

"Fasting is important, more important, perhaps than many of us have supposed. For all that it is not a major biblical doctrine, a foundation stone of the faith, or a panacea for every spiritual ill. Nevertheless, when exercised with a pure heart and a right motive, fasting may provide us a window opening up new horizons in the unseen world; a spiritual weapon of God's proving..."

It is obvious fasting was an important part of the life of many of God's leaders through the centuries. We have many Biblical examples of individuals fasting. Moses, David, Elijah, Daniel, Hannah, Anna, Paul, Barnabas all come to mind. Even our Lord began His public ministry with 40 days of prayer and fasting.

CHRIST'S TEACHING

Our Lord did not eliminate fasting from the disciplined spiritual life.

He took for granted any sincere believer would be fasting from time to time. He did not present fasting as an option. He taught that our pilgrimage of faith includes times of fasting. He did not say, "If you fast," but he confidently said, "When you fast..."

"Moreover when you fast, be not as the hypocrites, of a sad countenance...but thou, when thou fastest, anoint thine head and wash thy face," Matt. 6:16-18.

Jesus approached fasting as He did prayer and contributing to the needy. He simply took for granted that believers would fast.

He took this as much for granted as He did that believers would pray and that they would share what they have with others.

There were no "ifs" or "buts" about the spiritual discipline of fasting. Fasting and prayer were a part of our Lord's disciplined life and He wanted them to be a part of the disciplined life of His followers:

"And when thou prayest..." Matt. 6:5-7.
"...when thou doest alms...." Matt. 6:1-4.
"...when ye fast...." Matt. 6:16.

FOCUSED ON THE LORD

One of the practical aspects of fasting is it helps you to get your mind off of yourself and upon others and the Lord.

Many in our nation have so much they have become spiritually flabby. Overeating and improper eating habits can also lead to many problems in our physical body.

Lack of discipline in the midst of abundance in the things of the spirit can lead to spiritual heart trouble. Ultimately spiritual heart trouble is more devastating to you than is physical heart trouble.

Moses realized the spiritual dangers of abundance. He said, "...*lest when thou hast eaten and art full, hast goodly houses...herds and flocks multiply, thy silver* and *gold is multiplied,...then thine heart be lifted up, and thou forget the Lord thy God...*" Deut. 8:11-14.

The prophet Hosea graphically reveals the fears of Moses were not unfounded. He says, "...*they were filled, and their heart was exalted; therefore they have forsaken me,*" Hosea 13:6.

Misuse and abuse of abundance were sins of Sodom. We usually think only of their sin of homosexuality. Notice carefully the indictment of the prophet Ezekiel. He does not minimize the horrible sin of sodomy, but he puts his finger on a very real problem which is often neglected. "*Your sister Sodom's sins were pride and laziness and too much food, while the poor and needy suffered outside her door,*" Ez. 16:49 LB.

Fasting is doing by choice what many must do of necessity. It is abstaining from food. It goes further and permits the spiritual to be accented. It is a conscious effort to cease to always serve the flesh. It is for our day.

63

THE BIBLE AND FASTING

Fasting was definitely a part of the life of many of the individuals of Biblical times. It has been a spiritual practice on the part of the devout through the centuries.

The Church of our day needs to stress the positive privileges and power of fasting. It is my prayer Christians today will seek the Lord's forgiveness as never before for failing to fast.

TYPES OF FASTING

There are three basic types of fasting mentioned in Scripture. All are for a limited period of time and observed on many different occasions and for many different reasons. They are as follows:

1. The Normal Fast--This is the abstaining from all forms of food, but not from water.

2. The Absolute Fast--This involves the abstaining from all food and all liquids.

3. The Partial Fast--This is curtailing, but not completely eliminating one's intake of food and drink.

I have listed below some biblical references to fasting. You will find the references to be helpful for your own study as well as for teaching and preaching opportunities.

OLD TESTAMENT REFERENCES TO FASTING

1. Exod. 34:28 .... By Moses
2. Lev. 23:14 .... Until the wave offering
3. Num. 6:3, 4 .... The Nazarite Law
4. Deut. 9:9, 18 .... By Moses
5. Judges 20:26 .... By Israel
6. I Sam. 1:7, 8 .... By Hannah
7. I Sam. 7:6 .... At Mizpah
8. I Sam. 14:24-30 .... Saul's battle instructions
9. I Sam. 20:34 .... Jonathan grieved
10. I Sam. 28:20 .... Saul before his death
11. I Sam. 31:13 &
    I Chron. 10:12 .... By those who buried Saul
12. II Sam. 1:12 .... David and his men
13. II Sam. 3:35 .... David at Abner's death
14. II Sam. 12:16-23 ...... David at son's death
15. I Kings 13:8-25 .... By Prophet
16. I Kings 19:4-8 .... By Elijah
17. I Kings 21:9 .... When Naboth set on high
18. I Kings 21:12 .... By Ahab
19. II Chron. 20:3 .... Proclaimed by Jehoshaphat
20. Ezra 8:21-23 .... Proclaimed by Ezra
21. Ezra 10:6 .... By Ezra
22. Neh. 1:4 .... By Nehemiah
23. Neh. 9:1 .... By people of Jerusalem
24. Esther 4:3 .... By the Jews
25. Esther 4:16 .... Called by Esther
26. Esther 9:31 .... Feast of Purim
27. Psalm 35:13 .... Psalmist for the sick

28. Psalm 69:10 . . . . .The soul chastened
29. Psalm 109:24 . . . . .The cause of weakness
30. Isa. 58:1-14 . . . . .Fasting which pleases God
31. Jer. 14:10-12 . . . . .Fasting which displeases God
32. Jer. 36:5-10 . . . . .A Day of Fasting
33. Dan. 1:12-16 . . . . .Limited food consumption
34. Dan. 6:18 . . . . .By Darius
35. Dan. 9:3 . . . . .By Daniel
36. Dan. 10:2, 3 . . . . .Daniel's partial fast
37. Joel 1:14 . . . . .Sanctify a Fast
38. Joel 2:12 . . . . .When returning to God
39. Joel 2:15 . . . . .Sanctify a Fast
40. Jonah 3:5-9 . . . . .By people of Nineveh
41. Zech. 7:3-5 . . . . .Fifth & Seventh months
42. Zech. 8:19 . . . . .4th, 5th, 7th, 9th months

NEW TESTAMENT REFERENCES TO FASTING

1. Matt. 4:2, Luke 4:2 . . . . .By our Lord
2. Matt. 6:16:18 . . . . .Not as hypocrites
3. Matt. 9:14; Mark 2:18
   Luke 5:33 . . . . .John's disciples & Pharisees
4. Matt. 9:15; Mark 2:19;
   Luke 5:34 . . . . .When bridegroom departed
5. Matt. 11:18; Luke 7:33-- A disciple of John
6. Matt. 15:32; Mark 8:3--   The four thousand
7. Matt. 17:21; Mark 9:29-- Prayer and fasting
8. Luke 2:37 . . . . .By Anna
9. Luke 18:12 . . . . .By boastful Pharisee
10. Acts 9:9 . . . . .By Saul of Tarsus
11. (Acts 10:30) . . . . .By Cornelius
12. Acts 13:2, 3 . . . . .At Antioch
13. Acts 14:23 . . . . .Appointment of Elders
14. Acts 23:12-21 . . . . .Jews desiring to kill Paul
15. Acts 27:9 . . . . .Day of Atonement
    See: Lev. 16:29; 23:27, 32; Num. 29:7

16. Acts 27:21, 33 .... By those with Paul
17. (I Cor. 7:5) .... In marriage relationship
18. II Cor. 6:5 .... Part of a faithful ministry
19. II Cor. 11:27 .... Among Paul's sufferings

In ( ) are references to fasting in the King James Version, which are omitted by most later versions.

64

SPIRITUAL HEALING AND FASTING

Spiritual wholeness is a demanding life. In fact, physical, spiritual, and emotional wholeness demands dedicated devotion to God's laws.

One of the avenues to vitality of body, soul, and spirit is fasting. Sad but true, this discipline of the Christian life is often completely neglected by most believers.

I am one who believes the ministry of Spiritual Healing cannot be pursued to the fullest if fasting is neglected. It must be included. Saints through the ages have told us fasting helps cultivate the presence and power of the Lord.

WHAT IS FASTING?

The dictionary definition of fasting is abstinence from food, partial or total, or from prescribed kinds of foods, for a limited period of time.

The word, *"faest,"* meaning *"firm or fixed,"* is the Anglo-Saxon word from which our word, *fast*, is derived. Thus *fast* simply means to fasten or hold one's self from food.

THE BIBLE AND FASTING

There are dozens of references to fasting in the Bible. I call your attention to the following occasions of fasting as revealed in the scriptures:

a. Fasting in times of national crises (II Chr. 21:3; Esther 4:16).

b. To escape God's judgment (Jonah 3:5).

c. As a sign of repentance (I Sam. 7:6).

d. When in close fellowship with God (Ex. 34:28) --Moses.

e. In the face of personal dangers and difficulties (I Kings 19:20) - Elijah.

f. When burdened for others (Ezra 10:6).

g. For spiritual insight (Daniel 10:3).

h. As Church leaders are chosen and commissioned (Acts 13:2; 14:23).

i. As a practice endorsed by the Lord Jesus (Luke 4:1, 2).

Some Christians infer Jesus discouraged fasting. They teach that He did away with all rituals.

A careful study of the Scriptures will reveal otherwise. He practiced fasting. This was especially true during the 40 days of His temptation, and before He began His public ministry.

He gave a strong and positive endorsement of fasting. "*But thou, when thou fastest, anoint thine head, and wash thy face; that thou appear not unto men to fast, but unto the Father which is in secret...*" Matt. 6:17, 18.

These words indicate Jesus expected His followers to fast. He did not want them to do it for show, but for power. His intent was not to prohibit fasting, but to promote the proper aspects of fasting.

He admonished his followers to fast in private. It was another source of spiritual power for them. I must emphasize that although fasting was to be a private exercise, Jesus healed in public. Good works were to be evident before all.

"Let your light so shine before men, that they may see your good works, and glorify your Father which is in heaven," Matt. 5:16.

The exercises of prayer, fasting, and giving are to be done privately, but the release of His power is to be done publicly.

SOME RULES FOR FASTING

There are some guidelines concerning fasting which will help you. Please consider:

1. Set aside a definite day of the week or month when you will fast.

2. Observe a special fast in regard to a specific occasion such as a need in your life, in the life of a friend, a special event in your church, special problem facing our nation, etc.

3. Devote as much time as possible to the study of the Bible and of Christian literature during your times of fasting.

4. Decide today to soon devote yourself to a time of fasting and prayer. Fasting is for you and you should be fasting. Discover the power of this spiritual discipline.

PRAYER

65

PRAYER POWER

As far as the biblical record is concerned, the only thing the disciples ever asked the Master to teach them was how to pray.

"And it came to pass, that, as he was praying in a certain place, when he ceased, one of his disciples said unto him, 'Lord, teach us to pray, as John also taught his disciples,'" Luke 11:1.

We have several instances of Jesus teaching His disciples and other people concerning many things.

"And it came to pass, when Jesus had made an end of commanding his twelve disciples, he departed thence to teach and to preach in their cities," Matt. 11:1.

"And he began again to teach by the sea side; and there was gathered unto him a great multitude..." Mark 4:1.

"And when the sabbath day was come, he began to teach in the synagogue; and many hearing him were astonished," Mark 6:2.

"And Jesus, when he came out, saw much people, and was moved with compassion toward them, because they were as sheep not having a shepherd;

and he began to teach them many things," Mark 6:34.

"And he began to teach them, that the Son of man must suffer many things, and be rejected of the elders, and of the chief priests, and scribes, and be killed, and after three days rise again," Mark 8:31.

We are told in most cases what Jesus taught the people or the disciples. However, we have no record of the disciples asking Him to specifically teach them in greater detail about any of the things he proclaimed other than prayer. They, on ocassion, did ask Him to further interpret a parable, but not to teach them a specific thing. (See Matt. 13:36; Luke 8:9)

WHY AND HOW TO PRAY

I firmly believe they asked Jesus to be taught how to pray, because they saw what He was able to accomplish.

They knew He spent many hours in prayer. Consider the references: Morning (Mark 1:35); Evening (Mark 6:46); Alone (Luke 5:15, 16); All night (Luke 6:12); With His disciples (Luke 9:18); In the garden (Luke 22:41); In public (Matt. 6:9-13, 11:25-27; Luke 3:21, 11:2-4; John 11:41-42, 17:1-26).

They also knew that when He came in contact with individuals or the multitudes, He released the power of God. He healed and restored hope to those who were ill and downcast.

His disciples surely perceived the power which flowed from Him in a fashion they had never known before. They were fully aware that He wanted to have this same power flow through them. He specifically instructs them to go forth and to heal, (Matt. 10:1; Mark 6:7; Luke 10:1-9; John 14:12).

They certainly had perceived by this time that the Lord Jesus prayed in private and healed in public. There is no record of a long public prayer by our Lord. Neither is there a record of a private healing by our Lord. He always took two or three of His disciples into the room with Him or else He healed in the presence of many and often in the midst of a multitude. He would on occasion take a person a short distance from the crowd, but his friends obviously knew the person was with Jesus and certainly were immediately aware of his healing (Mark 8:22-26).

We are inclined to reverse the process and pray in public and heal in private, if we even seek to heal at all in the Name of Jesus Christ of Nazareth.

Further evidence that prayer was the avenue through which the Lord Jesus appropriated the power of God is seen in the incident following His transfiguration. He comes down from the mountain and is met by a distressed father with a son the disciples could not heal.

Now, they must have attempted to heal him. They must have sought to practice what Jesus had taught them. The people must have expected the disciples to be able to heal. All of this and more is evident from the comment of the father, "*I brought him to thy disciples, and they could not cure him,*" Matt. 17:16.

The fact that they had attempted to cure the child is further enhanced with the pertinent question the disciples asked Jesus. "*Then came the disciples to*

Jesus apart, and said, 'Why could not we cast him out?'"
Matt. 17:19.

If they had not tried, why this question? He answers in this fashion: "*Howbeit this kind goeth not out but by prayer and fasting,*" Matt. 17:21. Scholars tell us the word "fasting" is not present in ancient manuscripts. Prayer is really the key.

The results of prayer should be healings. Prayer is more than eloquence. It is more than liturgy. It is more than form. True prayer is appropriating the power of the living God into your life. Power should be released in your life and in the lives of those unto whom you minister with prayer.

Yes, the disciples saw the practical results of a life of prayer. They wanted prayer power, and asked Jesus to teach them to pray. It is still the believer's most worthy goal. "Lord, teach us to pray." Amen.

66

PRAYER AND HEALING

The Bible certainly conveys the importance of prayer. For instance:

"...*Men ought always to pray and not to faint,*" Luke 18:1.

"*Pray without ceasing,*" I Thess. 5:17.

"...*the effectual fervent prayer of a righteous man* availeth much," James 5:16.

DEEP COMMUNION

Prayer is the deep communion and precious fellowship of the believer with the Triune God. This relationship is essential. "It is Thee and not Thy gifts I crave," said Matheson.

NOT MAGIC

Prayer is more than seeking to move God to fulfill our selfish desires. It is not magic. It is not a tool to be used only in a "pinch."

It is not simply an avenue for seeking special favors from the Lord, nor the key to changing God's mind.

CONVERSATION

Brother Lawrence presents a beautiful insight concerning prayer when he speaks of it as a continual conversation with God.

"There is not in the world a kind of life more sweet and delightful than that of a continual conversation with God. Those only can comprehend it who practice and experience it."

BREATH OF THE SPIRIT

Prayer is more than passive contemplation. It is the Spirit of the Living God being very much a part of you. It is relating to the Lord in the most meaningful way possible.

William James has well said that prayer "is the very soul and essence of religion" and without prayer there "is no intimate commerce, no interior dialogue, no interchange, no action of God in man, no return of man to God."

ANIMAL OR CHILD OF GOD?

Tennyson so vividly conveys that if a believer does not pray, he/she is no better than an animal:

"More things are wrought by prayer
Than this world dreams of. Wherefore, let thy voice
Rise like a fountain for me night and day
For what are men better than sheep or goats
That nourish a blind life within the brain,
If, knowing God, they lift not hands of prayer
Both for themselves and those who call them
  friend."

ALWAYS PRAY

R.T. Richey eloquently conveys the truth of the Apostle Paul's statement that a believer should pray "without ceasing."

"Men ought to pray when clouds gather and rain descends in torrents; when birds have hushed their songs and flowers no longer bloom; when sorrow lays its crushing weight on the heart and all is wrong with the world. Men ought to pray when it seems God has forgotten to be gracious; when souls seem bleak and barren; when the flour bin is empty; when house rent is past due and there is not money to meet pressing bills; when the job is done and there is no other in sight, when health and hope are gone and friends are gone and money is gone and everything is gone - for God is not gone, He is ever near, He never changes."

PRAYER AND HEALING

Healing without prayer is like a body without the breath of life. Every believer must realize no one has done all he can about any problem or illness until he has prayed. Also, he should pray with others and be prayed for and ministered unto with prayer by others.

This emphasis upon prayer is in no way a suggestion that professional help should be ignored or neglected.

AID TO HEALING

Even in physical distress prayer is vital. Dr. Alexis Carrel has written, "A doctor who sees a patient give himself to prayer can indeed rejoice. The calm engendered by prayer is a powerful aid to healing. It appears indispensable to our highest development."

PRAYER SUGGESTIONS

Below are some practical ways to make prayer a vital part of healing in your life:

1. Each believer should spend time each day in prayer and meditation.

2. Develop and maintain a prayer group in cooperation with your church.

3. Form prayer chains for urgent requests.

4. Have intercessory prayer time at healing services or prayer groups.

5. Use my book, "Personal Prayer Diary," in which prayer requests may be entered as they are received and answers to prayer recorded.

6. Each believer should make the 30-Day Prayer Pilgrimage as outlined in this book.

IT WORKS

Prayer is a most practical and powerful force. It does work. Pray today!

67

PRACTICAL PRAYER

Prayer is essential. It is essential not because it enables us to do the work of the church. It is essential because it *is* the work of the church.

A VITAL PRAYER LIFE

You can develop a more vital prayer life. It is imperative you do so. It is the one aspect of Christian devotion which can be done anytime, anywhere, and by anyone.

Prayer knows no barriers. It can circle our globe in an instant. It is possible through prayer to enter prisons, lift distant loved ones unto the Lord, and to enter into impossible situations. This power should not be neglected by you or by any believer.

Below are two very practical prayers which will help you minister unto yourself and to others. I also include positive exhortation for the one unto whom you minister in prayer.

I. AFFIRMATION

The Lord has invited you unto Himself. You need to affirm in your own heart the faith the Lord has given to you. Therefore, I suggest this prayer:

"Precious Father, you are my Creator and Sustainer. You are Lord of my spirit, body, and soul. As your child I have been made alive in Christ Jesus. I am free from the law of sin and death.

"Holy Spirit, thank you for ever wanting to impart the assurance of your presence with me. Thank you for revealing to me the love, light, and peace of the Father. Thank you for continuing to cleanse, guide, and comfort me.

"Lord Jesus, I am grateful that I can give my life to you as an instrument of your healing life and love. Amen."

II. INTERCESSION

I strongly encourage you to minister unto others through intercessory prayer. Prayers in intercession do not have to be long. I suggest the following:

"Father of all mercies, I pray for your wholeness for ...(name)... May he/she know your love in its fullness. Set him/her free from fears, distresses, and infirmities. I pray for ...(name)... in the Name of Jesus Christ our Great Physician. Amen."

After praying the above I would encourage you to continue ministering unto the one in need. The following prayer will help you do this. It may even be used when the person you are ministering unto is not in your presence.

"...(name)..., as I lift you into the light and love of the Lord I pray you will commit your life unto your loving heavenly Father. May you realize He is more willing to forgive, restore, refresh, and revive than you are to ask. I pray you will know that our Lord does not give you the spirit of fear, but of power, and of love and of a sound mind.

"...(name)..., be of good cheer. The Lord's love surrounds you. May His ways become your ways. May His precious peace pervade your being. May you lift your eyes from your problems to your Problem Solver, Jesus Christ. May His joy be within you, His radiance around you, His glory above you, and His everlasting arms underneath you.

"...(name)..., may these truths be grasped by you. May you never forsake them. These things I pray in the Name of Jesus Christ our Great Physician and through the power of the Holy Spirit. Amen."

The words of the prophet Samuel are fitting to consider when thinking of intercessory prayer. He said, "*God forbid that I should sin against the Lord in ceasing to pray for you,*" (I Sam. 12:23).

68

PATTERNS OF PRAYER

One of my goals is to accent corporate and private prayer in our churches. The church is more than a building. It is really a group of believers meeting and serving in the Name of the Lord Jesus, the Head of His Church.

A person once said to me, "You certainly have a beautiful church," obviously referring to our truly beautiful colonial- style building.

My reply was, "We really do! And the building is nice too." I sought to convey that a church is actually the people. The building happens to be the place where we assemble for corporate worship, study, and fellowship.

The following I pray will help bring prayer to the forefront to a greater degree on the part of all who read and study this section.

IMPORTANCE OF PRAYER

Isn't it interesting that the only specific responsibility of Elders, as listed in the scriptures, is to pray for the sick and to anoint them? What was considered primary to the leaders of the early church has been relegated to almost last place by the contemporary church, or sometimes completely ignored.

You and I are called to a deep and abiding communion with the Living Lord. Please consider the following scriptures:

BELIEVING PRAYER

Mark 16:17   *"These signs shall follow those that believe..."*

John 14:12   *"He that believeth on me, the works that I do..."*

James 5:15   *"The prayer of faith shall save thee..."*

EXPECTANT PRAYER

Matt. 8:8   *"Speak the word only and..."*

Matt. 9:21   *"If I but touch..."*

ACCEPTING PRAYER

Matt. 14:36   *"As many as touched..."*

PRAYER OF THANKFULNESS

John 11:41   *"...Father, I thank thee that thou..."*

PRAYER OF PRAISE

Matt. 15:31   *"...And they glorified the God of Israel..."*

PRAYER OF CONFESSION

Rom. 10:9   *"If thou wilt confess..."*

James 5:16   *"Confess...pray...that ye may be healed."*

I John 1:9   *"If we confess our sins..."*

PRAYER OF ABSOLUTION

Rom. 10:13   *"Whosoever shall call..."*

I John 1:9   *"...He is faithful and just to forgive..."*

PRAYER OF RELINQUISHMENT

Mark 14:36   *"...Not what I will, but what thou wilt..."*

Luke 23:46   *"...Father, into thy hands..."*

Acts 7:59   *"...Lord Jesus, receive my spirit..."*

WITH LAYING ON OF HANDS

Mark 6:5   *"He laid hands on few..."*

Mark 16:18   *"...and they shall lay hands on the sick..."*

PRAYER WITH ANOINTING

Mark 6:13   *"...and anointed with oil many who were ill..."*

James 5:14   *"...anointing him with oil..."*

INTERCESSORY PRAYER

Luke 22:32   *"I have prayed for thee..."*

John 17:9   *"I pray for them..."*

Eph. 1:16   *"...making mention...in my prayers..."*

PETITIONARY PRAYER

Luke 18:13   *"...be merciful to me..."*

James 5:13   *"...and let him pray..."*

WHAT IS PRAYER?

I define prayer as believing, appropriating, and releasing the power of God into and through you as a believer.

It is my experience that often what is thought to be prayer is really only a pious recitation of our problems, or an exercise of begging God for favors. Frequently there is little expectation He will help. The point of His inward strength in the midst of all is often overlooked.

We must believe the Lord is willing and able to help in the situation of deep concern. The one praying must appropriate the power of the Lord by faith. The final step is believing the power of the Lord is being released for strength and solutions.

True prayer, not pious formality, leads to commitment. Commitment leads to great things. I like what H. M. Murray wrote concerning commitment.

"Until one is committed, there is a hesitancy, a chance to draw back. But the moment one commits oneself, then God moves too, and a whole stream of events erupts. All manner of unforseen incidents, meetings, persons and material assistance, which no man could have dreamed would come his way, begins to flow toward him."

CONCLUSION

It is the privilege of every believer to develop and to maintain a meaningful prayer life. May you discipline your life to that end.

69

A PATTERN OF PRAYER

I am frequently asked, "How do you pray for someone who is ill?" This is a very pertinent question and one I shall seek to answer.

I Cor. 12:9 speaks of the gift of healing. I like Dr. William Barclay's insights concerning this verse: "*The Church never altogether lost this gift of healing; and one of the biggest things that is happening today is that the Church is rediscovering it. The old Frenchman Montaigne, one of the wisest writers who ever wrote, said about a boy's education, 'I would have his limbs trained no less than his brains. It is not a mind we are educating nor a body; it is a man. And we must not split him in two.' For too long the Church has split man into a soul and a body, and has accepted responsibility for his soul but not for his body. It is one of the greatest recoveries of our time that once again we are learning to treat man as a whole, and the day will come when the doctor and the minister will once again work hand in hand.*"

It is my firm conviction that prayer is the work of the church. It is not simply a tool to be used to equip a person to do church work. Believers are workers together with God and not for God (I Cor. 3:9).

After decades of living the Christian life it was Dr. Albert E. Day who said, "*This half-century of pilgrimage has wrought deeply into my soul the conviction that the life of prayer is the most indispensable aspect of our career on earth. Without it, there cannot be either the personal holiness or social effectiveness for which earnest persons yearn and in which alone is there hope for a desirable future for mankind.*"

Dr. Alexis Carrel wrote, "*The influence of prayer on the human mind and body is as demonstrable as that of the secreting glands. Its results can be measured in terms of increased physical buoyancy, a greater intellectual vigor, moral stamina, and deeper understanding of the realities underlying human relationships. Properly understood, prayer is a mature activity indispensable to the fullest development of personality--the ultimate integration of man's highest faculties.*"

An unknown author has succinctly stated, "Of all the calls flung out across the world, the sovereign summons is to intercession."

The following is my personal pattern of prayer, as I present the pattern in my book, "Personal Prayer Diary." The six steps I suggest are linked to six portions of the Lord's prayer.

I have also included a scripture reference for each segment of the prayer pattern. This will enable you to study for yourself and to teach others concerning prayer and to base your teaching upon the Word of God.

STEP ONE - QUIET

STEP TWO - LIFT

STEP THREE - VISUALIZE

STEP FOUR - BELIEVE

STEP FIVE - PRAISE

STEP SIX - TRUST

I now want to expound on each of the above six steps in the rest of this chapter, and following chapters.

STEP ONE - QUIET

(Psalm 46:10)

"Our Father, which art in heaven, hallowed be Thy Name," Matt. 6:9.

Father, I seek to quiet my mind, emotions, body, spirit (Ps. 46:10) and:

* My quiet spirit rejoices that I am created to worship you (John 4:24)

* My entire being is strengthened as I hear the still small voice of the Lord Jesus saying, "*I died for you,*" (Eph. 2:13)

* I realize afresh the Holy Spirit is my strength (Rom. 8:11)

I lift up my hands without wrath and without doubt (I Tim. 2:8) and give thanks for:

* forgiveness of my sins (Col. 2:13)
* the power of the Holy Spirit in my life (I Cor. 3:16)
* divine health of body, soul, and spirit (III John 1:2)
* being able to believe for Your healing in all areas of my life (Isa. 53:5)
* deliverance from the curse of the law and freedom in Christ Jesus (Gal. 3:13)

STEP TWO - LIFT

(Matt. 11:28; John 8:12; I John 2:8)

"Thy Kingdom come, Thy will be done; in earth as it is in heaven," Matt 6:10

I lift myself, Father, into your light and love as I:

* claim the realities of Your Kingdom (Ps. 22:28)
* name and repent of any known sin in my life (James 5:16).

I lift my hands without doubt and without wrath (I Tim. 2:8) and release Your power in and through... (Do not hesitate to be very specific as you verbalize needs):

* my activity goals for today (I Tim. 4:8)
* my business affairs for today and the future (Joshua 1:7)
* my thoughts, temptations, passions (Luke 22:40)
* my dreams and ambitions (I Cor. 9:25)

* my seeking Your kingdom and Your righteousness (Matt. 6:33)

STEP THREE - VISUALIZE

(Proverbs 23:7)

"*Give us this day our daily bread,*"
Matthew 6:11

Father, I seek to visualize my needs met in such areas as:

* a meaningful prayer life (Luke 18:1; Matt. 21:13)
* fellowship with a local body of believers (Heb. 10:25)
* the necessities of life (Phil. 4:19)
* money to contribute to Your work throughout the world (Eph. 4:28)
* being able to rebuke Satan in all areas of life (Eph. 6:13)
* having restored many-fold the health and wealth Satan has stolen (Prov. 6:31)

I lift my hands without wrath and without doubt (I Tim. 2:8) as I face East, West, North, and South (Isa. 43:4-7) and as I face each direction I:

* release Your power (Matt. 10:8)
* bind Satan in the Name of Jesus (Luke 10:17)
* send forth my ministering angels (Heb. 1:14)
* believe blessings are coming from sources and people unknown (Matt. 7:7, 8)

STEP FOUR - BELIEVE

(Mark 9:23; John 14:12; Heb. 11:6)

"And forgive us our trespasses as we forgive those who trespass against us," Matt. 6:12

Father, I believe You as I seek:

* Your forgiveness for any unconfessed sin which I now confess (I John 1:9)

* a firm belief that Jesus Christ has paid for all my sins (II Cor. 5:21)

* strength to love even my enemies and those who persecute me (Matt. 5:44)

* to see those who speak evil of me as my "joy makers" and not as individuals permitted to depress and defeat me (Matt. 5:11, 12)

* a greater understanding of Your health care plan encompassed in the Fruit of the Spirit (Gal. 5:22-23): * love * joy * peace * longsuffering * gentleness * goodness * faith * meekness * temperance
I lift up my hands without wrath and without doubt (I Tim. 2:8) and:

* thank you that my debt of sin has been paid in full (Colossians 2:13)

* acknowledge that I am a person of unclean lips in the midst of a people of unclean lips (Isa. 6:5)

* accept Your willingness to forgive all of my sins be they real or imagined (Matt. 6:12)

STEP FIVE - PRAISE

(Heb. 13:15; I Peter 2:9; Ps. 22:3)

"And lead us not into temptation, but deliver us from evil," Matt. 6:13

I praise You, Lord, that I can:

* believe and possess victory in Jesus (Rom. 5:17)

* know You are my fortress and the One in whom I can trust (Ps. 91:2)

* have constant victory in Jesus (John 16:33)

* realize I am surrounded, upheld, and protected by You, the Almighty One (Psalm 91)

* know I can overcome any and all temptations (I Cor. 10:13)

I lift up my hands without wrath and without doubt (I Tim. 2:8) and put on Your full armour (Eph. 6:14):

* loins girded with truth (Eph. 6:14)

* breastplate of righteousness (Eph. 6:14)

* feet shod with the Gospel of peace (Eph. 6:15)

* shield of faith (Eph. 6:16)

* helmet of salvation (Eph. 6:17)

* sword of the Spirit (Eph. 6:17)

If praying alone, you may desire to read or repeat some favorite verses or portions of the Scripture. If in a group, participants may share favorite verses or passages from the Bible.

STEP SIX - TRUST

(Ps. 37:5; 118:8; Prov. 3:5; Isa. 26:3, 4)

"*For thine is the Kingdom, and the power and the glory for ever. Amen,*" Matt. 6:13.

Father, I rejoice my times are in Your hands (Ps. 31:15) and that:

* I can know Your Kingdom is not of this world (Rom. 14:17)

* You are stronger than any problem(s) that I face (name them) and I believe for victory (Phil. 4:13)

* I can trust You in all situations. (Name them) (Rom. 8:31, 37)

I lift my hands without wrath and without doubt (I Tim. 2:8) as I pray:

"Father, thank you for making it possible for me to be delivered from sin through Your only begotten Son, the Lord Jesus Christ. I praise Your Name that I have been set free to live in freedom.

"I thank you for my family. I claim each and every one of them for You. I thank You for Your precious promises concerning family members. I believe Your promises are for me and for them. I truly believe You stand firmly behind every one of Your promises without respect of persons.

"I am trusting in Your victory this very moment. You loved the world so much You gave Your only begotten Son for it. I want to love the world through You, and I want You to continue to love the world through me.

"Please receive my hearty and loud Amens as uttered in the Name of Jesus and through the power of the Holy Spirit. Amen, Amen, and Amen! Hallelujah, Hallelujah, Hallelujah!"

70

A PATTERN OF PRAYER - QUIETNESS

Most believers discover that prayer is a quieting force in their lives. They feel William James was correct when he said, "The exercise of prayer, in those who habitually exert it, must be regarded by us doctors as the most adequate and normal of all the pacifiers of the mind and calmers of the nerves."

Prayer really becomes effective when we learn to quiet our whole being in the presence of the Lord before we pray.

I believe the prayer of faith is most often prayed by the relaxed person, and best received by the relaxed person. I do not mean the indifferent, but the relaxed person is one whose confidence is in the Lord.

Dr. A.E. Day writes, "Right prayer demands a quieting of the whole being...the truest prayer begins when we pass beyond words into deep silence; when lips are hushed; when racing thoughts are stilled; when emotions are placid as the dawning over the waveless ocean."

The Bible calls for the quiet spirit.

"Be still and know that I am God..." Ps. 46:10.
"And that ye study to be quiet..." I Thess. 4:11 KJV.

STEPS TO QUIETNESS

You may ask, "How can a person arrive at this point of holy hush before the Lord? How can I bring others to this place?" Here is what I do.

When I begin to intercede for another I seek first to quiet my mind. I put forth conscious effort to still the racing mind and to contemplate upon the presence of the Lord. I then seek to quiet my heart and to bring my emotions to a placidity before God. I simply imagine His being with me and giving to me His Peace. Then I seek to quiet my physical body. I consciously imagine every cell of my body being open to His spirit. I desire to be clear and open to His power. I use this approach whether I am ministering to someone present with me or in some distant place. If the person is with me I lay my hands upon them and say the following:

"Now I want you to join with me in this ministry of prayer. I am laying my hands upon you and seeking to quiet my whole being before the Lord. I want you to do the same. I ask that to the best of your ability you quiet your mind. Also, I want you to quiet your heart, so that at least for these few moments you will be quiet in the Lord. Let your total emotions relax in the Loving Lord. I want you to seek to relax your body. Begin at the top of your head and let the relaxed spirit flow through your face, body, legs, to the very tip of your toes. You are now opening yourself completely to the power of the Lord and I am going to minister unto you with prayer."

It is amazing to me how many are so tense, and feel they must struggle with the Lord to receive His answer. It is hard for them to realize He is more willing to answer than they are to call.

CONFIDENCE IN THE LORD

I learned a long time ago that the Lord does not hear because we shout or carry on in prayer. In fact, as I searched the Scriptures I discovered it was not the believers who had to shout, but those who worshiped false gods (I Kings 18:28). Elijah prayed what I have affectionately termed a "Presbyterian prayer." It was short and to the point (I Kings 18:36, 37). The fire of the Lord fell and the sacrifice was consumed. Later Elijah learned even more dramatically that the Lord's presence is in quietness (I Kings 19:12).

THE STRENGTH OF QUIETNESS

A force, to be strong, does not have to be loud. In fact, the strongest force in the universe, other than God, is gravity. It holds the galaxies in place and keeps objects and people from chaos. Yet, you never hear gravity. No one has ever said to you, "What was that grating noise?" and you replied, "Oh, it is just gravity pulling a little harder for the moment." This is ridiculous. Gravity is never heard, but always experienced.

Evaporation is a powerful force. More water goes up each day throughout the world than comes down. The most ravaging flood in all history did not contain more water than evaporation lifted from the earth. Yet, you have never sat by the seashore and said, "Wow! Did you hear that? Evaporation is really heavy today." Nonsense, you will never hear the water ascending. It is a quiet force.

The power of growth which increases the size of a child, splits a rock wherein a seed has fallen, which becomes a tree, or the flourishing of a wheat field is silent. You do not hear your children or grandchildren grow. Tons of leaves are produced every year on the thousands of acres of forest land of our planet. Yet, never a sound is heard. Growth is silent.

The most sacred moments of life are usually the most quiet ones. Hushed is the soul in deep communion with the Lord. Further, in the most intimate moments of man and woman there is a holy quietness which prevails.

I often say the Lord frequently comes nigh in His holy "hush puppies!" The still soul is the one who detects His presence and power.

An exuberant worship service is wonderful, but you also need those moments of being quiet, ever so quiet before the Lord.

71

A PATTERN OF PRAYER - LIFT

After you have quieted yourself before the Lord, learn to lift yourself and those for whom you are concerned into the light and love of the Lord.

PROBLEM SOLVER

It is absolutely essential all of our prayer concerns be lifted unto the Lord. He alone is the Problem Solver.

It is impossible for me to solve anyone's problem or to heal anyone. Only the Lord can do this. His forces of wholeness must be received for any healing or help to come.

Therefore, when I lift someone into the light and love of the Lord, at least for the moment, I get my eyes off of the problem and onto the Problem Solver. If the individual is present when I pray I ask him/her to also imagine being in the light and love of the Lord. Thus together we seek to open ourselves completely for His wholeness to flow.

MY BURDEN BEARER

The Lord is more than willing for you to give your burdens to Him. He has asked that you do so.

"Come unto me, all ye that labour and are heavy laden, and I will give you rest," Matt. 11:28.

"Casting all your care upon Him, for He careth for you," I Peter 5:7.

I seek to lift myself and others into the light and love of the Lord. I want to bring myself and them to Jesus the Great Physician.

I do not, and cannot, visualize the resurrected King of Kings in mere human form. I best picture Him as light and love. This helps me to realize He is everywhere and able to penetrate every situation. He is willing to bring His touch to every segment of my life and your life.

Thus light and love are parts of the mental picture I paint to lift myself, and those unto whom I minister in prayer, unto the One who is the Great Physician and the Answer for you.

LIGHT

Light possesses so many beneficial characteristics that it is indeed an appropriate concept concerning our Lord.

Light dispels darkness, reveals, purifies, guides, makes growth possible, serves as a transmitter of voice, is a source of energy, etc.

Light is also the fruit of God's first recorded command. *"And God said, 'Let there be light; and there was light,"* Gen. 1:3.

Jesus often referred to Himself as light. "*...I am the light of the world: he that followeth me shall not walk in darkness, but shall have the light of life,*" John 8:12.

"*I am come a light into the world, that whosoever believeth on me should not abide in darkness,*" John 12:46.

There are many Scripture references which refer to Christ as light. "*In Him was life; and the life was the light of men,*" John 1:4.

"*To give light to them that sit in darkness...*" Luke 1:79.

"*A light to lighten the Gentiles and the glory of thy people Israel,*" Luke 2:32.

"*But if we walk in the light, as he is in the light, we have fellowship one with the other, and the blood of Jesus Christ His Son cleanseth us from all sin,*" I John 1:7.

"*And the city had no need of the sun, neither of the moon, ...and the Lamb is the light thereof,*" Rev. 21:23.

WASTE DISPOSAL

You may be assured the best waste disposal place for your problems is in the arms of Jesus. He is the world's first class garbage collector. He takes all your filth and concerns unto Himself. They are never returned by Him and they never can further polute the world. Thus, it is unto Him we should lift all of our needs and concerns now and forever.

72

A PATTERN OF PRAYER - VISUALIZE

Visualization is not a sinful activity nor is it contrary to the Word of the Lord. Some Christians feel if you stress this facet of prayer you are moving into some New Age territory. Nothing could be further from the truth. I am one who does not want to permit abuse by cults to keep me from utilizing Christian principles and procedures to the fullest.

I find the discipline of visualizing to be very helpful as part of my prayer life. I seek to visualize the wholeness of the Lord being transmitted to the one for whom I pray. The Lord is the Healer. However, as His child I can ask for His healing power. I am an instrument not because I have some very special power to heal, but because I have a very special heavenly Father.

POWER OF IMAGINATION

You have often heard the common appraisal, "His illness is all in his imagination." This is possible. Members of the medical profession tell us a large percentage of illnesses are emotionally induced.

Have you ever considered that you can also use your imagination to be well? There is emotionally induced wholeness as well as emotionally induced illness.

The writer of the book of Proverbs proclaimed a great truth when he said, "*For as he thinketh in his heart, so is he...*" Pro. 23:7.

Have you ever given time to visualize yourself as healthy, and/or visualize wholeness for the ones for whom you pray?

TANGIBLE HELP

Visualization is a most tangible step to really believing. You are using the wonderful brain God gave you, which directs the rest of your body. It puts power into your prayers.

This is the reason I suggest that when you pray for healing for yourself and others, you seek to visualize them healed. Whatever the illness or situation may be, visualize the Lord bringing His wholeness into the situation.

I know from experience that too often we spend our prayer time dwelling upon the problem. This only compounds the problem.

It was a number of years ago that I discovered this from personal experience. My illness at the time was such that there was no moment of the day I was not in pain. The only time I was not aware of pain were the brief moments when I was distracted by some activity or conversation. I was constantly praying for the Lord to take away the pain or at least to give me some relief.

I finally realized my praying for the pain to be relieved was simply concentrating more upon the pain. It was then, and in subsequent years, that I learned to pray for the wholeness which I sought to realize. No longer would I pray, "Lord, take away my pain." Now my prayers would be somewhat as follows:

"Father, may your presence prevail in every cell, nerve, and fiber of my being. Thank you for the comfort and the peace and wholeness which you are bringing to me. I bring my total being into your light and love."

This was a completely different and much more helpful approach. Instead of negatively praying for pain to be gone, I positively visualized my body as well. This got my mind off of my pain. I concentrated upon my body as well. I mentally pictured myself free of pain and free to function as I should.

I have since learned to go further and picture myself, or the one for whom I am praying, as using the afflicted organ.

HOW LONG AND HOW OFTEN

You may ask, "How often and for how long should I visualize wholeness?" My answer is, "all the time you possibly can." You will have your weak moments, and slide back into the rut of doubt. However, as much as possible, continue to visualize wholeness. A man was on the danger list in the hospital with cirrhosis. I ministered unto him with prayer and visualized the diseased liver cells as whole and the process of deterioration as reversed. I laid hands upon him as I prayed. He had an immediate and remarkable remission. The Lord gave him six more months and he was used to bring several people to Jesus. Prior to this time he had little or no use for the things of the Lord nor for His people.

Effective prayer takes time and practice. The Lord uses the vessel willing to follow His laws and to obey and believe His word. Start where you are to visualize the wholeness of the Lord entering into your situation.

73

A PATTERN OF PRAYER - BELIEVE

No pattern of prayer would be complete without emphasis upon the power of faith and the importance of believing.

There are many Bible references which impart the importance of belief. Please consider:

"...he that believeth on Me, the works that I do shall he do also..." (John 14:12).

"...all things are possible to him that believeth," (Mark 9:23).

"...for he that cometh to God must believe that He is, and that He is a rewarder of them that diligently seek Him," (Heb. 11:6).

FOR WHOM YOU PRAY

When I pray for someone I endeavor to lead them to really believe that the Lord is present and that He loves them.

This is not always easy to do. Most individuals come to me for prayer because of deep distress. They do not come because of great belief.

Emotionally and spiritually they can no more help themselves than can a seriously physically afflicted person. We who pray for others should realize this problem and face it. May I illustrate?

If you discovered someone on the floor with two broken legs and two crushed arms, you would not insist he get up and phone a physician. You would call the doctor for him. Now, many are just as critically crippled emotionally and spiritually. How can belief enter their situation?

YOU BELIEVE

There is power released when you believe as you minister unto someone with prayer. Jesus honored the faith of others in behalf of a friend.

"When Jesus saw their faith, he said unto the sick of the palsy, Son, thy sins be forgiven thee," (Mark 2:5). These words speak volumes.

BELIEVE FOR OTHERS

The Lord does not want you to wait until everyone in the world believes before you pray. He has called you to believe and to pray. Several of the greatest miracles I have witnessed have happened to individuals who had little or no faith.

For instance, I prayed for one who was physically afflicted because of a whiplash, depressed, spiritually dead, and who didn't even want someone to pray for her. Reluctantly she came for prayer ministry with her husband and friends.

She was instantly healed physically, emotionally, spiritually, and received the baptism of the Holy

Spirit and the gift of tongues. Quite a miracle for one who did not believe and did not want prayer and Laying-on-of-hands! What released the power of the Lord in her life? I believe it was the faith of those of us ministering unto her with prayer.

SHARE YOUR FAITH

I hope you will not feel I am minimizing the faith of the one for whom prayer is offered. I am trying to point out your responsibility even when the other person's faith is weak or absent, as the following demonstrates:

I was asked to visit a hospital patient. She was the most seriously ill individual I have ever met, who was restored to relatively good health. She was critically ill physically, emotionally, and spiritually. Her treatment included many weeks in the psychiatric ward and at times being shackled to her bed. Screaming and thrashing, she would curse God and man. She did not, and said she could not believe. As graciously as possible I told her that the Lord did care. She remonstrated with, "I have no faith and I don't and can't believe!" My reply was, "True, at this moment. However, let my faith undergird you. I believe the Lord loves you and He is going to heal you."

She was in no condition to have me present the theological implications of her believing. She needed to be undergirded by my faith. Her recovery has been a miracle. She has often mentioned how she was sustained by my prayer and others. She was much too ill to believe on her own. Your faith is important for you and for others.

Belief is more than a private, nice feeling on the inside of a person. Believing involves developing and maintaining a lifestyle in keeping with the teachings of our Lord Jesus Christ. It involves deeds more than doctrine, and action more than accepting certain beliefs of a denomination. Faith is the key which opens the door to the power and presence of the Lord for you and others.

74

A PATTERN OF PRAYER - PRAISE

The Lord has chosen His favorite place among believers in the midst of their praises. I want the Lord in my life and in the midst of those with whom I worship and journey with as believers. I love what the Psalmist stresses in the midst of a very tragic Psalm:

"But thou art holy, O thou that inhabitest the praises of Israel," (Psalm 22:3).

EMPHASIS UPON PRAISE

Praise is referred to often in the Bible and emphasis is placed upon it as one of the most important facets of victorious Christian living. Praise is contained in the Bible as follows:

Praise = 236 times,
Praised = 26 times,
Praiseth = 1 time,
Praising = 10 times
Praises = 27 times.

It is evident that believers are to praise the Lord and to rejoice in their relationship with Him. Your prayer life will be greatly enhanced if there is time devoted to conscious praise.

"By him therefore let us offer the sacrifice of praise to God continually, that is, the fruit of our lips giving thanks to his name," (Heb. 13:15).

Many feel true sacrifice is to give up some beloved habit or object. Others feel it is doing a super abundance of work, or to deprive themselves of something. All of these have some value, but the sacrifice the Lord seeks is praise.

It is relatively easy to praise the Lord when a healing has occurred. Frequently I am asked what I do for those for whom prayer is offered and there is no healing. My answer is that I seek to lead all people to praise the Lord. All of us need to praise God regardless of what happens at the moment of prayer, or what happens in the future.

Most of the healings I witness are not instantaneous. Healing is more of a pilgrimage than it is an incident. This is not to deny the validity of instantaneous healing, but to face the reality that most healings are gradual.

Thus, once I have ministered to an individual for healing I begin to encourage him/her to praise the Lord for the healing which is taking place. This delivers myself and the one for whom I am praying from continually "begging" the Lord for healing. It keeps individuals from dwelling upon their illness.

I believe the Lord knows the need and wants to meet your need. Thus, you are to praise Him for doing so and to put your trust in His wisdom and timing.

Many individuals attend healing services week after week and are not completely healed of their crucial problem of mind or body. Even if they are never healed in some areas, they are urged to develop a spirit of praise. This will change their entire outlook upon the Lord, their problem, and their prayer life, but most of all, they receive healing for their spirit, as God is a Spirit and the word of God instructs us to worship Him in "spirit and truth."

Those who develop a spirit of praise soon discover they have moved to a vital and positive life of prayer.

BENEFITS OF PRAISE

The first person who benefits from a life of praise is the one who is ill. He may not be healed in the area for which he first prays. But he will be healed in other areas. A good example of this is the person who came to me with great pain and physical discomfort. He developed a spirit of praise and although not cured physically, became a confident, rejoicing child of the Lord.

Another individual, as he suffered through what proved to be an incurable physical disease said, "I can now praise the Lord. Thanks be to Him for what He has done for me on the inside!"

Praise moves from our self-pity parties to times of rejoicing and victory. Murmurings and grumbling always turn inward and do harm to the one complaining. Consider the following:

"Caesar's servants prepared a great feast for his nobles and friends. It was such a terrible day that the whole affair had to be canceled. In a rage Caesar ordered his archers to shoot their arrows into the heavens at Jupiter, their chief god, to express anger at him for the horrible rainy weather. Of course, the arrows did not reach heaven, but all came right back to earth. A number of them hit archers and wounded many and killed some of them."

Murmurings have only one direction to go and that is back upon the one murmuring. Surely the Lord doesn't want them nor will He receive them. It is our praises which reach beyond us and keep us aglow for the Lord. It is with the sacrifices of praise that the Lord is well-pleased (Heb. 13:15; I Pet. 2:9).

The second way praise is beneficial is that it blesses others. Someone has said, "If Christians would praise the Lord more the world would doubt Him less." If you want to become powerful in prayer, then become faithful in praise. "The fragrant flower of thanksgiving, which blossoms in the heart of God's people, is the result of a little bud called 'praise' which is firmly affixed to the stem and stalk of Christian faith."

HOW DO YOU PRAISE THE LORD?

There is no "one" way to praise the Lord. However, I offer the following suggestions:

1. Keep your mind on the Problem Solver and often say, "Praise you, Jesus."

2. Read or recite from memory Scripture which praises the Lord: Ps. 33:2; 67:3; 100; 103:1, 2; 105:1, 2; 106:1; 107:1; 117:1, 2; 118:1, 2; 147:1.

3. Actually say aloud many times during the day, "Praise the Lord."

4. Praise the Lord for His victories and benefits. Keep your mind off of the apparent failures. We are not called to be beggars toward God, but to be His children who praise Him continually!

5. Realize you praise the Lord as you praise and speak well of others. This is a point many believers miss. Loved ones and acquaintances are often put down instead of being praised and lifted up in spirit and truth.

We are all familiar with the teachings of Jesus that we have done it unto Him when we have done it unto the least of the brethren (Matt. 25:40).

Christ is intimately part of His followers. Saul was asked by the Lord why he persecuted Him (Acts 9:4). Saul had never actually persecuted Jesus. He had never seen Him in the flesh. Saul was persecuting believers and Jesus is so much a part of all who believe that Saul was persecuting Him.

I feel the same thing is true of praise. When you praise those you see in the flesh you, in a sense, are truly praising the Lord. You might say we can paraphase and substitute the word, "praise," for the word, "love," as follows:

"If a man say, I praise God, and down grades his brother, he is a liar: for he that praiseth not his brother whom he hath seen, how can he praise God whom he hath not seen? And this commandment have we from him, That he who praiseth God praiseth his brother also," I John 4:20, 21.

Thomas Carlisle was a great writer and deep thinker. However, it is said that he was so attached to his mother that he made life miserable for everyone around him. Seldom, if ever, did he have a good word of praise for anyone. He especially ignored his wife. After her death the following entry was found in her diary. "Carlisle never praises me. If he says nothing, I have to be content that things are all right." The absence of any outward negative criticism had to be taken as a form of approval.

What a terrible way to live. She hungered for a little praise and received none. She longed for some recognition and appreciation and it was not forthcoming.

One of the ways you can praise the Lord today is to express some sincere praise unto someone you know. Express appreciation to a member of your family or to a close friend. Even if you must force yourself to do it, I would suggest that you verbalize appreciation to someone today. Surveys have proven again and again that many would gladly work for less money if they received more praise. Praise is desired and praise is desirable. An unknown author has written,

"If with pleasure you are viewing
Any work a man is doing,
If you like him or you love him tell him now,
Don't withhold your approbation till
The preacher makes oration
And he lies with snowy lilies on his grave.
For no matter how you shout it,
He won't know how many tear drops you have shed,

If you think some praise is due him,
Now's the time to slip it to him,
For he cannot read his tombstone when he's dead."
Kathryn II of Russia said, "I praise loudly! I blame softly." A Greek teacher observed, "Many men know how to flatter, but few men know how to praise." One of the sweetest sounds your ears will ever hear are the sounds of praise.

CONCLUSION

The above insights concerning praise leads us to the point where we can truly say I can and will praise the Lord at all times (See Psalm 150).

75

A PATTERN OF PRAYER - TRUST

The dictionary definition of trust is "to repose; trust in; rely upon; to commit to or as to the care of another with assurance; to put something in the care or keeping of; entrust."

Anyone who, in a sense, computerizes his petitions to the Lord and then endeavors to keep track of how many he thinks are answered and how many he feels are not answered is making a mockery of prayer. This is not to say we do not acknowledge His work in our lives and testify of that to others.

Believers are called to be committed followers who fellowship with the Lord. They are not cold calculators who keep track of positive and negative responses to their prayers. Prayer is an experience of fellowship with the Lord. It is not a means of using the Lord for your own selfish ends.

A little blind girl was taken from her father's arms by one of his friends. She showed no fear whatsoever. The father was a bit surprised and said, "Aren't you afraid my child?" She replied that she was not. Her father said, "But you don't know who has you." The

little girl's answer is classic and so beautifully conveyed trust as she responded, "No, but you do, Father."

WHENCE COMETH TRUST?

Trust is of the Lord. He imparts a spirit of trust to
you as you place your trust in Him. It is as if you must
trust, before you are given trust. You are given trust
in order that you might trust. I like the words of
Andrew Murray: "Never try to arouse faith from
within. You cannot stir up faith from the depth of
your heart. Leave your heart and look into the face
of Christ; and listen to what He tells you about how
He will keep you."

The Scriptures are so plain as to Whom you
should trust with all your heart:

*"It is better to trust in the Lord than to put confi-
dence in man,"* Ps. 118:8.

*"Trust in the Lord with all thine heart; and lean not
unto thine own understanding,"* Prov. 3:5. See also:
Isa. 26:4 and Isa. 26:3.

Learning to trust and to lean on the Lord is a
pilgrimage. I feel Brother Lawrence speaks for many
of us. It is evident it took many years for him to arrive
at a level of trust in the Lord which brought him great
joy.

*"I took a resolution to give myself up to God as the
best return I can make for His love and for the love of
Him to renounce all besides. Such was my beginning
and yet I must tell you that for the first ten years I
suffered much. The apprehension that I was not devoted to God as I wished to be, my past sins always*

present to my mind and the great unmerited favors which God did me were matter and source of my sufferings. During this time I fell often and rose presently--during this time I thought of nothing but to end my days and these troubles which did not at all diminish the trust I had in God and which served only to increase my faith. I found myself changed all at once and my soul which to this time was in trouble felt a profound inward peace as if she were in a center and place of rest."

HOW DO WE TRUST?

Trust is really leaving things in the hands of the Lord. Prayer is no more than vain verbalization if the element of trust is absent. The Lord is the One who must make the ultimate decisions concerning our prayers.

Frequently my disappointments in prayer have turned out to be great blessings. I may not have seen the hand of the Lord in the apparent answer. I certainly beheld the will of the Lord in the ultimate answer.

Psalm 73 is my kind of Psalm. The Psalmist's pilgrimage is my pilgrimage. How I love verse 23, *"Nevertheless I am continually with thee; thou hast holden me by my right hand."*

I believe that eternity will reveal a life pattern for each of us which will have been to the Lord's glory. As you minister to yourself and to others, may you keep this thought in mind. May you trust the Lord in all things and in all ways. Consider the following as you learn to trust the Lord:

1. Don't get up tight when you pray for others. Trust the Lord. You are not the healer. He is. May you look only unto Him and encourage others to do the same.

2. Leave the results of your prayers in the hands of the Lord. Many feel the Lord's reputation is at stake and thus they frantically seek to immediately see everyone whole. The Lord's reputation is not at stake. Jesus is Lord and always will be. Deep down you know it is your reputation you are concerned about and apparent failure defeats you. Your real calling is to be obedient and to let the ultimate results up to God.

3. Maintain your confidence in the Lord regardless of the circumstances of life. Many live a life of defeat and despair. They are as the one who wrote. "I entered this world in lowliness; I have lived it in anxiety; I shall leave it in fear." What a pathetic way to live and die. I like the prayer of the fishermen of Brittany, "Keep me my God; my boat is small and the ocean wide." The Living God is with you always (Matt. 28:20).

CONCLUSION

Our consistent trust in the Lord should not be determined by circumstances, but by the fact we are in Him. The desire, ability, and reality of trust is not determined by your outward circumstances. This depends upon your inward spiritual depth. The storms of life may buffet, but the ship of trust will never sink. It will remain afloat by the grace of God.

Our trust results in His peace being ours at all times and in all ways. Two artists were commissioned to paint a picture of trust and confidence in the Lord. The one painted a beautiful pastoral scene. The meadow was green and aflame with blooming flowers. The sky was an exotic blue and dotted with playful clouds. Cows grazed in the distance and a happy family sat on their back porch serenely surveying the tranquility of the moment.

The second picture depicted one of the most devastating storms imaginable. The sky was ominous, the lighting sharp and terrifying. The heavy rain was lashing against the rocks and added force to the raging waterfall. The trees nearly touched the ground as they bent before the onslaught of the wind.

A close inspection revealed a small bird in the cleft of a rock unruffled by the storm. Underneath the picture was the one word--PEACE. This one was chosen because it depicted the peace of God in the midst of the turmoil of life. You can trust Him at all times and in all ways.

76

HEALING AND PRAYER PILGRIMAGE

I have included a 30-Day Prayer Pilgrimage guide in this HEALING HANDBOOK. One of the reasons this is done is because I am thoroughly convinced you cannot separate prayer and healing. The two go hand-in-hand. You have not really learned to pray as effectively as possible if you do not believe for healing through prayer. In like manner, you cannot heal in some cases without the prayer power Jesus appropriated in His own life.

JESUS AND PRAYER

Jesus put tremendous emphasis upon the place and power of prayer in the life of a believer. This is graphically conveyed in the 17th chapter of Matthew.

Jesus is transfigured in the presence of Peter, James, and John (Matt. 17:1-13). They return from the experience and discover the disciples have been unable to bring a healing in the life of a young man (Matt. 17:14-16). Jesus proceeds to heal the young man (Matt. 17:17-18). The disciples privately ask

Jesus why they were unable to heal this afflicted person, (Matt. 17:19-21).

BELIEVERS ARE TO HEAL

Jesus did not rebuke the father for bringing his son to the disciples to be healed. Jesus did not tell the disciples they should not expect to cure everybody. Jesus did not say some situations are too difficult for His followers. He did not say the only one who could heal certain people was Himself.

NO! Jesus said their unbelief prevented the healing. Notice carefully, He did not say the unbelief of the son or the father prevented this healing. He put the blame on the disciples because of their unbelief, (Matt. 17:20).

Jesus went on to say that prayer was essential. *"Howbeit this kind goeth not out but by prayer."* The earliest manuscripts do not include the word fasting. They only mention prayer.

APPROPRIATING THE POWER

Jesus conveyed the message that prayer is not only rightly relating to God, but also includes appropriating the power of God. Jesus never separated prayer from healing and healing from prayer.

His lifestyle depicts the message that prayer without signs following is only pious performance. True prayer releases the power of the Lord. It is not long and fancy verbalization.

True prayer helps to build and release the faith of the one praying. Belief is secured and maintained through proper prayer.

Many believers act as if prayer is simply saying the proper words in the proper position and proper place. Jesus was not one to spend time with words in public prayer. HE PRAYED IN PRIVATE. HE HEALED IN PUBLIC.

This point is further reinforced on the day of His Triumphant entry into Jerusalem. Matthew records Jesus entering the temple and casting out all who sold and bought. Further, He overturned the tables of the moneychangers and those who sold doves (Matt. 21:12).

It was then He proclaimed, "*My house shall be called a house of prayer; but ye have made it a den of thieves,*" Matt. 21:13.

After this pronouncement what did Jesus do? Did He get down on His knees and pray for a long time? Did He have all the people join Him in a time of prayer? Did He teach for an hour concerning the importance of prayer?

NO! He did none of these things. What did He do? He healed! "*And the blind and the lame came to Him in the temple; and he healed them,*" Matt. 21:14. He released the power of God in their midst and healings took place.

Jesus knew prayer, to be prayer, must be power! Prayer, true prayer, equals power; and power, God-given and God-used power, equals prayer.

Most books concerning prayer never touch the area of healing. Isn't this strange? Jesus never separated prayer from healing nor healing from prayer. He definitely told His disciples if they learned to pray they would be able to heal. Can we infer from this, if healings are not taking place, we have failed to learn to pray? I think that we can.

God does not simply want us to relate properly to Him to enable us to feel good and to have us make His day. No, a resounding "no" to this! Rather, He wants us to learn to pray to enable us to receive His blessings. He wants to release His power. Prayer can make this possible.

Yet, traditionally the church has looked at prayer as being "properly" done instead of being the power source for healings. I desire to do what I can to change this approach and to help myself and others to see the hand of God at work in our midst.

Prayer should be much more to believers than the method of opening and closing meetings, piously seeking God's approval for what we already intend to do, or seeking to quiet our nerves. Prayer is power appropriated from the One Who has chosen to have prayer the instrument of releasing His power. Prayer is securing, undergirding, and enhancing belief in the life of each Believer.

NEGATIVE REACTION

Religious leaders are often prone to react negatively to prayer as the release of the Lord's power, as well as relating unto Him. The chief priests, and the scribes were angry at Jesus and even people being healed did not assuage their animosity (Matt. 21:15). It appears prayer to them was important, but certainly they reacted as if it should never accomplish anything of immediate benefit to others. Jesus felt, taught, and demonstrated otherwise. I cannot emphasize enough times that one of the reasons He could powerfully heal in public was that He earnestly and correctly prayed in private.

77

SCRIPTURE AND PRAYER

If prayer is so important, then we should learn all we can about it. Therefore, I shall include in this chapter many biblical references to prayer. A prayerful and careful study of the following will be of help to you:

"THOU shalt make thy prayer unto Him, and He shall hear thee, and thou shalt pay thy vows," Job 22:27.

"SEEK ye the Lord while He may be found, call ye upon Him while He is near..." Isa. 55:6.

"AND it shall come to pass, that before they call, I will answer: and while they are yet speaking, I will hear," Isa. 65:24.

"BUT thou, when thou prayest, enter into thy closet, and when thou hast shut thy door, pray to thy Father which is in secret; and thy Father which seeth in secret shall reward thee openly. But when ye pray, use not vain repetitions, as the heathen do; for they think that they shall be heard for their much speaking. Be not ye therefore like unto them: for your Father knoweth what thing ye have need of, before ye ask him," Matt. 6:6-7.

"IF two of you shall agree on earth as touching any thing that they shall ask, it shall be done for them of my Father which is in heaven," Matt. 18:19.

"ALL things, whatsoever ye shall ask in prayer, believing, ye shall receive," Matt. 21:22.

"WHATSOEVER ye shall ask in my name, that will I do, that the Father may be glorified in the Son," John 14:13.

"ASK, and it shall be given unto you; seek, and ye shall find; knock, and it shall be opened unto you; for every one that asketh receiveth; and he that seeketh findeth; and to him that knocketh it shall be opened," Matt. 7:7.

"THE Lord is nigh unto all them that call upon Him, to all that call upon Him in truth. He will fulfill the desire of them that fear him: he also will hear their cry, and will save them," Ps. 145:18-19.

"PRAY without ceasing," I Thess. 5:17.

"IN every thing give thanks: for this is the will of God in Christ Jesus concerning you," I Thess. 5:18.

"I EXHORT therefore, that, first of all, supplications, prayers, intercessions, and giving of thanks, be made for all men; for kings, and for all that are in authority; that we may lead a quiet and peaceable life in all godliness and honesty," I Tim. 2:1.

"I WILL therefore that men pray every where, lifting up holy hands, without wrath and doubting," I Tim. 2:8.

"LET us come boldly unto the throne of grace, that we may obtain mercy, and find grace to help in time of need," Heb. 4:16.

"THE eyes of the Lord are over the righteous, and His ears are open unto their prayers...." I Pet. 3:12.

"BE ye therefore sober, and watch unto prayer," I Pet. 4:7.

"IS any among you afflicted? Let him pray. Is any merry? Let him sing psalms. Is any sick among you? Let him call for the elders of the church; and let them pray over him, anointing him with oil in the name of the Lord: and the prayer of faith shall save the sick, and the Lord shall raise him up; and if he have committed sins, they shall be forgiven him," James 5:13-15.

"THE effectual fervent prayer of a righteous man availeth much," James 5:16.

"THIS is the confidence that we have in Him, that, if we ask any thing according to His will, He heareth us: and if we know that He hear us, whatsoever we ask, we know that we have the petitions that we desired of Him," I John 5:14.

SOME SHORT PRAYERS

The Bible does not contain long prayers. Prayer is presented more as a lifestyle than hours of verbalizing problems unto the Lord. The following brief prayers will be of interest to you:

ADORATION - PRAISE

"BE Thou exalted, O God, above the heavens; let Thy glory be above all the earth," Ps. 57:5.

"BLESSED be the Lord for evermore. Amen and Amen," Ps. 89:52.

"I WILL love Thee, O Lord, my strength," Ps. 18:1.

"BLESSED are they that dwell in Thy house: they will be still praising Thee," Ps. 84:4.

"BLESS the Lord, O my soul: and all that is within me, bless His holy name," Ps. 103:1.

THANKSGIVING

"I WILL give thanks unto Thee, O Lord...I will sing praises unto Thy name," II Sam. 22:50.

"O GIVE thanks unto the Lord, for He is good: for His mercy endureth for ever," Ps. 107:1.

"BLESS the Lord, O my soul, and forget not all His benefits," Ps. 103:2.

"BLESSED be the Lord, because He hath heard the voice of my supplications," Ps. 28:6.

"VERILY God hath heard me: He hath attended to the voice of my prayer. Blessed be God, which hath not turned away my prayer, not His mercy from me," Ps. 66:19-20.

"THANKS be unto God for His unspeakable gift," II Cor. 9:15.

"THANKS be to God, which giveth us the victory through our Lord Jesus Christ," I Cor. 15:57.

ACKNOWLEDGMENT

"THOU, Lord, hast not forsaken them that seek Thee," Ps. 9:10.

"I WAITED patiently for the Lord; and He inclined unto me, and heard my cry," Ps. 40:1.

"IN the day when I cried Thou answeredst me, and strengthenedst me with strength in my soul," Ps. 138:3.

TRUST

"IN the Lord put I my trust," Ps. 11:1.

"PRESERVE me, O God: for in Thee do I put my trust," Ps. 16:1.

"THE Lord is my shepherd: I shall not want," Ps. 23:1.

TO BE HEARD

"LET my prayer come before Thee: incline Thine ear unto my cry," Ps. 88:2.

HELP-GUIDANCE

"GIVE us help from trouble: for vain is the help of man," Ps. 108:12.

"SHOW me Thy ways, O Lord: teach me Thy paths," Ps. 25:4.

"NOW therefore, O God, strengthen my hands," Neh. 6:9.

"MAKE haste, O God, to deliver me; make haste to help me, O Lord," Ps. 70:1.

"HOLD up my goings in Thy paths, that my footsteps slip not," Ps. 17:5.

"LORD, save us: we perish," Matt. 8:25.

"THOU Son of David, have mercy on us," Matt. 9:27.

"JESUS, Master, have mercy upon us," Luke 17:13.

FOR GRACE

"I STRETCH forth my hands unto Thee: my soul thirsteth after Thee," Ps. 143:6.

FOR MERCY

"LET Thy mercy, O Lord, be upon us, according as we hope in Thee," Ps. 33:22.

"I SAID, Lord, be merciful unto me; heal my soul; for I have sinned against Thee," Ps. 41:4.

FOR GOD'S PRESENCE

"FORSAKE me not, O Lord: O my God, be not far from me," Ps. 38:21.

"ARISE for our help, and redeem us for Thy mercies' sake," Ps. 44:26.

MOUTH AND LIPS

"SET a watch, O Lord, before my mouth; keep the door of my lips," Ps. 141:3.

"O LORD, open Thou my lips; and my mouth shall show forth Thy praise," Ps.51:15.

FOR FORGIVENESS

"HAVE mercy upon me, O God, according to Thy loving-kindness: according unto the multitude of Thy tender mercies blot out my transgressions," Ps. 51:1.

"GOD be merciful to me a sinner," Luke 18:13.

IN DISTRESS

"OUT of the depths have I cried unto Thee, O Lord. Lord, hear my voice: let Thine ears be attentive to the voice of my supplications," Ps. 130:1-2.

TO LEARN

"TEACH me to do Thy will; for Thou art my God," Ps. 143:10.

78

PRAYERS FROM THE OLD TESTAMENT

The art of prayer did not begin with the earthly ministry of our Lord Jesus Christ. It had been developed through the years and was a part of the lives of believers from the beginning. The Old Testament abounds with references to prayer and examples of prayer:

Aaron and Priests	For Benediction........................	Numbers 6:24-26
Abraham	For a Son.................................	Genesis 15:2,3
	For Ishmael..............................	Genesis 17:18
	Intercession for Sodom and Gomorrah, Genesis 18:23	
Asa	For God's Help before Battle..	II Chronicles 14:11
Boaz	For Ruth...................................	Ruth 2:12
Daniel	Blessing and Thanksgiving.......	Daniel 2:20-23
	Confession and Plea for Forgiveness, Daniel 9:4-19	
David	For the Perpetuation of His House, II Samuel 7:18-29	
	For Solomon.............................	I Chronicles 29:19
	For His People..........................	Psalm 25:22, Psalm 28:9
	Confession-For Forgiveness....	Psalm 51
	Confession...............................	II Samuel 24:10
	Confession-Intercession for His People, II Samuel 24:17	
	Thanksgiving............................	I Chronicles 29:10-19
	For the Righteous.....................	Psalm 7:9, Psalm 36:10
Eliezer	For the Success of His Mission, Genesis 24:12-14	
	Thanksgiving for God's Help, Genesis 24:27	
Elijah	For the Widow's Son.................	I Kings 17:20,21
	At Carmel.................................	I Kings 18:36,37

PRAYERS FROM THE PSALMS

(Traditionally these prayers have been attributed to David)

79

PRAYERS FROM THE NEW TESTAMENT

The life style of Jesus was one of prayer. Therefore, as we consider the prayers from the New Testament, it is logical to begin with the prayers of Jesus.

PRAYERS OF JESUS

The Lord's Prayer . . . . Matthew 6:9-13, Luke 11:2-4
To the Father . . . . John 12:27,28
A Thanksgiving . . . . Matthew 11:25,26
At Lazarus' Grave . . . . John 11:41,42
The High Priestly Prayer . . . . John 17
In Gethsemane . . . . Matthew 26:39,42
On the Cross . . . . Luke 23:34,46; Matthew 27:46

PRAYERS UNTO JESUS

The Woman of Canaan For Her Daughter. Matthew 15:22
The Father For His Possessed Son . . . . Matthew 17:15
The Leper . . . . Mark 1:40
Jairus . . . . Mark 5:23
James and John . . . . Mark 10:37
The Thief on the Cross . . . . Luke 23:42

APOSTLES' PRAYERS

The Apostles for Divine Direction . . . . Acts 1:24,25
The Apostles' and Believers' Prayer . . . . . . Acts 4:24-30
STEPHEN For His Murderers . . . . Acts 7:60
PAUL His First Plea Acts9:6
Thanksgiving for the Faith
   of the Roman Christians . . . . Romans 1:8

CONCLUSION

It is my prayer the chapters concerning healing and prayer will help undergird your 30-Day Prayer Pilgrimage.

If prayer is essential to fulfilling our high calling as labourers in the harvest field of sin and disease and to securing others to help us with the harvest, how can we neglect it? (Luke 10:2).

Thus, devoting 30 days developing a lifestyle of prayer is indeed a worthwhile venture. I truly believe many, many people are going to be helped as they blend the message of healing and prayer as presented in this HEALING HANDBOOK.

80

HOW TO TEACH YOURSELF AND OTHERS TO PRAY

The 30-Day Prayer Pilgrimage is included in this Healing Handbook because prayer and healing go together. You cannot separate the two. The prayer of faith is an integral part of the healing of the sick (James 5:15).

PURPOSE

The purpose of the 30-Day Prayer Pilgrimage is to help develop disciplined Christians. It seeks to strengthen believers and to lead unbelievers to accept Jesus Christ as Lord and Saviour.

GOALS

The 30-Day Prayer Pilgrimage is designed to help you achieve several worthwhile and desirable goals. They are:

1. To deepen your devotional life.

2. To learn how to more effectively minister unto yourself and others through prayer.

3. To provide a means of teaching others how to pray as you lead them through this Prayer Pilgrimage.

4. To help you appreciate how healing and prayer are intricately related.

5. To provide guidance for a lifestyle of prayer for the rest of your life.

6. To enable you to effectively and consistently practice His presence.

OTHER RESOURCES

There are other resources available which will enhance your 30-Day Prayer Pilgrimage. They are especially effective in developing your prayer life, deepening your understanding of the month-long topics, and facilitating the Pilgrimage for groups.

1. PERSONAL PRAYER DIARY - This is the booklet I developed in which you may list hundreds of prayer concerns and/or answers. Included in this book is a pattern of prayer which has proven to be an inspiration to many.

2. SECOND MILE RESOURCES - The Second Mile Resources consist of 30 recorded messages. This sixteen-cassette series amplifies the reading topics for each day through the use of teaching and prayer. It also includes the devotions cassette for the group meeting and suggestions for the Leader.

3. LEADER'S GUIDE - The Leader's Guide is for the Pastors and lay people desiring to take a group through the Pilgrimage. It provides the guidance needed to promote and implement the Pilgrimage in a church or group. There is guidance for:

a. Enrollment and Evaluation forms
b. Group meetings
c. Questions to be discussed
d. Cluster Leaders' Guidelines
e. Participants relating to one another
f. Retreat at the close of the Pilgrimage
g. And much more.

4. DEVOTIONAL CASSETTE - This 60-minute cassette consists of a seven-minute devotional message by Pastor Bartow for each of the five Group Meetings and for the Retreat. It also has guidance "For The Leader" to successfully launch and conduct the 30-Day Prayer Pilgrimage.

81

THE PATTERN OF YOUR 30-DAY PILGRIMAGE

The following are all part of your daily devotional exercise. You are encouraged to participate to the fullest extent possible. Some will discover it possible to do all the suggestions, while others will not be able to do everything in the 30 minutes. Each must set his/her own pace and maintain the goal of devotional development, not the goal of making sure you do every suggestion each day. Each of these sections are contained in this Healing Handbook.

PRAYER FOR GUIDANCE

The brief prayer which begins each day's guide is to help set the spirit of devotion and openness. It is an acknowledgement of your dependence upon the Lord for His help.

SCRIPTURAL STUDY

The suggested daily scripture study has been chosen with the intention of helping you understand truths which speak to your everyday experiences.

You are asked to briefly summarize the truths you have gleaned from His Holy Word.

VERSE OF THE DAY

The verse of the day helps you to concentrate upon the Word of God. Seek to plant it in your heart and mind to the best of your ability during this Pilgrimage.

READING

The daily readings were selected to help you develop the skill and power to minister to your own needs and to the needs of others. You are asked to summarize what you read so as to put the truths into your own words and ultimately into your life. I do not desire that you merely have something to do for 30 days, but that you learn things which will be helpful to you for the rest of your life.

PRAYER MINISTRY

You are encouraged to expand your ministry of prayer. This is done by having you specifically pray for some area of concern each day. The suggested concerns are:

Each Monday - Your family and relatives.
Each Tuesday - Government leaders.
Each Wednesday - Missionaries.
Each Thursday - For the unbelievers.
Each Friday - Churches and Denominations.
Each Saturday - For your own church.
Each Sunday - Prayer and Praise.

The above does not limit you to only these concerns on any special day. However, it does help to expand your concerns and to realize all of life is in need of prayer.

The time of concentration in prayer is more than moments of begging God. This is a time of ministering unto others through prayer. Prayer is work. It is ministry.

The entire Experience is designed to help you discover a life style of constant prayer. Herein lies the victory for believers in Christ Jesus.

You should make daily use of your PERSONAL PRAYER DIARY book during this 30-day Pilgrimage. Enter the suggested prayer requests in it, as well as the requests which are uniquely yours.

ACTION TIME

The optional action time suggestion each day is presented only as a guide for you. You may choose to do some other kind deed and in ways I could never imagine. Use your creativeness to minister unto others.

You may find this to be a difficult aspect of your daily devotions, but do the best you can and receive many blessings from so doing.

THEME FOR THE DAY

The theme for the day is an effort to challenge you to consider ways you can change or revamp your thinking. It will help you attain and maintain a victorious life in the Lord. Hopefully it will help lead you to a style of living which will keep you triumphantly aflame for Jesus.

TITHING

Are individuals and families able to tithe in these difficult times? Yes, they are. However, do not let this become such a distracting problem that you miss the impact of the Pilgrimage. At the same time, it would be a spiritually rewarding experience for you to seek to tithe during this 30-day Pilgrimage. It is an adventure which has proven a blessing to believers through the ages.

TIME FOR CHURCH

Many who will be participating in this Pilgrimage are already doing a great deal for their local church. However, there will be those who have not thought of a tangible expression of service to their church each week. Your prayer life and spiritual development will be enhanced as you give of your time and effort for your church.

PRACTICING HIS PRESENCE

It is essential to practice the presence of the Master every day. It is an art developed over a period of time. Each day put forth conscious effort to behold the presence and power of the Lord being manifested in your life.

DAILY QUESTION

The daily question seeks to help you consider at greater depth some facet of the topic. There are no right or wrong objective answers to the questions, but they are asked to ascertain your feelings and insights.

SECOND MILE RESOURCES

Experience has revealed that when you listen to the Second Mile Resources each day there is much greater spiritual growth. The cassettes have been prepared to help you in your personal relationship with the Lord. These resources should not be neglected by the leader or participants. They may be secured from the publisher.

DO IT AGAIN

Many have discovered their second or third time through the Pilgrimage to be the most fruitful. Plan now to participate in the Pilgrimage again in the not-too-distant future.

WHAT NEXT?

After you have experienced the 30-Day Prayer Pilgrimage is an excellent time to encourage others to participate in it. There are probably more of your fellow church members and friends interested in prayer than you realize. I received a letter concerning a person who thought he would have 3 in his group. He ended up with 18. A church averaging 65 in worship each Sunday had 17 participate in this prayer experience. Another congregation which averaged about 85 in worship each Sunday had 22 in their first group. You can start by being enthused about the idea and encouraging others to join you.

The Leader's Guide for the Prayer Pilgrimage is available from the publisher. It presents many helpful insights for enlisting and leading a group on the Pilgrimage.

WHEN TO BEGIN

The Pilgrimage should begin on a Monday. It is 30 days in length and it doesn't matter which Monday of the month you begin.

TIME INVOLVED

The Pilgrimage necessitates a minimum of one-half-hour per day for the 30-day period. If you use the optional resources you will be involved approximately an hour per day.

The specific task for your church will involve perhaps several hours one week, and very little another week. Each participant must make this decision.

It does take some time, but very little compared to the benefits derived.

FASTING

Fasting is a discipline frequently associated with prayer. The Lord Jesus did not make fasting an option, but stated it as a spiritual discipline to be observed by His followers. He said "when" you fast and not "if" you fast.

Your fast may be for one or more meals or for an entire day. It may be longer. If it is, you should use good judgment as to how long and how complete the fast will be.

Many have been blessed by observing a special day of the week for fasting. Each individual must determine when and how long he/she will fast.

During this 30-day Pilgrimage I suggest Wednesday as the day of fasting for each participant. You will have to determine if you desire to fast for one meal or for the entire day. You will determine if it be a total fast throughout the day or simply cutting back on your food intake.

Some may choose to use another day for their fasting experience. The important thing is that you observe some type of fasting during this 30-day period.

PERSISTENCE IS THE KEY

The average person usually begins a new activity with great enthusiasm. However, in a few days or weeks the initial thrill is gone. Interest wanes and so does participation. You are urged to be doggedly persistent with this Pilgrimage. The typical pattern is a first week of great enthusiasm of blessings and experiences. During the second week many will discover they have hit a let-down period.

It is at this time you need to really apply yourself. Once you get through the second week doldrums, you will discover things will become much better for you.

It will be an encouragement and relief to you to know that others have the same second week blues as you. Hang in there and discipline yourself even more. The prize comes to the persistent and not to the one who starts and does not finish.

One of the prime aims of the Pilgrimage is to get all participants to complete it. We want everyone who starts the Pilgrimage to finish, if at all possible. It is not a program to test your spiritual intelligence. Rather, it is a program with purpose. It is an effort to teach you to pray, not only for the moment, but for the rest of your life. It is a Pilgrimage of power.

Your spiritual journey and exercises are like physical exercise. You may become very sore if you have not exercised regularly. However, keep at it and the soreness will depart and you will soon be doing more than you thought you could.

You will gain from this Pilgrimage only what you are willing to put into it. You probably have never devoted an entire month to such rigid devotional practices. Therefore, take advantage of your fine intentions. Don't come to the end of the 30 days saying, "I wish I would have done more." Plan from the beginning to really give yourself to this Pilgrimage to the fullest.

IF YOU FAIL

Perhaps this section should be entitled "when" you fail. It is not a matter of "if" you fail. No one is perfect. It is simply a matter of "when" and "how."

What do you do when you miss a day of devotional time? What do you do when you fail to be aware of His presence, to do a kind act, to minister in prayer, etc.?

You try again. You simply go on from there. You go on seeking to renew and refresh your prayer experiences.

The Apostle Paul summed things up very well when he wrote, "*And let us not be weary in well doing; for in due season we shall reap, if we faint not,*" Gal. 6:9.

THE 30-DAY PRAYER PILGRIMAGE ENROLLMENT FORM

Each participant should carefully read the following prior to enrolling in the Pilgrimage.

Disciplines

The required disciplines of the Pilgrimage to which you are asked to commit are:

1. Spend at least 30 minutes each day in devotions.
2. Attend the Orientation meeting and meet with the group once per week.
3. Seek to practice His presence each day.
4. Tithe your income during this 30-day period.
5. Give time each week in a task for His Church and to do it for your local church or for some Christian group or movement.

Optional

The optional disciplines to which you may also commit are:

6. Seeking to do a kind deed each day.
7. Using the Second Mile Resources.

Enrollment

Having made my commitment to follow the disciplines of the Pilgrimage to the best of my ability, I desire to enroll in the 30-Day Prayer Pilgrimage.

Personal Information

My Name_____ Phone_____

Address_____

City/State/Zip_____

My birthday_____(Year may be omitted)

My vocation_____

My church_____

My pastor_____

What I view as my calling in life:_____

_____

_____

_____

_____

_____

_____

NOTE: You may make as many extra copies of this page as needed to give to individuals for their enrollment.

82

THE 30-DAY PRAYER PILGRIMAGE

The daily readings for the 30-Day Pilgrimage are all in this Healing Handbook and are listed by page number.

1. Use the Enrollment Form on page 405 to understand and make your commitment.
2. Use the Verse of the Day list on page 473 to meditate upon the daily scripture.
3. Use the Evaluation Form beginning on page 469 to assess how well you did in accomplishing the Pilgrimage and also how well the Pilgrimage ministered to you.
4. Use the certificate on page 471 to conclude a worthwhile and fruitful month of your life.

Contained within these next few pages are the daily tools for your spiritual growth.

You are about to enter into a wonderful experience in your devotional life.

I pray the Lord be with you as you begin.

FIRST DAY -- MONDAY,_____19__

Prayer For Guidance -- *Father, as I begin this Prayer Pilgrimage, I pray for your wisdom, guidance and strength. Amen.*

Scripture Study -- Mark 11:20-26. Summarize:

_____

_____

_____

Verse For The Day -- Mark 11:24.

Reading -- Page 550, "How To Receive God's Blessing." Briefly summarize.

_____

_____

_____

Prayer Ministry -- Pray specifically for your family members and at least some of your relatives. List some or all of them in your *PERSONAL PRAYER DIARY.* You may desire to list several names on each request line, and to pray for them by name.

Action Time -- Today seek the Lord's guidance as to which family member or relative you will reach out to with a special act of kindness. It may be someone who has been a special blessing to you recently. Write below the person's name and how you intend to act. Prayerfully follow through with your intentions.

_____

_____

_____

Theme For The Day -- Write below the attitude you would like to possess or impart during the day or tomorrow if you have afternoon or evening devotional time.

_____

_____

Time For His Church -- How do you feel about giving some time each week working for His church this month?

_____

_____

Practicing His Presence -- Through what incident or person did you sense the presence of Christ yesterday? How did it make you feel?

_____

_____

_____

Question -- Do you believe God wants to bless you? Explain.

_____

_____

_____

Second Mile Resource -- Cassette Lecture No. 1, _How To Receive God's Blessing._ Summarize what the lecture meant to you.

_____

_____

_____

_____

SECOND DAY -- TUESDAY,_____19__

Prayer For Guidance -- *Heavenly Father, I do thank you for your Son who gave His life for my life. Amen.*

Scripture Study -- Philippians 4:4-9. Summarize:

_____

_____

_____

Verse For The Day -- Philippians 4:7.

Reading -- Page 567, "Emotionally Induced Wholeness." Briefly summarize.

_____

_____

_____

Prayer Ministry -- Today you minister through prayer unto government leaders. You will want to list local, county, state, national, and world leaders in your *PERSONAL PRAYER DIARY.* You cannot list them all, but only the ones for whom you feel a special burden, ask the Lord to grant them wisdom, courage, health, and direction.

Action Time -- Today your prayer concerns zero in on government officials. You may never have contacted someone like this before. Why not today pray for the Lord to reveal to you someone in government leadership you should write, phone, or talk to in person. Write the name of this person below and follow through on what has been laid upon your heart.

_____

_____

Theme For The Day -- Below write the attitude you would like to possess or impart during the day or tomorrow if you have afternoon or evening devotions.

_____

_____

Practicing His Presence -- Through what incident or person did you sense the presence of Christ yesterday? How did it make you feel?

_____

_____

_____

Time For His Church -- List below the specific task you did for His Church yesterday, the approximate time it took, and how you felt about it.

_____

_____

Question -- How do you feel your mental outlook affects your health?

_____

_____

_____

Second Mile Resource -- Cassette lecture No. 2, *Emotionally Induced Wholeness.* Summarize:

_____

_____

_____

_____

THIRD DAY -- WEDNESDAY,_____19__

Prayer for Guidance -- *Father, help me during the devotional time and throughout the day to be yielded to the things of the Spirit. Amen.*

Scriptural Study -- Psalm 46:1-11. Summarize:

_____

_____

Verse For The Day -- Psalm 46:10.

Reading -- Page 345, "A Pattern Of Prayer - Quietness." Briefly summarize.

_____

_____

Prayer Ministry -- You cannot physically go to all parts of the world. You can spiritually minister in prayer to all corners of the world. List in your *PERSONAL PRAYER DIARY* the names of missionaries and organizations which minister throughout the world. Pray for whom you desire to minister unto through prayer.

Action Time -- There may be a very worthy local mission in your community. Yet, have you ever contacted anyone related to it as to your concern and appreciation for their efforts? Today minister unto someone in your community who is involved in Christian mission. Write them a letter, or phone them, or visit them. Write below the person you will minister unto and how you will do this. Follow through on these good intentions.

_____

_____

Theme For The Day -- Write below the attitude you would like to possess or impart during the coming day.

_____

_____

Time For His Church -- List below the specific task you did for your church yesterday, the approximate time it took, and how you felt about having done it.

_____

_____

Question -- What makes it so difficult for you to quiet yourself in the Lord's presence?

_____

_____

_____

Practicing His Presence -- Through what incident or person did you sense the presence of Christ yesterday? How did it make you feel?

_____

_____

_____

Second Mile Resource -- Lecture No. 3, _A Pattern Of Prayer - Quiet._ Summarize:

_____

_____

_____

_____

FOURTH DAY -- THURSDAY,_____19__

Prayer For Guidance -- *Father, I give to you this day and all that it includes and entails. Amen.*

Scripture Study -- Matthew 11:25-30. Summarize:

_____

_____

_____

Verse For The Day -- Matthew 11:28.

Reading -- Page 349, "A Pattern Of Prayer - Lift." Briefly summarize:

_____

_____

_____

Prayer Ministry -- Today minister through prayer unto family members, relatives, and friends whom you desire to come to a personal knowledge of Christ as their Lord and Saviour. Also, minister through prayer unto some of the countries of the world.

Action Time -- The world hears of horrors and problems every day. Someone must bring to people good news. The best news you can bring to a person is the message that God loves them. Write below the person you want to convey the love of God unto today and how you intend to do this. Your actions pursued will bring blessings to you and the one unto whom you minister.

_____

_____

_____

Theme For The Day -- Write below the attitude you would like to possess or impart during the coming day.

_____

_____

Time For His Church -- List below the specific task you did for your church yesterday, the approximate time it took, and how you felt about having done it.

_____

_____

Practicing His Presence -- Through what incident or person did you sense the presence of Christ yesterday? How did it make you feel?

_____

_____

_____

Question -- Did you fast yesterday? How do you feel about fasting?

_____

_____

_____

Second Mile Resource -- Lecture No. 4, *A Pattern Of Prayer - Lift.* Summarize:

_____

_____

_____

_____

FIFTH DAY -- FRIDAY,_____19__

Prayer For Guidance -- *Help me, Father, to always give the glory to you for your many blessings.*

Scripture Study -- II Corinthians 5:16-21. Summarize:

_____

_____

_____

Verse For The Day -- II Corinthians 5:17.

Reading -- Page 352, "A Pattern Of Prayer - Visualize." Briefly summarize.

_____

_____

_____

Prayer Ministry -- Fridays are devoted to a ministry of prayer unto the churches of your own community. Also, for unity among denominations throughout the world. List in your *PERSONAL PRAYER DIARY* the churches of your community and also the different denominations that you feel should be of prayer concern for you.

Action Time -- Seek the Lord's guidance as to ways you can bear witness to another person of the Oneness which is in Christ Jesus. Let one of your Christian friends know how much you appreciate their dedicated life even though they belong to another denomination. Your good intentions will be lost in the activity of the week unless you follow through on your guidance.

_____

_____

Theme For The Day -- Write below the attitude you would like to possess or impart during the day or tomorrow if you have afternoon or evening devotional time. This may deal with the approach you desire to take toward some problem or situation you now are facing.

_____

_____

_____

Practicing His Presence -- Through what incident or person did you sense the presence of Christ yesterday? How did it make you feel?

_____

_____

_____

Question -- How does a person see with the heart?

_____

_____

_____

Second Mile Resource -- Lecture No. 5, _A Pattern Of Prayer - Visualize._ Summarize:

_____

_____

_____

_____

SIXTH DAY -- SATURDAY,_____19__

Prayer For Guidance -- *Father, my mind often wanders from your presence. Show me how to keep my thoughts on you. Amen.*

Scripture Study -- John 14:1-14. Summarize:

_____

_____

_____

Verse For The Day -- John 14:12.

Reading -- Page 356, "A Pattern Of Prayer - Believe." Briefly summarize.

_____

_____

_____

Prayer Ministry -- Each Saturday I encourage you to minister with prayer unto your own local church. Your church is important. Prayer is the work of your church. Your pastor, officers and fellow members need your prayer ministry. List in your *PERSONAL PRAYER DIARY* specific names for whom you have a ministry of prayer within your local church.

Action Time -- Perhaps today you will want to consider a way you can express your appreciation to your pastor. Write below the way and when you plan to do this. Follow through on your good intentions.

_____

_____

Theme For The Day -- Write below the attitude you would like to possess or impart during the day or tomorrow if you have afternoon or evening devotions.

_____

_____

_____

Group Meeting -- What was your reaction to the resource material given to you at the first group meeting?

_____

_____

_____

Practicing His Presence -- Through what incident or person did you sense the presence of Christ yesterday? How did it make you feel?

_____

_____

_____

Question -- What does it mean to believe?

_____

_____

_____

Second Mile Resource -- Lecture No. 6, _A Pattern Of Prayer - Believe._ Summarize:

_____

_____

_____

SEVENTH DAY -- SUNDAY,_____19_

Prayer For Guidance -- *Father, reveal to me how I can have more confidence in your love for me. May I see your hand at work in my life. Amen.*

Scriptural Study -- Psalm 150:1-6. Summarize:

_____

_____

Verse For The Day -- Psalm 150:6.

Reading -- Page 360, "A Pattern Of Prayer - Praise." Briefly summarize:

_____

_____

_____

Prayer Ministry -- Let this seventh day of the week be one of praise and thanksgiving. Your ministry through prayer today will praise the Lord for your church and for the Head of your church, the Lord Jesus Christ. List in your *PERSONAL PRAYER DIARY* many of the activities and programs of your church for which you praise the Lord.

Action Time -- It is suggested during this 30-day Pilgrimage that Sundays be days of praise unto the Lord. You praise Him most effectively by praising His children. Write below the name of a person to whom you want to express thanks for some action or concern. Let them know that you praise God because of them. Also, write how you plan to do this. Follow through.

_____

_____

Theme For The Day -- Write below the frame of mind and heart you hope to maintain today or tomorrow if you have afternoon or evening devotions.

_____

_____

Time For His Church -- List below the specific task you did for your church yesterday, the approximate time it took, and how you felt about having done it.

_____

_____

_____

Practicing His Presence -- Through what incident or person did you sense the presence of Christ yesterday? How did it make you feel?

_____

_____

_____

Question -- In what situation or circumstance did you praise the Lord yesterday? How did it make you feel?

_____

_____

Second Mile Resource -- Lecture No. 7, _A Pattern Of Prayer - Praise._ Summarize:

_____

_____

_____

_____

EIGHTH DAY -- MONDAY,_____19__

Prayer For Guidance -- *Father, thank you for helping me through this first week of the Prayer Pilgrimage. Forgive where I failed and help me to be faithful throughout this second week. Amen.*

Scripture Study -- Psalm 118:1-9. Summarize:

_____

_____

_____

Verse For The Day -- Psalm 118:6.

Reading -- Page 367, "A Patter Of Prayer - Trust." Briefly summarize.

_____

_____

Prayer Ministry -- Today you again minister in prayer unto members of your family and other relatives. Pray for a wholeness of relationships which will make your family more devoted to each other and relationships with relatives more pleasant.

Action Time -- There may be a family member or relative who is going through an illness or grieving because of the loss of a loved one. Your reaching out to them will be an act of kindness on your part and an encouragement to them. Write below the person you feel led to contact and how you intend to do this. It may be by phone, a letter, card, or perhaps a personal visit. Do follow through your good intentions.

_____

_____

Theme For The Day -- Write below the attitude you would like to possess or impart during the day or tomorrow if you have afternoon or evening devotions.

_____

_____

Tithing -- How do you feel about having tithed last week?

_____

_____

Time For His Church -- What is your reaction concerning your work for your church this week?

_____

_____

Question -- In what areas of your life are you trusting the Lord this very day?

_____

_____

Practicing His Presence -- Through what incident or person did you sense the presence of Christ yesterday? How did it make you feel?

_____

_____

Second Mile Resource -- Lecture No. 8, _A Pattern Of Prayer - Trust._ Summarize:

_____

_____

_____

NINTH DAY -- TUESDAY,_____19__

Prayer For Guidance -- *Father, sometimes my life gets so busy and full. Help me to sort out what I really ought to be doing. Help me do it. Amen.*

Scripture Study -- Isaiah 58:1-7. Summarize:

_____

_____

Verse For The Day -- Matthew 6:18.

Reading -- Page 316, "Spiritual Healing And Fasting." Briefly summarize.

_____

_____

Prayer Ministry -- Your ministry through prayer unto government leaders today could be in the area of peace. Peace is a worthy goal for our world, but it must begin with local leaders and peoples and permeate all of society. Peace in a township, for instance, is essential for ultimate peace in the world.

Action Time -- Your newspaper, radio and TV newscasts and news magazines abound with the names of government officials who are responsible for decisions which will affect the lives of many people. Seek the Lord's guidance as to which one of them you should contact today. Write below this person's name and how you intend to follow through your good intentions.

_____

_____

_____

Theme For The Day -- Write below the attitudes that you feel you are developing as you practice the disciplines of this 30-day Pilgrimage.

_____

_____

_____

Time For His Church -- List below the specific task you did for His Church yesterday, the approximate time it took, and how you felt about it.

_____

_____

Question -- What is your reaction to some time for fasting during this 30-day Pilgrimage?

_____

_____

Second Mile Resource -- Lecture No. 9, *Spiritual Healing And Fasting.* Summarize:

_____

_____

_____

TENTH DAY, -- WEDNESDAY,_____19__

Prayer For Guidance -- *Father, I want this day to be completely yours. Please reveal to me how I can do this and give me your grace to do it. Amen.*

Scripture Study -- Psalm 51:1-12. Summarize:

_____

_____

Verse For The Day -- Psalm 51:10.

Reading -- Page 113, "Inner Illness." Briefly summarize.

_____

_____

Prayer Ministry -- As you minister in prayer unto missionaries today may it be that they will sense your prayer burden for them. The assurance of your concern means so much to those who serve the Lord in other lands and unto other people. Prayer buoys a person in spirit as water buoys your body.

Action Time -- Have you ever written a missionary? Have you ever taken the time to appreciate the price they pay for their faithful service? Why not get a letter off to one of them today? You may even want to enclose a contribution to let them know you appreciate them representing you in the Lord's work in their chosen field. Write below the person you will minister unto and how you intend to do this. Your thoughts will be of little value until you follow through concerning them.

_____

_____

_____

Theme For The Day -- Write below, in light of your personal joys and sorrows, the attitude you would like to possess or impart during the coming day.

_____

_____

_____

Practicing His Presence -- Through what incident or person did you sense the presence of Christ yesterday? How did it make you feel?

_____

_____

_____

Question -- How do you feel Inner Illness is a part of your life?

_____

_____

_____

Second Mile Resource -- Lecture No. 10, *Inner Illness.* Summarize:

_____

_____

_____

_____

ELEVENTH DAY -- THURSDAY,_____19__

Prayer For Guidance -- *Father, I have been aware of your presence. Help me to live in the realities of this awareness. Amen.*

Scripture Study -- John 3:16-21. Summarize:

_____

_____

_____

Verse For The Day -- John 3:16.

Reading -- Page 195, "Inner Healing Through God's Love." Briefly summarize:

_____

_____

_____

Prayer Ministry -- The leadership and people of other countries need our ministry of prayer. Also, remember the individuals you have listed for prayer on Thursdays.

Action Time -- There are many wonderful tracts and books available to help individuals understand the love of God. Today is a good time for you to pass on to another person some of this worthwhile material. Pray for guidance as to whom you will share uplifting reading and how you intend to do this. The fruit of your efforts will only be forthcoming if you follow through on your good intentions.

_____

_____

_____

Theme For The Day -- Write below the frame of mind and spirit you would like to maintain throughout the coming day.

_____

_____

Tithe -- How do you feel a Christian should spend the 90% of his/her money after giving the tithe?

_____

_____

Time For His Church -- List below the specific task you did for your church yesterday, the approximate time it took, and how you felt about having done it.

_____

_____

Question -- Why do you feel fasting is difficult?

_____

_____

Practicing His Presence -- Through what incident or person did you sense the presence of Christ yesterday? How did it make you feel?

_____

_____

_____

Second Mile Resource -- Cassette lecture No. 11, _Inner Healing Through God's Love_. Summarize:

_____

_____

_____

TWELFTH DAY -- FRIDAY,_____19__

Prayer For Guidance -- *Heavenly Father, I need you every moment of this day. Help me to believe that you will be with me every moment. Amen.*

Scripture Study -- Romans 12:1-8. Summarize:

_____

_____

_____

Verse For The Day -- Romans 12:2.

Reading -- Page 199, "Inner Healing Of The Memories." Briefly summarize.

_____

_____

_____

Prayer Ministry -- Today minister through prayer to the members of the local churches of your community. Also, remember the leadership of the denominations seeking to bring unity to the worldwide Church.

Action Time -- Your acceptance of other denominations and appreciation of the variety of worship is important to you and others. Today share with some pastor of another denomination in your community your love for him/her and appreciation of his/her ministry. Write below who this person will be and how you plan to do this. Follow through.

_____

_____

_____

Theme For The Day -- Write below the spirit in which you hope to face the biggest problem that is facing you at this moment.

Group Meeting -- What do you feel you would like to share with your group at the next meeting?

Question -- What memories do you have which need the healing touch of the Lord?

Practicing His Presence -- Through what incident or person did you sense the presence of Christ yesterday? How did it make you feel?

Second Mile Resource -- Cassette lecture No. 12, *Inner Healing - The Memories.* Summarize:

THIRTEENTH DAY -- SAT.,_____19__

Prayer For Guidance -- *Dear Father, it is sometimes such a struggle to fulfill my vows to you. Please help me to understand you love me as I am. Amen.*

Scripture Study -- Psalm 103:1-13. Summarize:

_____

_____

Verse For The Day -- Psalm 103:10.

Reading -- Page 207, "A Prayer For Inner Healing." Briefly summarize.

_____

_____

Prayer Ministry -- Prayer helps you to identify with your fellow church members. Today as your ministry of prayer includes your local church may you be led to rejoice with those who rejoice, weep with those who weep, feel for those who hurt. Identify with your church through prayer today.

Action Time -- Today you may want to express your appreciation for others of your church by planning to attend a function or meeting you have never attended. This will let others know you appreciate their efforts and that you are interested in their area of concern. It might be the children's Sunday School class, the women's circle, a youth activity, etc. Write below what function or meeting you plan to attend and when you will do this. The fulfilling of your good intentions will do much for you and your church.

_____

_____

Theme For The Day -- Write below the attitude you would like to possess or impart during the day or tomorrow if you have afternoon or evening devotions.

_____

_____

Question -- What is your reaction to the prayer for Inner Healing?

_____

_____

Time For His Church -- List below the specific task you did for your church yesterday, the approximate time it took, and how you felt about having done it.

_____

_____

Practicing His Presence -- Through what incident or person did you sense the presence of Christ yesterday? How did it make you feel?

_____

Second Mile Resource -- Cassette lecture No. 13, _A Prayer For Inner Healing._ Summarize:

_____

_____

_____

FOURTEENTH DAY -- SUN.,_____19__

Prayer For Guidance -- *Father, on this day help me to rejoice with others in your presence. Give me the desire and the wisdom to worship you aright. Amen.*

Scripture Study -- Colossians 3:1-17. Summarize:

_____

_____

_____

Verse For The Day -- Colossians 3:14.

Reading -- Page 203, "Some Steps To Inner Healing." Briefly summarize:

_____

_____

_____

Prayer Ministry -- Your ministry through prayer today includes praising God for the challenge of being a member of your church. There are things to be accomplished, obstacles to be overcome, obnoxious individuals to be loved, and goals to be achieved. Praise the Lord for all of them and accept the challenge of being a devout and faithful church member.

Action Time -- Your feelings of praise unto the Lord will be enhanced as you share your good spirit with others. Write below how you plan to greet others at your Sunday School and/or worship service today. May you go out of your way to extend a glad hand and a warm word to many of your fellow worshippers today. Follow through on your good intentions.

_____

Theme For The Day -- Write below how you feel you can maintain a spirit of praise unto the Lord throughout the next week.

_____

_____

_____

Time for His Church -- List the task you did for your church yesterday, the approximate time it took and how you felt about having done it.

_____

_____

_____

Question -- What are some steps toward Inner Healing which you should take?

_____

_____

_____

Practicing His Presence -- Through what incident or person did you sense the presence of Christ yesterday? How did it make you feel?

_____

_____

Second Mile Resource -- Cassette lecture No. 14, *Some Steps To Inner Healing.* Summarize:

_____

_____

_____

FIFTEENTH DAY -- MON.,_____19__

Prayer For Guidance -- *Father, as I begin the third week of this Pilgrimage, I need your help as never before. Please reveal your truths unto me. Thank you. Amen.*

Scripture Study -- Luke 7:19-23. Summarize:

_____

_____

_____

Verse For The Day -- Acts 10:38.

Reading -- Page 214, "Christ's Ministry." Briefly summarize.

_____

_____

_____

Prayer Ministry -- This is the day to specifically minister with prayer unto your family members and to relatives. I suggest that you seek to be a channel for the power of the Lord to flow to them to help in their ministry through each one's particular vocation. May each come to see ways to glorify God through his/her work and other activities.

Action Time -- Has a member of your family received a special award or attained special recognition in his/her work? Consider someone near to you who has received special attention recently and let them know how proud you are of them. Write below the person you will be ministering unto and how you plan to do this. Don't fail to follow through the action the Spirit has laid on your heart.

_____

Theme For The Day -- Write below the way you believe this week is going to go for you.

_____

_____

Tithing -- How do you feel about having tithed last week's income?

_____

_____

Time For His Church -- List the task you did for your church yesterday, the approximate time it took, and how you felt about having done it.

_____

_____

Question -- Do you agree that the lifestyle of Jesus was one of bringing wholeness? Explain.

_____

_____

Practicing His Presence -- Through what incident or person did you sense the presence of Christ yesterday? How did it make you feel?

_____

_____

Second Mile Resource -- Cassette lecture No. 15, _The King of The Kingdom._ Summarize.:

_____

_____

_____

SIXTEENTH DAY -- TUES.,_____19__

Prayer For Guidance -- *Father, I thank you for the still small voice within me which speaks of your love. Help me to believe and to obey your Spirit. Amen.*

Scripture Study -- I Peter 3:7-12.

_____

_____

Verse For The Day -- I Peter 3:8.

Reading -- Page 241, "God's Health Care Plan - Compassion." Briefly sumarize.

_____

_____

Prayer Ministry -- The leadership of government officials on all levels is an important factor in the well-being of all. Your ministry of prayer for government leaders today can be for wisdom in ministering to the poor and oppressed. We need prophetic leadership today if everyone is going to be fairly treated and justly respected.

Action Time -- The peace of the world seems to rest in the hands of government leaders. The local, state, and national peace is essential to world peace. Today consider some political leader you feel is a key person as far as peace among peoples is concerned. Express your interest in them and let them know of your undergirding prayer support. Write below the person you have in mind and how you will pursue your concern. Don't fail to follow through on your concern.

_____

_____

Theme For The Day -- Write below how you would like to see your life change to be able to face today.

_____

_____

_____

Practicing His Presence -- Through what incident or person did you sense the presence of Christ yesterday? How did it make you feel?

_____

_____

Question -- Unto whom and how did you show compassion yesterday?

_____

_____

Time For His Church -- List the task you did for your church yesterday, the approximate time it took, and how you felt about having done it.

_____

_____

Second Mile Resource -- Cassette lecture No. 16, *God's Health Care Plan - Compassion.* Summarize:

_____

_____

_____

_____

SEVENTEENTH DAY -- WED.,_____19__

Prayer For Guidance -- *Father, I want to understand your Word. Reveal your truth unto me today. Amen.*

Scripture Study -- I John 4:8-21. Summarize:

_____

_____

_____

Verse For The Day -- I John 4:11.

Reading -- Page 244, "God's Health Care Plan - Love." Briefly summarize.

_____

_____

_____

Prayer Ministry -- Today you are asked to minister through prayer unto missionaries and outreach organizations. May you seek to be a channel of the flow of the Spirit unto the people to whom the missionaries minister. Their task is difficult and often the harvest seems meager if not barren.

Action Time -- The action time each day is an optional discipline of this Pilgrimage. The blessings you receive if you act are not optional. They are guaranteed. Today may you let some missionary know of your prayer support for them. Write below the person you will contact and how you intend to do this. Do not stop with writing down your guidance, but follow through on your good intentions.

_____

_____

Theme For The Day -- Write below, in the light of your personal joys and sorrows, the attitude you would like to possess or impart during the coming day.

_____

_____

Practicing His Presence -- Through what incident or person did you sense the presence of Christ yesterday? How did it make you feel?

_____

_____

Group Meeting -- How do you feel about the last group meeting?

_____

_____

Question -- How do you define love?

_____

_____

Your Witness -- List below at least two people with whom you will share the love of God in the next three days.

_____

_____

Second Mile Resource -- Cassette lecture No. 17, *God's Health Care Plan - Love.* Summarize:

_____

_____

_____

_____

EIGHTEENTH DAY -- THURS.,_____19__

Prayer For Guidance -- *Father, I ask for your Spirit to lead me in the path of righteousness. May I faithfully seek to do your will. Amen.*

Scripture Study -- John 16:16-24. Summarize:

_____

_____

_____

Verse For The Day -- John 16:24.

Reading -- Page 248, "God's Health Care Plan - Joy." Briefly summarize.

_____

_____

Prayer Ministry -- The lines between believers and un-believers are becoming more sharply drawn each day. Every unbeliever is a mission field worthy of your prayer ministry. Pray today for unbelievers to submit their lives to the Lord Jesus Christ. Revise your *PERSONAL PRAYER DIARY* for this day as needed.

Action Time -- You surely have a friend or acquaintance you feel needs to come to a knowledge of Christ as personal Saviour. Why not invite that individual to a worship service at your church or to some special service at your church or in your community? Write below the person you will invite and how and when you intend to do this. Follow through with your plan.

_____

_____

Theme For The Day -- Write below the attitude you would like to possess or impart during the day.

_____

_____

Time For His Church -- List below the specific task you did for your church yesterday, the approximate time it took, and how you felt about having done it.

_____

_____

Question -- Were you able to fast yesterday? How do you feel about your answer?

_____

_____

Practicing His Presence -- Through what incident or person did you sense the presence of Christ yesterday? How did it make you feel?

_____

_____

Second Mile Resource -- Cassette lecture No. 18, _God's Health Care Plan - Joy._ Summarize:

_____

_____

_____

_____

NINETEENTH DAY -- FRI.,_____19__

Prayer For Guidance -- *Father, I pray you would help me to really pray. May I learn to pray to your glory and to the good of those unto whom I minister in prayer. Amen.*

Scripture Study -- John 14:25-31. Summarize:

_____

_____

_____

Verse For The Day -- Romans 5:1.

Reading -- Page 251, "God's Health Care Plan - Peace." Briefly summarize.

_____

_____

Prayer Ministry -- The pastor and other staff members of the churches of your community need your ministry of prayer. May you be a channel of God's grace to release His power in and through these dedicated workers. Revise your *PERSONAL PRAYER DIARY* as needed.

Action Time -- Every community has leadership devoted to efforts which involve many denominations and many churches. This is sometimes very difficult and frustrating work. Write below someone you can encourage who is working with the different churches of your community. Write below the person you will encourage and how you plan to do this. Your good intentions will mean much when then are pursued and completed.

_____

_____

Theme For The Day -- Write below the spirit in which you hope to face the biggest problem that is facing you at this moment.

_____

_____

Group Meeting -- What have you experienced this week that you would like to share at your next group meeting?

_____

_____

Question -- How important is the peace of the Lord to a believer?

_____

_____

Practicing His Presence -- Through what incident or person did you sense the presence of Christ yesterday? How did it make you feel?

_____

_____

Second Mile Resources -- Cassette lecture No. 19, _God's Health Care Plan - Peace._ Summarize:

_____

_____

_____

_____

TWENTIETH DAY -- SAT.,_____19__

Prayer For Guidance -- *Father, I have so many areas to improve in my life. Reveal to me how I can best do this. Amen.*

Scripture Study -- James 1:1-8. Summarize:

_____

_____

_____

Verse For The Day -- James 1:4.

Reading -- Page 255, "God's Health Care Plan - Patience." Briefly summarize.

_____

_____

_____

Prayer Ministry -- The world would be a better place by far if every believer worshipped regularly in his/her church. Your ministry of prayer today should be for the faithfulness of all of your fellow members.

Action Time -- Express to someone in your church how much you appreciate what they are doing. They deserve to know that someone appreciates their efforts. Write below the person you intend to contact concerning their faithful service in your church and how you intend to do this. Do not neglect to follow through your inner feelings.

_____

_____

_____

Theme For The Day -- Write below the attitude you would like to possess or impart during the day or tomorrow if you have afternoon or evening devotions.

_____

_____

Tithing -- What is your reaction to the statement, "I cannot afford NOT to tithe"?

_____

_____

Question -- In what areas of your life do you need patience?

_____

_____

_____

Practicing His Presence -- Through what incident or person did you sense the presence of Christ yesterday? How did it make you feel?

_____

_____

_____

Second Mile Resource -- Cassette lecture No. 20, _God's Health Care Plan - Patience._ Summarize:

_____

_____

_____

TWENTY-FIRST DAY -- SUN.,_____19__

Prayer For Guidance -- *Father, as I begin my last week of this 30-day Pilgrimage, please help me to make the most of it. Amen.*

Scripture Study -- Ephesians 4:20-32. Summarize:

_____

_____

_____

Verse For The Day -- Ephesians 4:32.

Reading -- Page 259, "God's Health Care Plan - Kindness." Briefly summarize.

_____

_____

Prayer Ministry -- Praise is the key aspect of your ministry of prayer today. Praise the Lord for the hardships encountered in your local church participation and see them as stepping stones to victory in Jesus.

Action Time -- Praise God today by praising someone of your local church. Write below who and how to express appreciation for the person's part in the worship service of your church. It may be the person who presented special music, it might be the choir director, an usher, and pastor, or even the custodian. Write below who you want to minister unto with a word of praise in the Name of Jesus and how you plan to do this. Do not let your good intentions go unheeded.

_____

_____

Theme For The Day -- Write below how you feel you can maintain a spirit of praise unto the Lord throughout the next week.

_____ _____

_____

_____

Time For His Church -- List the task you did for your church yesterday, the approximate time it took, and how you feel about having done it.

_____

_____

Question -- How do you react when someone is kind to you?

_____

_____

Practicing His Presence -- Through what incident or person did you sense the presence of Christ yesterday? How did it make you feel?

_____

_____

Second Mile Resource -- Cassette lecture No. 21, _God's Health Care Plan - Kindness._ Summarize:

_____

_____

_____

_____

TWENTY-SECOND DAY -- MON.,_____19__

Prayer For Guidance -- *Father, quiet my mind and heart. Let me hear your still small voice, and give me the desire and wisdom to respond. Amen.*

Scripture Study -- Psalm 23:1-6. Summarize:

_____

_____

_____

Verse For The Day -- Psalm 23:6.

Reading -- Page 263, "God's Health Care Plan - Goodness." Briefly summarize.

_____

_____

Prayer Ministry -- Your family members and relatives are worthy of your prayer ministry. Today as you specifically lift them unto the Lord may your desire be that each grow in the ways of the Lord and the things of the Spirit.

Action Time -- There may be a member of your family or relative that you have not seen for a long time and yet they have been upon your heart in recent days. Why not let them know of your love for them and that they are in your mind and upon your heart. Write below the name of this person and how you intend to be in touch with them. You will be blessed if you follow through on your good intentions.

_____

_____

_____

Theme For The Day -- Write below the way you believe this week is going to be for you.

_____

_____

_____

Tithing -- How do you feel about having tithed last week's income?

_____

_____

Time For His Church -- Are you satisfied with the specific time you are giving to your church?

_____

Practicing His Presence -- Through what incident or person did you sense the presence of Christ yesterday? How did it make you feel?

_____

_____

_____

Question -- How do you feel the Lord's goodness has been with you?

_____

_____

Second Mile Resource -- Cassette lecture No. 22, _God's Health Care Plan - Goodness._ Summarize:

_____

_____

_____

TWENTY-THIRD DAY -- TUES.,_____19__

Prayer For Guidance -- *Father, it has been hard to spend 30 minutes in devotions each day. I seek your help for me to keep this discipline. Amen.*

Scripture Study -- Luke 16:10-13. Summarize:

_____

_____

_____

Verse For The Day -- Luke 16:13.

Reading -- Page 266, "God's Health Care Plan - Faithfulness." Briefly summarize.

_____

_____

Prayer Ministry -- Leadership in government demands many sacrifices. One aspect deserving of your ministry of prayer is the family life of our leaders. May you minister in prayer to the well being and stability of the family life of government leaders.

Action Time -- The amount of time and energy needed to serve in a political office often leaves the person's family neglected. Today you may desire to inform some local, state, national, or world leader your prayers are with this person's family. Write below the name of the person you feel led to encourage and how you are planning to do this. Follow through on this concern.

_____

_____

_____

Theme For The Day -- Write below how you would like to see your life change to enable you to face your tomorrows.

_____

_____

_____

Practicing His Presence -- Through what incident or person did you sense the presence of Christ yesterday? How did it make you feel?

_____

_____

Question -- Faithfulness -- How do you feel when you know you have been unfaithful in some area of life?

_____

_____

_____

Time For His Church -- List the task you did for your church yesterday, the approximate time it took, and how you felt about having done it.

_____

_____

_____

Second Mile Resource -- Cassette lecture No. 23, _God's Health Care Plan - Faithfulness._ Summarize:

_____

_____

_____

TWENTY-FOURTH DAY -- WED.,_____19_

Prayer For Guidance -- *Father, I want to love your Word. Reveal its truth to me. Amen.*

Scripture Study -- Titus 3:1-8. Summarize:

_____

_____

_____

Verse For The Day -- II Timothy 2:24.

Reading -- Page 270, "God's Health Care Plan - Gentleness." Briefly summarize.

_____

_____

Prayer Ministry -- There is constant need for new recruits in the missionary outreach of the church. Today pray the Lord of the harvest to send laborers into the fields ripe unto harvest. Also, minister in prayer unto your missionary list.

Action Time -- Do you have a favorite mission project or organization? If so, have you ever shared your feelings with others? Today think of someone who may be interested in knowing of your support and interest in a particular mission enterprise. Write below the person you will inform concerning your interest and how you will do it. Do not fail to follow through with your intentions.

_____

_____

_____

Theme For The Day -- Write below, in the light of your personal joys and sorrows, the attitude you would like to possess or impart during the coming day.

_____

_____

Practicing His Presence -- Through what incident or person did you sense the presence of Christ yesterday? How did it make you feel?

_____

_____

Group Meeting -- How do you feel you can develop a more gentle spirit?

_____

_____

Your Witness -- List below the person(s) with whom you desire to share what this Prayer Pilgrimage has meant to you. Seek to enroll the one(s) you list in a future Pilgrimage.

_____

Second Mile Resource -- Cassette lecture No. 24, _God's Health Care Plan - Gentleness._ Summarize.

_____

_____

_____

TWENTY-FIFTH DAY -- THURS.,_____19__

Prayer For Guidance -- *Father, help me to live out in daily life what I am learning in my devotional life. Amen.*

Scripture Study -- Galatians 6:1-10. Summarize:

_____

_____

_____

Verse For The Day -- Galatians 6:7.

Reading -- Page 274, "God's Health Care Plan - Self-Control." Briefly summarize.

_____

_____

Prayer Ministry -- Your ministry of prayer unto unbelievers today should ask the Lord to help Christian believers to have a strong, wise and fruitful outreach to unbelievers. The gospel is preached through sharing of material things as well as spiritual teachings. Caring and sharing leads to believing on the part of many.

Action Time -- It is not easy to get our unbelieving friends to accept the message of the Lord Jesus Christ being their Saviour. Often acts of kindness will open a heart more than words of admonition. Write below a person you would like to see come to Christ and a kind act you want to extend toward him/her. Follow through on your decision.

_____

_____

_____

Theme For The Day -- Write below the attitude you would like to possess or impart during this day.

_____

_____

Time For His Church -- List below the specific task you did for your church yesterday, the approximate time it took, and how you felt about having done it.

_____

_____

Question -- Are there areas of your life in which you need more self-control? Has fasting helped your spirit of self-control?

_____

_____

Practicing His Presence -- Through what incident or person did you sense the presence of Christ yesterday? How did it make you feel?

_____

_____

Second Mile Resource -- Cassette lecture No. 25, _God's Health Care Plan - Self-Control._ Summarize:

_____

_____

_____

TWENTY-SIXTH DAY -- FRI.,_____19__

Prayer For Guidance -- *Father, teach me to pray. Keep me in close communion with you. Amen.*

Scripture Study -- Matthew 8:1-4. Summarize:

_____

_____

_____

Verse For The Day -- James 1:17.

Reading -- Page 529, "According To Thy Will." Briefly summarize.

_____

_____

Prayer Ministry -- The local congregations exist to reach out with the Good News. Your ministry through prayer today for the churches of your community should include their outreach ministry. The world is huge. The message is hope. Prayer is needed to bring this hope to the hopeless.

Action Time -- Today contact a leader of your denomination and express your appreciation and prayer support to this person. The concern and prayer of members of a denomination for the leaders is essential to wholesome growth and spiritual maturity. Write below the person you intend to contact and how you will do this. Your fulfilling these good intentions will result in a blessing for you and for the one you contact.

_____

_____

_____

Theme For The Day -- Write below the spirit in which you hope to face the biggest problem that is facing you at this moment.

_____

_____

Group Meeting -- What have you experienced throughout this Pilgrimage that you would like to share at your next group meeting?

_____

_____

Question -- Do you truly believe it is God's will for you to be well and to be blessed?

_____

_____

Practicing His Presence -- Through what incident or person did you sense the presence of Christ yesterday? How did it make you feel?

_____

_____

_____

Second Mile Resource -- Cassette lecture No. 26, _According To Thy Will._ Summarize:

_____

_____

_____

_____

TWENTY-SEVENTH DAY -- SAT.,_____19__

Prayer For Guidance -- *Father, my earnest prayer is to do your will. Show me the way and help me to walk in it. Amen.*

Scripture Study -- John 10:10. Summarize:

_____

_____

_____

Reading -- Page 479, "What Is Spiritual Healing?" Briefly summarize.

_____

_____

Prayer Ministry -- The Holy Spirit reveals the importance of the church to believers. May your ministry of prayer for your local church today include the point of every member giving of time, talent, and treasure to his/her church as the Lord directs. None can do all in a local church, but all can do something.

Action Time -- Have you ever considered an open letter to members of your church concerning your appreciation for your church? This could be published in your Sunday bulletin or in your parish letter. It could even be read from the pulpit at a worship service. There surely are many things for which you are grateful as far as your church is concerned. Write below some of the things for which you are grateful as far as your church is concerned and when and how you will express this spirit to your fellow members. Follow through on this leading.

_____

_____

Theme For The Day -- Write below the attitude you would like to possess or impart during the day or tomorrow if you have afternoon or evening devotions.

_____

_____

Tithing -- What has been your feeling about tithing your income this month?

_____

_____

Question -- Do you find it difficult to believe in Spiritual Healing?

_____

_____

Practicing His Presence -- Through what incident or person did you sense the presence of Christ yesterday? How did it make you feel?

_____

_____

Second Mile Resource -- Cassette lecture No. 27, *What Is Spiritual Healing.* Summarize:

_____

_____

_____

_____

TWENTY-EIGHTH DAY -- SUN.,_____19__

Prayer For Guidance -- *Father, help me to realize as never before that I need your help. May I believe you want to give it to me. Amen.*

Scripture Study -- Isaiah 53:1-6. Summarize:

_____

_____

Verse For The Day -- Isaiah 53:5.

Reading -- Page 281, "How Does God Heal Today?" Briefly summarize.

_____

_____

Prayer Ministry -- Praise the Lord through your prayer ministry today for the hope you have in Christ and through His Church. Praise Him that your local church can be a part of the total world church in bringing hope to individuals and to nations. Seek to actually enumerate some of the things in your local church for which you should praise God.

Action Time -- How many activities and how many people in your church are a blessing to you? Write a number of them below and spend time praising the Lord for them. You may praise Him in private prayer, or while driving to church, or while busy with activities of the day. The important point is that you develop a spirit of praise for the many facets of your local church and for the many blessings the Lord bestows upon you and yours. Follow through on your good intentions as listed below.

_____

_____

Theme For The Day -- Write below how you feel you can maintain a spirit of praise unto the Lord throughout the next week.

_____

_____

Fasting -- What has been your reaction to times of fasting during your Pilgrimage?

_____

_____

Question -- Do you agree the Lord uses many channels for healing?

_____

_____

Practicing His Presence -- Through what incident or person did you sense the presence of Christ yesterday? How did it make you feel?

_____

_____

Second Mile Resource -- Cassette lecture No. 28, _How Does God Heal Today._ Summarize:

_____

_____

_____

HEALING HANDBOOK #1

TWENTY-NINTH DAY -- MON.,_____19__

Prayer For Guidance -- *Father, help me to see your will being worked out in my life. Amen.*

Scripture Study -- Romans 8:31-39. Summarize:

_____

_____

_____

Verse For The Day -- Romans 8:31.

Reading -- Page 47, "Action or Alibis?" Briefly summarize.

_____

_____

Prayer Ministry -- Your family members and relatives need your support. Your ministry through prayer unto them today should seek to help you rejoice with those who are rejoicing, grieve with those who sorrow, and to put yourself in the shoes of each in an understanding and loving way.

Action Time -- These are difficult days for many people. You may have a family member or relative who is out of work or in dire need for some other reason. Your prayer and loving concern could be the highlight of the week for them. Write below the person you feel led to express concern and how you plan to do this. Do not let your good intentions die on the vine, but bring them to fruition with action.

_____

_____

_____

Sharing -- What have the Sharing Times meant to you?

_____

_____

Time For His Church -- List the task you did for your church yesterday, the approximate time it took, and how you felt about having done it.

_____

_____

Question -- Do you feel there are times you make excuses for failures on your part?

_____

Practicing His Presence -- Through what incident or person did you sense the presence of Christ yesterday? How did it make you feel?

_____

_____

Second Mile Resource -- Cassette lecture No. 29, _Action or Alibis._ Summarize:

_____

_____

_____

THIRTIETH DAY -- TUES.,_____19__

Prayer For Guidance -- *Father, I thank you for your guidance through this Pilgrimage. May I apply what I have learned and live to your glory. Amen.*

Scripture Study -- Matthew 28:16-20. Summarize:

_____

_____

_____

Verse For The Day -- Matthew 28:19.

Reading -- Page 302, "The Healing Community." Briefly summarize.

_____

_____

Prayer Ministry -- Today you again minister to government leaders through prayer. Our world desperately needs moral and spiritual leadership. Today would be a good time to lift the leaders unto the Lord with the thought of their spiritual commitment deepening each day.

Action Time -- The spiritual fiber of our world is the missing factor in many actions and decisions. Believers need to encourage leaders to depend upon the Lord for strength and wisdom. Today pray for the person you should encourage in the things of the Spirit. You may be led to send to them some material which you have found especially helpful. It might be the very thing which will help them in the days ahead. Write below the person you will minister unto and how you plan to do this. Follow through.

_____

Theme For The Day -- Write below how you feel you will handle your devotional life following this 30-day Pilgrimage.

_____

_____

Time For His Church -- What has been your reaction to giving specific time to your church?

_____

_____

Your Witness -- List below the person(s) you desire to talk to about making this Pilgrimage in the future.

_____

Question -- Have you felt a sense of community with others during this Pilgrimage?

_____

Practicing His Presence -- Through what incident or person did you sense the presence of Christ yesterday?

_____

_____

Second Mile Resource -- Cassette lecture No. 30, _The Healing Community._ Summarize:

_____

_____

_____

EVALUATION OF THE 30-DAY PRAYER PILGRIMAGE

The 30-Day Prayer Pilgrimage is designed to achieve several goals. How well do you feel you achieved them?

GOALS	100%	To Great Degree	Partially	Not At All	No Opinion
1. To deepen your devotional life.					
2. To learn how to more effectively minister unto yourself and others through prayer.					
3. To provide a means of teaching others how to pray as you lead them through this Prayer Experience.					
4. To help you appreciate how healing and prayer are intricately related.					
5. To provide guidance for a lifestyle of prayer for the rest of your life.					
6. To enable you to effectively and consistently practice His presence.					

The MINISTRY OF PRAYER Pilgrimage has five disciplines all were requested to fulfill. There were two optional disciplines. To what degree were you able to fulfill the disciplines?

DISCIPLINES					
1. Spend at last 30 minutes each day in devotions.					
2. Attend the Orientation meeting and meet with the group once per week.					
3. Seek to practice His presence each day.					
4. Tithe your income during this 30-day period.					
5. Give time each week in a task for His church and to do it for your local church or for some Christian group or movement.					
OPTIONALS					
6. Seeking to do a kind deed each day.					
7. Using the Second Mile Resources.					

What was the most meaningful part of this Pilgrimage to you?_____

_____

What was the least helpful part of the Pilgrimage to you?_____

_____

Please use the following evaluation scale to appraise the following 20 items. 10 - excellent, 9 - very good, 8 - good, 7 - average, 6 - fair, 5 - poor, 4 - very bad, 3 - terrible, 2 - of little value, 1 - no value, 0 - wash out.

Item	Evaluation
1. The daily prayer for guidance	
2. The daily scripture study	
3. The daily verse for the day	
4. The daily reading suggestion	
5. The daily prayer ministry	
6. The daily optional action time	
7. The writing of a theme for each day	
8. The fasting emphasis	
9. Days of fasting	
10. The daily practicing His presence	
11. The daily optional Second Mile Resources	
12. The weekly group meeting	
13. The recorded devotional by Pastor Bartow	
14. The retreat	
15. The refreshments following group meetings	
16. The cluster talk-it over experiences	
17. The group singing	
18. The cluster prayer experiences	
19. The book, Healing Handbook #1	
20. The book, Personal Prayer Diary	
Total	

Do you feel you would like to be a leader of a Prayer Pilgrimage in the future?   __ Yes   __ No   __ Maybe

Signed_____Date_____

Address_____

City, State, Zip _____

Phone_____

My Church_____

My Pastor_____

Certificate of Achievement

This is to certify that

completed the

30-DAY
PRAYER PILGRIMAGE

Signed

Signed

Date

30-DAY PRAYER PILGRIMAGE
VERSE OF THE DAY

-1-
Therefore I say unto you, What things soever ye desire, when ye pray, believe that ye receive them, and ye shall have them.
Mark 11:24

-2-
And the peace of God, which passeth all understanding, shall keep your hearts and minds through Christ Jesus. Phil. 4:7

-3-
Be still and know that I am God: I will be exalted among the heathen, I will be exalted in the earth. Ps. 46:10

-4-
Come unto me, all ye that labor and are heavy laden, and I will give you rest.
Mt. 11:28

-5-
Therefore if any may be in Christ, he is a new creature: old things are passed away; behold, all things are become new.
II Cor. 5:17

-6-
Verily, verily, I say unto you, he that believeth on me, the works that I do shall he do also; and greater works than these shall he do; because I go unto my Father.
John 14:12

-7-
Let every thing that hath breath praise the Lord. Praise ye the Lord.
Ps. 150:6

-8-
The Lord is on my side; I will not fear: what can man do unto me? Ps. 118:6

-9-
That thou appear not unto men to fast, but unto thy Father which is in secret: and thy Father which seeth in secret, shall reward thee openly. Mt. 6:18

-10-
Create in me a clean heart, O God; and renew a right spirit within me. Ps. 51:10

-11-
For God so loved the world that He gave His only begotten Son, that whosoever believeth in him should not perish, but have everlasting life. John 3:16

-12-
And be not conformed to this world: but be ye transformed by the renewing of your mind, that ye may prove what is that good, and acceptable, and perfect, will of God.
Rom. 12:2

-13-
He hath not dealt with us after our sins; nor rewarded us according to our iniquities.
Ps. 103:10

-14-
And above all these things put on charity, which is the bond of perfectness.
Col. 3:14

-15-
How God anointed Jesus of Nazareth with the Holy Ghost and with power: who went about doing good, and healing all that were oppressed of the devil; for God was with him. Acts 10:38

-16-
Finally, be ye all of one mind, having compassion one of another, love as brethren, be pitiful, be courteous. I Pet. 3:8

-17-
Beloved, if God so loved us, we ought to love one another. I John 4:11

-18-
Hitherto have ye asked nothing in my name: ask, and ye shall receive, that your joy may be full. John 16:24

-19-
Therefore, being justified by faith, we have peace with God through our Lord Jesus Christ. Rom 5:1

-20-
But let patience have her perfect work, that ye may be perfect and entire, wanting nothing. James 1:4

-21-
And be ye kind one to another, tenderhearted, forgiving one another, even as God for Christ's sake hath forgiven you.
Eph. 4:32

-22-
Surely goodness and mercy shall follow me all the days of my life: and I will dwell in the house of the Lord forever. Ps. 23:6

-23-
No servant can serve two masters: for either he will hate the one, and love the other; or else he will hold to the one and despise the other. Ye cannot serve God and mammon. Luke 16:13

-24-
And the servant of the Lord must not strive; but be gentle unto all men, apt to teach, patient. II Tim. 2:24

-25-
Be not deceived; God is not mocked: for whatsoever a man soweth, that shall he also reap. Gal. 6:7

-26-
Every good gift and every perfect gift is from above, and cometh down from the Father of lights, with whom is no variableness, neither shadow of turning.
James 1:7

-27-
The thief cometh not, but for to steal, and to kill, and to destroy: I am come that they might have life, and that they might have it more abundantly. John 10:10

-28-
But he was wounded for our transgressions, he was bruised for iniquities; the chastisement of our peace was upon him; and with his stripes we are healed.
Isaiah 53:5

-29-
What shall we then say to these things: if God be for us, who can be against us?
Rom. 8:31

-30-
Go ye therefore, and teach all nations, baptising them in the name of the Father, and of the Son, and of the Holy Ghost.
Mt. 28:19

83

AFTER THE 30-DAY PRAYER PILGRIMAGE

After the 30-Day Pilgrimage, you may not pursue as rigid a devotional life as during the Pilgrimage. However, it is hoped you will have been helped to the point of maintaining a deeper and more exciting devotional life than prior to your 30-day Pilgrimage.

DAILY DEVOTIONS

It is important you have a daily devotional time. My daily devotional book, Healing Handbook #2, The Ministry Of The Master, is one you will find helpful.

This daily devotional book follows the pattern of prayer as presented in the 30-Day Pilgrimage. It has a daily promise from God's Word, a prayer for the day, a sermonette, suggested prayer concerns, emphasis upon practicing His presence, and a joke for each day. All of it blends together to make this one of the best and most useful devotional guides of our day.

CASSETTES

I have prepared many audio and video cassettes in the area of prayer and healing. They will help you in your daily walk with the Lord. Your deepened experience with Him has only begun. Discipline your life to deepen your walk and to creatively use your gifts to His glory.

You may write the publisher for information concerning these and other resources.

DEVOTED TO CHRIST

The most important thing after your 30-day Prayer Pilgrimage is to remain devoted to the Lord Jesus Christ.

Also, remain active in His Church. This is your high calling. There are no pious particles in the Christian faith. Each believer is a part of the body of Christ, His Church.

Prayer is the avenue of strength for you to be faithful unto the end. It is not that we begin which is so important as it is that we continue to be faithful. *"And ye shall be hated of all men for my name's sake: but he that shall endure unto the end, the same shall be saved."* (Mark 13:13).

III

WHOLENESS
A TO Z

There is no end to the insights available concerning healing for our day. Plus, I simply do not know everything there is to be known about healing!

However, I am familiar with many insights which can help individuals to believe God heals today. I also know many things which help assure a meaningful ministry of wholeness within an individual's life, as well as within the life of a congregation.

Jesus said the Kingdom of God is at hand. I believe with all my heart it is. His desire is that we experience His kingdom as fully as possible on earth today.

The following 26 chapters contain a wealth of biblical, theological and practical guidance concerning healing. They are written to be of help to the beginner as well as to the more seasoned believer of God's healing power.

I feel these chapters will be of special interest to those who have completed the 30-Day Prayer Pilgrimage. Prayer and healing cannot be separated. They truly go hand-in-hand.

A

WHAT IS SPIRITUAL HEALING?

What is a meaningful and workable definition of Spiritual or Divine Healing? How should a person look at a reasonable approach for the church and healing? These and other questions arise when considering healing.

A DEFINITION

Spiritual Healing is wholeness. It is the healing of the whole person. It is soundness of body, soul and spirit.

METHODS

The methods of Spiritual Healing include prayer, laying-on-of-hands, anointing with oil, confession, the sacraments, etc. All of these things become significant by the power of the Holy Spirit in response to faith in God through Jesus Christ.

NO SUBSTITUTE FOR MEDICINE

Although it may result in physical healings, Spiritual Healing is not a substitute for medicine or surgery. It makes no claims to prescribe in the areas of medicine, surgery, psychiatry, or psychology. It works closely with all involved in these allied professions dedicated to healing. Members of the allied professions of healing realize and appreciate the great value of faith in the healing process. All healing is of God. Individuals are but His instruments regardless of their profession in the area of healing.

THEOLOGICALLY SOUND

Spiritual Healing is theologically sound and is in harmony with:

1. Orthodox Christian theology,
2. The teaching and life-style of Jesus Christ,
3. The practice of the Apostolic Church.

It is an obedient response to the Commission given by Jesus to "go preach and heal."

BASED ON GOD'S LAWS

Spiritual Healing is not magic, sleight of hand, or hocus pocus. It is based on God's laws of faith and love just as medical healing is based on God's physical laws. The many miracles of Spiritual Healing do not break natural laws, but are the result of higher laws which many times we do not understand.

THE TERM, "SPIRITUAL HEALING"

Spiritual Healing is sometimes called "Christian Healing" because it comes from Christ and its meaning and its ends are Christian.

Some refer to it as "Faith Healing." This term falls short because often there is no clear understanding in whom faith is placed. This is not always made plain by some so-called "faith healers."

Spiritual Healing has, by some, been called, "Divine Healing." This is too broad of a term because, in a sense, all healing is divine.

Spiritual Healing differs from Christian Science as it acknowledges the reality of pain, disease, and evil.

A SANE, SENSIBLE APPROACH

The church's healing ministry has often been in disrepute because of abuses by charlatans and those seeking their own gain. These individuals and experiences are deeply regretted, but are not the criteria to determine the validity of Spiritual Healing.

Perhaps the major Protestant Churches have frowned on the healing ministry because of emotional excesses, the extreme theological views of some, and the over-emphasis upon physical healing to the neglect of the spirit.

However, today an approach to healing is developing which is thoroughly based upon Christian concepts and acceptable to leaders of all major denominations.

WIDELY ACCEPTED TODAY

Hundreds of congregations now conduct regular Spiritual Healing services. Each month many others begin this adventure of faith. Also, in 1989 the Presbyterian Church (U.S.A.) included in its Constitution, "Services for Wholeness" (W-3.5400). This official endorsement has helped further the message of healing in our day.

I conducted my first public service of healing May 6, 1959. The years have added excitement to my effort to proclaim the wholeness the Lord has for each of us.

It has been my pleasant experience to discover that the practice of Spiritual Healing has three main benefits:

1. It inspires individuals to greater devotion.

2. It leads people to richer experiences in worship.

3. It deepens understanding of the Bible.

B

THE GOAL OF SPIRITUAL HEALING

It would be great if I could convey to all that the GOAL of Spiritual Healing is Jesus Christ. There are far too many who feel that a physical healing is the chief aim of the healing ministry. Nothing could be further from the truth.

KNOWING THE GREAT PHYSICIAN

The true GOAL of Spiritual Healing is knowing the Great Physician and not simply being physically healed by Him. Jesus never did say you must be physically perfect. He did say you *"must be born again,"* John 3:7. It is only through the Spirit you can discern the things of the Spirit (I Cor. 1:10-14).

It is a thrill to see individuals healed in body and emotions. However, it is a greater thrill to see them come to personally know the One who is the Great Physician. It is great for you to receive His gifts. It is even more important you receive Him who is the greatest Gift.

ACCEPTING CHRIST

A letter from a good friend who is a Presbyterian Pastor sums up the essence of Spiritual Healing. He had attended one of our Clergy-Lay Conferences on Healing. This influenced his actions concerning the incidents discussed in his letter as follows:

"In the light of the Conference on Spiritual Healing I preached a sermon on the Healing Power of Christ. One couple was in church who average about one Sunday a month in church. The Friday after they heard that sermon their eight-year-old son was hit by a car while riding his mini bike on the highway. The boy was unconscious in the hospital, so I went in and had prayer and laying-on-of-hands for him with his parents. The boy regained consciousness Monday night, and has improved steadily ever since. Needless to say, the parents went through quite an emotional experience. The father, who did not join the church when the rest of the family did, vowed with his wife in the hospital to accept Jesus Christ."

The little boy received a healing. The father received an even more wonderful healing!

I feel the following, author unknown, gets to the heart of the message of healing:

"He for whom the martyrs died is He by whom we must live. That is what Christianity is and almost nothing else at all. That main, if not the sole, purpose of Healing Evangelism is to give people a supreme opportunity of encountering Jesus Christ and of binding themselves ever more closely to Him

through faith. We must be desperately serious in this. Spiritual Healing means more than physical cure by spiritual aids. It is the outcome of union with God in Christ Jesus the Healer.

"So the creed of the believer in Spiritual Healing today is Jesus Christ as Healer. Not primarily being well or doing good, not good health or even good behavior, but God Himself in focus in Jesus Christ. We do not teach sufferers to believe in healing, but in Jesus Christ. The believer in Spiritual Healing is therefore never disappointed, because he is seeking, not things, but God. Christianity for the first disciples was not primarily a matter of behavior, but of belief. They believed that Christ was of God and that He believed in them. What could be more exciting than that? They did not discuss or hold conferences about Spiritual Healing; they preached and healed. When we believe what they believed we achieve in miracles of healing what they received. They practiced Healing Evangelism and 'turned the world upside-down.' We can do the same."

I believe many people today are saying as the Greeks of old, *"we would see Jesus,"* (John 12:21).

All efforts of the ministry of healing should be expended to lead individuals to Jesus. It is He you need. May you accept Him now and in His fullness.

C

WHY A SPIRITUAL HEALING SERVICE?

I said the following years ago and I still believe it. "If I were the only one willing to be present, I would still hold a regular Spiritual Healing Service. It is a source of strength to me and a worthwhile discipline in my life."

THE HUB

I know the public Spiritual Healing Service is the hub of any strong emphasis concerning healing. It is the visible means through which the local church says to its entire membership and to the community that God is in the healing business.

Some will say, "Should not every worship service be a healing service and thus what is the need of a special one?" This is a good question. However, we all know the average worship service is not one in which individuals are made aware of God's healing power.

All aspects of our Christian Faith should be a part of every worship service. Yet, congregations have special times for evangelism, missions, stewardship, etc. We need this special emphasis on healing for us to know and to remain aware of our church's ministry to individuals.

A public service of healing will enable a congregation to more adequately say:

I. GOD WILLS WHOLENESS

You can categorically believe the Lord wills wholeness. He even made your body to ingeniously combat disease. The very forces of nature cry for your wholeness.

Jesus did not hesitate to heal the sick. He demonstrated again and again the heavenly Father desires wholeness for His children.

The promises of scripture confirm the Lord's desire for your wholeness. They are promises upon which we can base our hope for our healing.

II. MAN - UNITY

An individual cannot be considered as a being having a separate soul, separate body, separate spirit.

These three are not independent entities. They cannot be dealt with in isolation.

What you think influences how your body feels. In like manner the tone of your spiritual health determines the state of your emotional and mental outlook.

How you feel physically will even affect your spiritual vitality. You are a unity and must be treated and considered in this light.

III. WHOLENESS INVOLVES
ALL THINGS

You are affected by all of your relationships. Your attitude toward other people and the world about you deeply influences your well-being.

The attitudes and relationships with others must also be a part of the fact of wholeness in your life. There is more to you than your own soul, body, and spirit. The total "you" involves all the people in your life.

The message of Spiritual Healing is more than simply, "Lord, heal me!" of some bodily affliction. It is the realization that all aspects of our lives need the healing touch of the Lord.

IV. POSITIVE POWER AVAILABLE

The positive, healing, reconciling, God-provided spiritual forces are available to you. They can especially be applied to areas of your needs through the presence and prayers of God's people.

Indeed, prayer is better understood as a focusing of spiritual power rather than the verbalizing of one's requests unto the Almighty.

I implore you to permit every aspect of your life to be open to the powerful presence of the Lord. There is no aspect too small or too large for the Lord to consider.

V. ATTEND A HEALING SERVICE

This fifth point is obvious if you agree with the above four. You should put forth effort to attend a healing service.

If your church has no healing service, why not begin to pray and work toward starting one? In the meantime, perhaps you can attend one in a nearby church.

I present the above reasons for a healing service. I can't think of any reasons not to have one.

VI. PRESBYTERIAN CONSTITUTION

The Presbyterian U.S.A. Denomination in its constitution (W-3.5400) encourages healing services in all of its churches. Every local church would be wise to pursue this sacred call.

D

WHEN TO BEGIN A HEALING SERVICE

Often I am asked, "When should a congregation begin conducting healing services?" I answer this question on pages 198-200 of my book, "Creative Churchmanship." A summary follows:

ARE YOU WILLING?

"The basic question is, 'Are you willing to start?' If you are a pastor, dare to lead your people. If you are a lay person, dare to challenge your pastor and, together, go forward in the healing ministry."

NO PERFECT TIME

"It can be debated at length whether or not the time is right for the local congregation to begin conducting a public healing service. There is no perfect and complete answer to this problem. I have been privileged to speak to clergy and laity in many denominations regarding the blessings, pitfalls, and mechanics of the healing ministry. The preponderance of them have reacted with, 'Our people are not quite ready for this.'

"To our shame, although the Church has existed for nearly two thousand years, most congregations are not quite ready in many areas--complete stewardship commitment, a sensible program of evangelism, worship services that speak to the heart, or public healing services."

NEVER WILL ALL AGREE

"I do not want to say that every congregation should plunge blindly into a program of public healing ministry. I cannot answer for a particular congregation; but I can say that, in some instances, ten years from now will be no different--that is, some churches will still be discussing, investigating, studying, praying for guidance, attending seminars and conferences to decide whether or not there should be a public healing service in their local church.

"If lay people and pastors wait until everyone in their church is convinced of the validity of the healing ministry, they will never start.

"This is illustrated by the fact that if any church waited until all its members showed up at a Sunday morning worship service, they would never open the doors. If they waited until only half their members showed up, few churches would experience corporate worship on any given Sunday, including Easter. If Paul had waited until all the pagans pleaded for the power of the Gospel in their lives, he never would have proclaimed the riches of the Redeemer."

LEARN AS YOU GO

"Much time can be spent laying the foundation for an event and then moving forward from the findings. There is the other side of the coin--where the event takes place and you learn as you go along. In most churches, the latter approach is the best.

"It is simply true that, when something happens, you learn! How many would be married, and have children, if they were required to have to know all about it before the event took place? I took child psychology in college, but, believe me, you can't put in a book what God puts in a little life. I knew some of the aspects of personality development, but I learned a great deal more the first week after a little girl blessed our home. I have learned more from her than I did studying psychology and writing term papers concerning child development."

EXPERIENCE - EDUCATION

"This is not to minimize education, but simply to say that education without experience leads only to untried book knowledge.

"Experience without education and instruction leads only to feelings without adequate foundation. Christian creativity blends experience with education; education with experience.

"As long as we say we are not quite ready, we can never be blamed for failing. As long as a person is in preparation, he cannot be held responsible for what he is not doing.

"In a spirit of prayer, unity, and dedication, the congregation should seek to go forward in the Spirit of the Lord."

TRUST THE LORD

"No pastor or layperson can claim to know all about God and His ways. At the same time you cannot say you are really trusting the Lord until you have made a venture of faith, and discovered the joy of adventures beyond yourself as found in Christ."

LOOK TO JESUS

"We know not the end of what we begin, but we know Him who is the beginning and the end.

"We know not what blessings He has in store, but we know He has many blessings to bestow upon us.

"We know not what opposition we shall encounter, but we know what inner strength we have found.

"We do not choose to look back and become a pillar of salt, but to look ahead and to be the salt of the earth.

"Thus, looking unto Jesus, the Author and Finisher of our Faith, we worship, praise, and trust Him.

"The big secret is to get-going for the Lord. Now!"

E

LAYING-ON-OF-HANDS (LOH)

Throughout the Bible there are many references to the laying-on-of-hands on the part of the believers.

THE OLD TESTAMENT

There are two reasons for LOH (laying-on-of-hands) as mentioned in the Old Testament:

1. The blessing of an heir (Gen. 48:14)
2. Empowering of a leader, Joshua (Deut. 34:9), and Joash (II Kings 13:16)

THE NEW TESTAMENT

The LOH is included among the foundations of faith along with repentance, faith, baptisms, resurrection, and judgment (Heb. 6:1-3). Yet, how many have ever heard a Sunday morning sermon concerning the LOH? I ask this question to groups unto whom I am speaking. Very few have ever heard such a message even though the LOH is one of the foundations of the faith.

W-6.3011: "Prayer enacted by the laying-on-of-hands and anointing calls upon God to heal, empower, and sustain."

AN EXPRESSION OF BELIEF

Laying-on-of-hands is a tangible expression of one's belief in the Great Physician. The one administering and the one receiving this ministry of the Church are both acknowledging dependence upon the Triune God for all healing.

God uses many concerned hands for our well-being. He uses the human touch whether it be the hands of skilled surgeons, a dedicated nurse, a sympathetic physician, the pastor, or a concerned lay person. His healing is extended through each.

The sad tragedy is far too often the Church has abandoned the power of spiritual forces and left all ministry unto the ill to science. Science may complement spiritual ministries, but can never replace them.

THE FOCAL POINT

The focal point of laying-on-of-hands with prayer is the Lord Jesus Christ. The power does not come from the one laying on hands. The power is from the One in whose Name the prayer is offered. The believer serves only as an instrument of Christ's power.

WHO IS WORTHY?

Worthiness does not lie in the individual, but in the Lord Jesus. No one will ever arrive at the point of spiritual commitment which will make him or her worthy. One's willingness to minister through the laying-on-of-hands comes out of our obedience and not our purity.

There are some who feel only the professional clergy should lay on hands. I was in a large church conducting a healing service and the Pastor told me they did not encourage lay people in this ministry.

This, to me, is teaching which will stifle the healing ministry. Lay persons can and should be instructed in this vital ministry and provided opportunity to fulfill this ministry.

I seek to teach lay persons to minister with the laying-on-of-hands. They should not be denied this opportunity of service unto the Lord and to others.

HOW OFTEN?

How often should one receive laying-on-of-hands with prayer? At least weekly is the best answer I know. During periods of serious illness or problems, some will desire this ministry daily.

We haven't done all we can for ourselves and others until we have received this ministry of the Church. Since everyone constantly faces problems and also has deep concern for many friends and acquaintances, taking advantage of an opportunity to pray and to receive laying-on-of hands with prayer regarding these situations is an act of wisdom as well as obedience.

Your prayer and devotional life will be enhanced and your faith and trust increased as you minister unto others and others minister unto you through the laying-on-of-hands with prayer.

F

GOD'S DESIRE

God wants the very best for you. He does not delight in your illnesses, afflictions, and problems. On the contrary, His message is to obey His laws and be spared many of these things. The Kingdom of Heaven is at hand and you are invited to enter and to abide there. Most people believe God is able to create a vast universe. However, they have difficulty believing He can care for their little problems. I encourage you to accept this fact: The Lord of Creation is the Lord of every detail of your life!

BELIEVE JESUS IS YOUR SOURCE

The Lord may use many and varied instruments to meet your every need. However, He is the Source of all. Your apparently unsolvable problems or incurable disease is solvable or curable in God's sight. Jesus has power and resources available you never dreamed existed and will never experience until you believe He will supply your every need (Phil. 4:19). The person ministering wholeness unto you is not your source of help and healing, but only the instrument of God's power and purpose.

CONFESS YOUR NEED

Confession is a two-sided coin. First, it speaks of your inability to heal yourself. This you must acknowledge and accept. It may be obvious that physically you fall short of perfection and wholeness, but true confession acknowledges falling short of the Glory of God in all areas. Honesty is one of the biggest steps toward healing of body, soul, and spirit.

Pride keeps many from God's wholeness. Confession is not only good for the soul, but also for the body. The publican's prayer could very well be paraphrased, *"God be merciful to me the sick one,"* Luke 18:13.

CONFESS YOUR FAITH

The other side of the coin of confession is your witness to others. LOH is a confession to others of your faith in the Triune God. Your receiving the LOH is an outward confession of your inward belief that you realize the Lord is the Healer.

Jesus has promised to honor, now and in the world to come, your public confession of Him (Matt. 10:32).

LOH is not given or received for show, but is a public expression of inward faith. It is one way, among many, whereby you can say to the Church and the world you are not ashamed of the Master nor His methods. His desire is your wholeness. Believe Him today!

G

HEALING - GOD'S GIFT

Each year we celebrate the Birthday of our Lord. We do not claim that He was born December 25th. No one can be certain as to the exact day or date.

One thing we do know is that Jesus was and is the Son of God. We need to be reminded again and again that He was born into this world for each of us.

GOD'S GIFT

The Babe in Bethlehem's manger was God's gift to the world. Thus Jesus is God's gift to you and to people everywhere and for all time.

God desires His gift be received in each heart. It is through Jesus Christ you receive the gifts of redemption, forgiveness, and healing. None of these are earned. They are freely given by the Father of all love.

"Every good gift and every perfect gift is from above, and cometh down from the Father of lights, with whom is no variableness, neither shadow of turning," James 1:17.

"If ye then, being evil, know how to give good gifts unto your children, how much more shall your

Father in heaven give good things to them that ask Him?" Matt. 7:11.

"I am come that they might have life, and that they might have it more abundant," John 10:10.

The abundant life includes health of body and soul and spirit.

Wholeness, healing, and health have the same basic root meaning in Greek. The Apostolic Church knew and believed that one of God's gifts was healing:

"...to another the gifts of healing by the same Spirit," I Cor. 12:9.

The first Christians believed and lived-out the divine commission to preach, teach, and heal. They believed in the Power of God and thus possessed the Power of God.

RECEIVING THE GIFT

If healing is a gift of the Lord, the natural question is, "How do I receive this gift?"

A big step toward the receiving of the gift of healing is to understand the spiritual laws. They have been given to us to help us appropriate the blessings of the Lord.

"But his delight is in the law of the Lord; and in his law doth he meditate day and night," Psalm 1:2.

The spiritual laws are not temporarily suspended just for you. The natural laws are not changed with our whims and fancies. It would be foolish to jump from a tall building believing gravity would be altered. The Lord tells us there are spiritual laws which are essential to our wholeness and receiving all He has for us. I mention two of them.

1. BELIEF

Belief is a spiritual law of utmost importance. Jesus said,

"All things are possible to him who believes," Mark 9:23.

"What things soever ye desire, when ye pray, believe that ye receive them, and ye shall have them," Mark 11:24.

2. FORGIVENESS

Another spiritual law is forgiveness. This is the only point which Jesus expounded upon after He had given His disciples His model prayer: *"For if ye forgive men their trespasses, your heavenly Father will also forgive you: But if ye forgive not men their trespasses, neither will your Father forgive your trespasses,"* Matt. 6:14-15.

THE GIVER

I feel a valid healing ministry must keep focused upon the Lord Jesus Christ. It must be firmly grounded on the Word of God as revealed in scripture and especially as revealed in the Living Word, Jesus. I have met individuals who almost pride themselves with the fact their hands begin to shake when they minister unto an ill person. Others tell of great heat flowing through them, etc. It is my humble opinion a healing ministry built on outward signs is built on the sand of human experiences and not the Rock, Christ Jesus.

There have been a few times, but very few, in my ministry when an outward sign was evident. For instance, I was called to the hospital to pray for a man who was in the throes of terminal cancer. One of our Elders, a good friend of his, had paved the way for my visit.

After a few moments of casual conversation, I explained to him concerning the ministry of Laying-on-of-Hands with prayer. He eagerly accepted this ministry.

Following the LOH he lay with his eyes closed for some time. It was then that he softly said, "Pastor, I felt a great warmth flow though my body the moment you laid your hand on my head, and it remained all the time you were praying for me."

Later that day he experienced a vision of the Lord. He saw Christ appear at the foot of his bed and smile at him. He received a peace of spirit beyond description.

Several days later he passed from this life, but he had a wonderful witness of grace. The Lord used this to greatly touch members of his family in a spiritual way.

ELECTRIC SHOCK

On another occasion several of us laid our hands upon a man and were praying for him. We were standing on a tile floor. After we had been praying for a few minutes a sensation like an electric shock went through our hands.

NOT SIGNS

I mention the above incidents because many people feel these are the things they must experience if the healing message is to be a part of their ministry.

Nothing could be further from the truth. We are not called to seek signs. We are called to serve Christ. He is the Healer. You and I are to be His obedient followers. The outward signs cannot be our measure of effectiveness.

I have been involved in the healing ministry since 1959. I can assure you instances like the above are very rare in my life. Further, I never seek outward manifestations as confirmation of my calling to the ministry of healing.

GUIDELINES

I believe there are some general guidelines to keep in mind as you begin and continue a ministry of healing.

1. It is true there are a few individuals with special gifts of healing, just as there are a few with unique gifts of evangelism, etc. But every believer is not an Oral Roberts or Kathryn Kuhlman. Every believer is not a Billy Graham or James Kennedy in the area of evangelism. Would we leave all evangelism or healing ministry to these nationally known leaders? Perish the thought! All believers are called to a life of obedience as much as they are. We can't all be generals. The lowly private is still a vital part of the army.

2. The disciple of the Lord is to go forth with His message of wholeness (Mark 6:13; Luke 10:1-3; 17-20; Acts 8:4-8).

3. Leave the results and outward signs up to the Lord. You are not the Healer. You, nor anyone else, are called to change the Lord's mind concerning someone's condition. You are a believer called to always cooperate with the Lord's plan of wholeness for individuals.

4. The gift you are really seeking is the gift of wholeness for the one for whom you pray. It is not the gift of some outward manifestation to prove you are a so called "healer."

CONCLUSION

The bottom line is that God's Gift, His Son, is not received to be selfishly used or misused. You receive the Giver that you may impart the Gifts.

Share God's Gift for your health's sake.

H

PAUL'S THORN IN THE FLESH

Paul says, "...*There was given to me a thorn in the flesh*," II Cor. 12:7. This has been a controversial statement through the centuries.

A PHYSICAL MALADY?

The commonly accepted interpretation of this verse is:

1. Paul had a physical malady.
2. The Lord gave the problem.
3. The Lord refused to remove it.

I feel this verse can be either a stumbling block or a stepping stone as far as the message of healing is concerned. It all depends upon your interpretation of the total message of the Bible.

SEARCH THE SCRIPTURES

A careful consideration of Scripture provides provocative material for another insight concerning Paul's "thorn in the flesh."

Does "thorn in the flesh" necessarily mean a physical illness? The answer is a resounding "NO!"

The Old Testament has three references using similar language as Paul does in II Cor. 12:7:

1. Num. 33:55 speaks of "...*thorns in your sides*"

2. Josh. 23:13 says, "*scourges in your sides and thorns in your eyes*"

3. Judg. 2:3 refers to "...*thorns in your sides*"

It is evident from the context these three references do not imply physical illness. They very definitely refer to the pagan and carnal inhabitants of the land Israel is to conquer.

Paul had great knowledge of the Old Testament and was steeped in Jewish ways of expression. It would be natural for him to use this familiar phrase to refer to those who troubled him and hindered the advance of the Good News.

THE FLESH

The word translated "flesh" in II Cor. 12:7 is the same as the word for "flesh" used by Paul in many other places. He meant by "flesh" any and all things which were contrary to the nature and will of God (Rom. 7:5, 18; 8:1-3). Thus, "flesh" does not necessarily mean one's body.

PROBLEM PEOPLE

Paul, like the early Hebrew children, was plagued with problem people. They very well could have been his "thorn in the flesh."

It was because of them that he often had great difficulty preaching the Gospel. He was never completely delivered from those who followed him wherever he went and constantly fermented strife. (Acts

13:45, 14:19, 17:5, 18:12, 20:3, 21:27, 22:22, 23:2, 23:12, 24:1, 25:1-3, 25:7) They may have served to keep him humble, but they were also a hindrance to the advancement of the Church.

Paul's human weaknesses were more pointedly manifested in the face of opposition from such people. This concept certainly brings an understanding to II Cor. 12:10. *"Therefore I take pleasure in infirmities, in reproaches, in necessities, in persecutions, in distresses for Christ's sake, for when I am weak, then I am strong."*

SATAN - THE MESSENGER

Anyone who wants to defend his illness by hiding behind the "thorn in the flesh" theory faces another problem. Some leave the impression that God has made them ill to keep them humble and dependent upon Him.

This is a subtle way for a person to infer they may be a "special case" before the Lord. Thus the illness is almost turned into proof of the person being a favorite in the Lord's sight. What a strange twist to the total message of Scripture!

The verse, II Cor. 12:7, plainly identifies the messenger of the "thorn of the flesh" as Satan. If one interprets that the "thorn in the flesh" is a physical illness, then he must acknowledge it is from Satan. God's gift and God's will is not illness!

WHOLENESS - GOD'S WILL

I pray you will believe and acknowledge that illness is not from God. God wants to defeat illness, not deliver it. Jesus faithfully fulfilled the Father's will and He "...*healed them all*," Luke 6:19.

I

HERALDS OF HEALING

Christ has revealed His desire for your wholeness. It is wholeness of body, mind, and spirit which He wants to impart to you and to others.

It is tragic many have not heard this glad and good message. The following two comments illustrate that countless thousands have not heard the good news that Jesus Christ is the Great Physician:

"If I had known of Spiritual Healing years ago, I could have survived some very frustrating working conditions of the past."

"It seems to me that this area (healing) has been sadly neglected by many churches. I was reared in a church and never heard the subject discussed as being relevant to our day."

AN EFFECTIVE HERALD

Each believer should strive to become an effective herald of the message of healing. You have the opportunity to learn and to share concerning God's desire for wholeness. The following suggestions will serve to guide you in your pilgrimage of being a herald of His healing presence and power.

BOOKS

There are many good books concerning healing. I would urge you to read them. Your knowledge of healing will be increased and you can share your knowledge and books with others.

This Healing Handbook is an excellent book to share with others. It presents insights for the novice as well as for anyone advanced in their knowledge of healing.

INVITATION

There is no more effective teaching than experience. Therefore, I suggest you invite your friends to attend a healing service with you. During Jesus' earthly ministry many were healed because they were brought to Jesus (Matt. 4:24, 8:16, 9:2, 9:32, 12:22, 17:16; Mark 1:32, 9:17, 9:20, 10:13; Luke 4:40, 5:18, 18:15, 18:40; John 1:42; Acts 5:15). You are called to bring the sick to Him today.

A CONFERENCE

You can be a herald of healing by inviting individuals to attend a healing conference. It would be great if you paid the expenses of your pastor to a healing conference.

COURSE ON HEALING

Many congregations have discovered a course on healing has helped provide a firm foundation for a healing ministry. The course may be presented during Sunday School or at any convenient hour. My

Healing Handbook would be useful as the text for the course.

GUEST SPEAKERS

You and your church will be blessed by guest speakers in the area of healing. They can share their experiences. Some can effectively present strengths and blessings, pitfalls and problems, mechanics and methods of a healing ministry.

PUBLICITY

You and your congregation can be more effective heralds of healing through good publicity.

The church bulletin, parish paper, pulpit announcements, newspaper releases, tracts, pamphlets and books all are avenues for letting others know the Lord heals today.

SPIRITUAL HEALING SUNDAY

A Spiritual Healing Sunday can be a time of learning for a large percentage of the active members of your congregation.

Sunday School teachers and others will have to study concerning healing to present it to their students on this day. Thus it serves as a marvelous tool for a deeper understanding of healing by our youth.

THE SCRIPTURES

I encourage you to study the scriptures in the light of the healing message. You will be surprised how the Bible comes alive when you begin to really believe that the Great Physician heals today.

PRAYER

I hope you will pray for the Lord to guide you in the area of healing. Pray for yourself, for others who minister healing, for those unto whom you and others will minister. Invite others to make the 30-day Pilgrimage as presented in this book.

CONCLUSION

You and all believers are to be faithful heralds of healing. Our calling is to be faithful unto the Lord. Our privilege is to fulfill our responsibilties unto others through the ministry of healing. Some will never know greater wholeness unless we are faithful in our own sphere of influence and contacts.

J

ANOINTING WITH OIL

Anointing is mentioned many times in the Bible:

	Old Testament	New Testament
Anoint	30 times	5 times
Anointed	86 times	12 times
Anointest	2 times	0 times
Anointing	25 times	3 times

WHY ANOINT?

It is obvious anointing with oil was very much a part of Biblical practices. The following are some of the reasons for anointing:

1. Consecration of leaders - Ex. 28:41; I Sam. 16:12.
2. God's chosen ones - Ps. 2:2, 18:50.
3. Empowerment - Isa. 61:1.
4. Spirit of gladness - Heb. 1:9.
5. The sick - Mark 6:13; James 5:14.

POST-APOSTOLIC CHURCH

It is a shame the post-Apostolic Church declined spiritually. This decline resulted in many of the prac-

tices of the early Christian community being neglected, ignored, or distorted.

For instance, the anointing with oil became associated with death rather than with healing. Anointing became a last rite before death instead of a
sacred act of faith leading to restoration of health.

The Council of Florence in 1435 gave the kiss of
death to the true significance of anointing with oil.
It ruled oil could only be used for the sacrament of
Extreme Unction. Through the centuries most
Catholics and many Protestants have accepted this
position.

NEW INTEREST

I am thrilled at the intense interest in healing
which is in all branches of the Christian church today.
Basically this is happening because of the outpouring
of the Holy Spirit and the new awareness of His
presence and power. There is a new eagerness to
know the scripture and to renew the practices of the
early Church.

DON'T GET SIDETRACKED

Biblically, anointing with oil has strong support.
Practically, anointing with oil tangibly speaks to the
ill and troubled of the love of Christ and His desire
to heal.

Anointing also brings more meaning and significance to intercessory prayer.

It is sad to note some become sidetracked in this
ministry because they become entangled in details
and controversy. They become more disturbed as to

who should do it, how, when, where, etc. These real or imagined barriers hinder people from administering this sacred rite.

I feel the heart of the matter is every effort should be expended to inform individuals of the value and efficacy of anointing with oil. Lay persons and clergy should be involved in this important and biblical ministry.

ASK TO BE ANOINTED

Every believer bears the responsibility of requesting to be anointed when ill. You have not done all you can for yourself or an ill loved one if you neglect being anointed with oil.

Few pastors or officers of a congregation will refuse to honor a sincere request for anointing. As a believer you have the privilege and responsibility to call upon the leadership of your congregation for anointing (James 5:14).

TEACH ANOINTING

Pastors and other church leaders must teach concerning anointing with oil. Some pastors and lay persons may say, "If someone were to ask me to anoint with oil, I would. I never suggest or encourage it." This is a cute cop-out.

How can anyone ask for what they do not know exists? How can members of a congregation know of anointing with oil unless someone teaches them?

The disciples of our Lord had no hesitancy to use oil (Mark 6:13). He instructed them to do so.

If a person refuses to request anointing after being informed, he bears the burden of neglect. If a person is never enlightened, then his teacher or pastor bears the burden of guilt.

THE PRESBYTERIAN CHURCH AND ANOINTING WITH OIL

The Directory of Worship, which became a part of the Constitution of the Presbyterian Church USA in 1989 encourages anointing with oil.

Section W-3.3607 refers to the "anointing with oil" at the time of baptism if desired by the participants.

Section W-3.5403 states that during a healing service *"Enacted prayer in the form of the laying on of hands and anointing with oil is appropriate,"* James 5:14.

Section W-3.5405 stresses the need of education in the area of anointing with oil. "When a service for wholeness includes anointing and the laying on of hands, these enacted prayers should be introduced carefully in order to avoid misinterpretation and misunderstanding."

K

SPIRITUAL HEALING AND HOLY COMMUNION

There are many Christians who believe the Holy Communion is a beautiful service to be occasionally observed. It is, to them, more pageantry than power.

We need to be reminded again and again of the proper understanding of Holy Communion.

The Bible says, "*My people are destroyed for lack of knowledge...*" Hosea 4:6. There is no area where knowledge seems to be lacking more than with Holy Communion.

St. Paul points out the seriousness of improperly receiving the elements. He says it results in illness and sometimes even death (I Cor. 11:29, 30).

KORBANA

Communion is a word derived from the Aramaic word "Korbana." It means "offering or sacrifice" and it comes from an Aramaic root which means "draw near."

You never draw nearer to the source of all power than you do when you partake of the Holy Commun-

ion. How important to you and yours that you draw
near in a worthy manner.

NOT AN OPTION

Holy Communion is an open invitation to power
and wholeness. It is not an option for a believer.

It is a visible expression of the deep inward assur-
ance of the love and power of the Lord Jesus Christ
(Matt. 26:26-29; Mark 14:17-25; Luke 22:14-23; I
Cor. 11:17-30).

NOT MAGIC

The ordinances and practices of the Christian
faith are never matters to be mechanically observed.
They were instituted to help us appropriate the
power of the Lord.

There is no magic in the Holy Communion or any
other aspect of Christian worship. We are called unto
the Lord and not to ritual.

CHRIST YOUR STRENGTH

Christ's body was a healthy body. It was a Spirit-
filled body. He was a vessel of complete honor to His
Father.

Christ is your healer. The prophet tells us that in
His body He bore even our diseases. "*But he was
wounded for our transgressions, he was bruised for our
iniquities: the chastisement of our peace was upon him;
and with his stripes we are healed,*" Isa. 53:5. "*Who his
own self bare our sins in his own body on the tree, that
we, being dead to sins, should live unto righteousness:
by whose stripes ye were healed,*" I Pet. 2:24.

WHEN YOU COMMUNE

The next time you partake of Holy Communion please keep the following in mind:

1. The purpose of Christ--Christ came that you might have wholeness in all areas of life (John 10:10). This wholeness includes the forgiveness of your sin (Mark 10:45). He also desires your wholeness of body and mind (Mark 1:21-28).

2. The power of Christ--Christ made this vast universe from nothing (Heb. 11:3). All the forces of nature and even Satan are subject unto Him (Matt. 8:27; Mark 4:41, 1:27). He is coming again in power to reign forever and ever (Acts 1:11).

3. The presence of Christ--Christ is more than someone who lived, expressed His feelings, pro-pounded His theology and theories and then died. He is alive forever more. Jesus is the only begotten Son of God. He is One with God. He lives within each believer. He will be with His church to the end of this age and beyond (Matt. 28:20).

The presence of Christ is more than a nebulous thought. It is a real experience and assurance of His love. You are in Christ and He is in you.

The Holy Communion is a continuing life-line to Life Himself. Appropriate His healing power as you receive the Bread and the Cup.

L

HEALING OF THE SPIRIT

One of the most puzzling things to me in the area of the healing ministry is the reaction of individuals who are healed physically or emotionally.

It is a mystery to me for instance why...

...when someone is healed miraculously the person so often fails to really give the Lord the credit,

...an individual who has been healed so often does not continue to attend healing services and faithfully bear witness as one whom the Lord has touched,

...often the person healed does not really become a faithful follower of the Lord and an ardent participant in His Church,

...so many are willing to accept His gifts, but are hesitant to accept and to confess Him as the Giver,

...those who say they believe God heals in many ways including doctors, medicine, etc., react negatively when someone gives the Lord credit for her/his healing.

AN ANSWER

It was while prayerfully dealing with the above puzzle I came to realize unless a person is truly changed on the inside, their lifestyle will not change a great deal. The only healing which can produce profound change in a life is a spiritual healing.

In the light of this insight, I began to search the scripture and to appraise the ministry of healing. The following insights have proven helpful to me and I trust will be of value to you.

PHYSICAL HEALINGS

The message of healing is essential to the proclamation of the full gospel. However, it must be stated sometimes the emphasis upon healing leaves the impression that only physical healings are involved.

I have even been accused of neglecting the Spirit because of my emphasis upon the availability of total healing. This accusation falls short of the message I seek to convey.

WHOLENESS

The wholeness Jesus proclaimed included body, soul, and spirit. We must be careful not to neglect any one of these areas. He healed the body, forgave sin, and brought soundness of mind and balance of emotions. He gave us eternal life. He ministered to the whole person.

BORN AGAIN

Jesus said to Nicodemus, "*You must be born again,*" John 3:3, 7. This experience is needed by all not only to be properly related unto the Father through the Son, but also because a person cannot rightly perceive the things of God outside of the Kingdom.

Spiritual things are perceived by spiritual people. The Kingdom is a sacred mystery unto a believer, and a most baffling mystery to one who stands on the outside.

It is as a member of the Kingdom a person perceives miracles can and do happen. Entering the Kingdom by way of the New Birth, a believer beholds the reality of His power and purpose.

PHYSICAL ONLY

The healing many receive of the body does not necessarily lead to a deeper devotion unto the Lord. Nor does a physical healing necessarily lead to a life devoted to advancing the message of the Good News.

Ponder the fact we have no biblical record of a person physically healed who became a great proclaimer of the Gospel. For instance, we hear nothing more from the centurion whose servant was healed (Matt. 8:5-13); the man whose withered hand was restored (Matt. 12:9-14); the one leper who returned to thank Jesus for his healing (Luke 17:11-19); or even Lazarus who was restored to life after being dead four days (John 11:1-4). Nor does the Bible record a meaningful ministry by any of the five thousand miraculously fed (Matt. 14:15-21). There is no record of an attendee at the wedding feast where water became wine becoming a great witness of our Lord (John 2:1-11). Malchus whose ear was restored by Jesus seemed to take it in stride and to go on in his pagan ways (John 18:10). Those who witnessed it still took Jesus prisoner and turned Him over to the officials.

In fact, you can review the miracles of the New Testament as listed in Chapter 6 and you will discover there is no biblical record of any of those physically healed becoming great witnesses for the Lord.

The physical healing did not necessarily move a person to make a commitment to proclaim the healing power of the Lord. It led to telling others about Jesus for the moment (Matt. 9:31), but none of them left a lasting imprint that we know of on the Church. There are several references to others bringing individuals to Christ to be healed. The point I am striving to make is there is no record of any of them becoming one of the remembered disciples, or writers of the Word.

Another interesting insight is there is no record of any of the 12 disciples or of the 70 other disciples receiving a physical or emotional healing prior to their being willing to follow Jesus. The apostle Paul was not raised from the bed of affliction and because of the healing turned to Jesus. NO! All of these great leaders experienced a "spiritual" healing which resulted in a new and committed lifestyle of obedience unto the Lord.

EMOTIONAL HEALINGS

There were a few who made positive steps toward proclamation of the Good News after being emotionally healed. The woman at the well went and told the entire town a prophet was in their midst (John

4:28-30). The demon-possessed man delivered by Jesus wanted to become a disciple (Mark 5:18); but Jesus simply told him to go tell others (Mark 5:19, 20).

HOLY SPIRIT

The individuals having a lasting and profound effect upon the Church were those filled with the Holy Spirit. Jesus appeared after the resurrection with the news that all power had been given unto Him (Matt. 28:18). He tells His disciples they shall receive power (Luke 24:49; Acts 1:8).

The day of Pentecost involved the power being imparted unto the faithful (Acts 2). It was after this experience the followers of our Lord became bold, fruitful, and fearless.

All the healings of the body and emotions in the world could not suffice to impart what was needed on the inside for a person to fearlessly serve the Lord. The Spirit had to bear witness with one's spirit before devotion unto the end was possible (I John 5:10).

The first elected church leaders were filled with the Holy Spirit (Acts 6:3). Paul was filled with the Holy Spirit (Acts 9:17).

Peter, Paul, Phillip, and many others set the example of faithfulness. They did this not because they had been physically healed, but because they had been spiritually filled. The early church, and the church today, does not move on those "healed" of body, but on those "filled" with the Spirit.

M

ACCORDING TO THY WILL

"*...I will; be thou clean,*" are the words of Jesus to the leper who approached Him saying,"*...if thou wilt, thou canst make me clean.*" Christ's response was "*I will!*" Matt. 8:2, Mark. 1:40.

The Church today needs to emphasize that our Lord desires wholeness for His children.

ACCORDING TO THY WILL

It is going to take a great deal of teaching to counteract the centuries of false teaching of "If it be Thy will." This statement by our Lord dealt with total commitment to His high calling. It was never used by Him in relation to an illness.

SUFFERING

Some will say, "But so many are ill and there is so much suffering in the world. It must be God's will." I do not want to gloss over the misery in this world. However, do we lay the blame for it at the feet of God?

I feel to blame God for this is a basic misunderstanding of the Creator and Sustainer of all life.

Man's ignorance, failure to believe and to practice spiritual laws, and many other factors are involved in illness of body, soul and spirit.

It is God's will we seek and expect His wholeness. This is as true as to believe He wants all to come to repentance.

"The Lord is not slack concerning his promise, as some men count slackness; but is longsuffering to us-ward, not willing that any should perish, but that all should come to repentance," II Pet. 3:9. All do not come, but we do not accuse God of not wanting them.

GOOD HEALTH - GOD'S WILL

Jesus never said to anyone, "I'm going to make you ill so you will come to know the love of God in your life." How ridiculous! On the contrary, He healed the multitudes of their illnesses. Below are some good reasons why you can be certain God wants you well.

I. OUR FATHER

The very nature of our heavenly Father is that He is more concerned for our well-being than even we ourselves, or our parents and friends. *"If ye then, being evil know how to give good gifts unto your children, how much more shall your father which is in heaven give good things to them that ask Him?"* Matt. 7:11.

II. JESUS CHRIST

The very nature of Jesus Christ necessitates His ministering to meet your needs. He not only wants to forgive your sins, but He also wants to heal your diseases.

Jesus saw both illness and sin as of the Evil one and thus to be defeated. He not only told the paralytic his sins were forgiven, but also told him to rise and walk (Mark 2:1-12).

The Christian Church has always taught that Christ perfectly obeyed the Father. He would not do anything contrary to His Father's will. Since much of His ministry was healing, how can anyone say wholeness is not God's will?

III. THE BODY

Your very body is made for wholeness. Attacked by an alien substance, the defenses of your body immediately go into action. They strive to ward off disease and to restore wholeness.

An infection in your body is the alarm alerting your lymphocytes to pour out antibodies and to call upon other cells to help. There may be as many as a million antibodies in your body. They are available when needed and each is equipped to fight a particular disease. Amazing, isn't it?

IV. APOSTOLIC CHURCH

The ministry of the Apostolic Church was one of helping and healing. It was not a ministry of helplessness and hopelessness in the face of illness.

Physical, mental and spiritual healings were an integral part of the Apostolic Church. The "if it be thy will," approach crept into the life of the church as her faith and power faded. It was not part of its initial thrust, but a part of its later deficiencies and decay.

V. SCRIPTURE

The scriptural promises and instructions of the Lord Jesus attest to His desire for your wholeness (Matt: 10:1; Mark 16:18; Luke 9:1, 10:9).

The Good News was a message accompanied with much power. This is evident in the life of the followers of our Lord (Rom. 15:18, 19; II Cor. 12:12; Heb. 2:4; I Cor. 12:9, 12:28-30; I Pet. 2:24; Rev. 22:2).

The power is also evident in many of the events experienced by His followers (Acts 3:6-7, 4:29-31, 4:16, 22; 6:8, 8:6-8, 9:39-42, 19:11-12, 28:3-6, 8; Rom. 8:11; I Cor. 1:18, 2:4-5, 4:20).

The early Church often used anointing and prayer to heal the sick (James 5:14).

God's will is your health. Good health is God's will. Believe Him today! Your wholeness is according to His will. Amen.

N

THE HEARER'S RESPONSIBILITY

Several times throughout His ministry the Lord Jesus Christ said, "*He that hath ears to hear, let him hear,*" Matt. 11:15, 13:9, 13:43; Mark 4:9, 4:23, 7:16; Luke 8:8, 14:35.

Jesus made it very plain that the "hearer" has a grave responsibility. It is not simply that the "proclaimer" has a burden to proclaim the Good News. The "hearer" must be willing to *hear* the Good News.

WHAT SHOULD YOU HEAR?

It seems to me Jesus made it abundantly clear what He wants us to hear. It is recorded in all four of the Gospels and plainly imparted to His 12 disciples, to the other 70 disciples, and to all believers in all ages.

PROCLAIM THE KINGDOM-- HEAL THE SICK

He specifically and plainly said to His followers, "*Go and proclaim the Kingdom of God is at hand and heal the sick,*" Matt. 10:7, 8 ; Mark 6:7, 13; Luke 9:1, 2; John 14:12.

It is evident that His disciples sought to do as He did. A man brought his son to the disciples to be healed (Matt. 17:16). This man would not have done this if he were not aware of what the disciples did and how they did it. For instance, we have no record of people being brought to John the Baptist to be healed. The reason is simple. John did not know of the power which could be released, and he did not proclaim a message of wholeness. Jesus knew the power and how to release it. He taught His disciples of the power of God and how to release it in their lives and in the lives of others.

The disciples acknowledged that they tried to do as they were being taught by the Master. They asked Jesus why they could not cast the devil out of the young man. They would not have asked this question if they had not tried to accomplish this task (Matt. 17:19).

In every Gospel, He told His disciples what they should do and the message they should proclaim. It is a mystery to me why the Church has neglected to do what Jesus told His followers to do.

It is even stranger to me that many in the Church feel the message in John 3:7 is the only one to be proclaimed. In fact, some accuse me and others who are proclaiming the message of healing of neglecting the "born again" experience. How strange.

I thoroughly believe a person must be born again. However, the proclamation of the Good News is not an esoteric experience. It is not confined to those who have been born again, but it is for the entire world. The message of wholeness is for all.

THE SETTING

Please consider that the words of Jesus, *"ye must be born again,"* John 3:7 were uttered to one man, at night, in secret. Nicodemus was never told he should tell this to everybody. It appears that a large segment of the Church has come to believe the message "you must be born again" is the only message which should be made public.

To me it is strange that the seven times the followers of Jesus are told what should be taken public means so little to many pastors and lay people. Jesus made no bones about the fact that God wants to bless individuals and to set them free from sin and sickness. He specifically instructs His disciples to proclaim this message. How many times must we be told by our Lord to do something? How many times must we be told before we obey?

HIS CHURCH - HIS METHODS

Jesus said, *"...and I will build My Church,"* Matt. 16:18. It is His Church, and He has His method of building it. All too often His Church has turned from and rejected His methods and pursued their own. Rationalization and human reasoning have replaced revelation and God's ways. Is it any wonder there are millions who have never heard, and millions of those who have heard have turned away from the Church's message? The One who founded the Church also gave the methods for furthering and nurturing His Church.

Having established what message should be proclaimed, I want now to present what is expected of those who hear. Jesus makes it very plain. He simply and matter-of-factly says, if they do not hear and heed the message that the Kingdom of God is at hand, and that God desires to heal, then their end will be *"worse than that of Sodom and Gomorrah,"* Matt. 10:15; Luke 10:12.

This seriousness of hearing what is proclaimed is mentioned not once, but several times: Matt. 10:14, 15; Mark 6:11; Luke 9:5, 10:10-16.

The virgin birth of our Lord is mentioned but once in the Gospels, and it is considered a crucial doctrinal point. This is as it ought to be. But if something is mentioned 3, 4, 5, or 7 times, should it not definitely be a part of the teaching and practice of His Church?

The bottom line, it seems to me, is, "are you hearing what Jesus is saying?" You are being held responsible for your reaction to His message of hope and healing. You cannot lightly reject the essential facet of His ministry in your midst. It is not a matter to be taken lightly. It is not an option or a "take it or leave it" proposition. Jesus sternly said, if they will not hear, judgment is upon them.

WHAT SHOULD YOU HEAR?

Hear what? Hear that the Kingdom of God is at hand! Hear that the Lord is willing to heal! Hear that

His message of healing and hope is for you, NOW! It is so simple.

The devil comes to steal, to kill, and to destroy. He does not want the message of hope in this life to be proclaimed by the Church of our Lord Jesus. He loves to keep every good gift of God hidden from the world. He wants to keep our minds on the hereafter and to rule us in the now.

However, in spite of him, Jesus says, "*I am come that you might have life and that you might have it more abundant,*" John 10:10. He wants His people to be blessed now, as well as in the future.

Further, He says to His disciples that those who hear this message of hope are obligated to receive it with eagerness. The "hearer" has a responsibility.

You have heard the Word. You have a responsibility as a "hearer" to respond to it and to believe God for greater things in your life. You cannot continually blame the proclaimer for not proclaiming the message, or for not proclaiming it right. You are responsible for how you hear. "...*He that hath ears let him hear.*" Amen.

O

TITHING AND THE SPIRITUAL HEALING MINISTRY

"Bring ye all the tithes into the storehouse, that there may be meat in mine house, and prove me now herewith, saith the Lord of hosts, if I will not open you the windows of heaven, and pour you out a blessing, that there shall not be room enough to receive it," Malachi 3:10.

This verse is used by some to teach that all tithes should go to an individual's local church. In fact, I received a magazine from a famous evangelist and there was a paragraph stating all tithes should be given to one's local church, and that his evangelistic ministry was supported only by offerings above the tithe.

Is this teaching valid and is it to be taught and pursued by believers? I say it is not. I feel stressing that the complete tithe should always be given to the local church is not valid and is not in keeping with the scripture. Some pastors teach this as a means to make sure their members do not support other ministries. Some pastors use it to seek to place a guilt trip upon any who might share their tithes with ministries beyond their church.

You may choose to give all of your tithe to the local church, but Malachi 3:10, in my opinion, does not absolutely teach that you must do so.

Why do I feel teaching the local church is the only "storehouse" for one's tithe is biblically unsound and from a practical standpoint, inappropriate?

TIME AND PLACE DIFFERENT

It is biblically unsound because the situation which prompted the statement in Malachi 3:10 was entirely different than what exists today. Malachi lived in a day when there was only one "storehouse." The Lord's Word in his day was associated with one nation, Israel, and one sacred place, the Temple.

This is no longer true. There is no central temple for all the believers of the world. Today there are a multitude of spiritual "storehouses" ranging from local churches and single purpose ministries, to 24-hour-a-day Christian television and radio.

MANY STOREHOUSES

It is unsound in a practical sense because today there are many places where you may secure your spiritual food. Most believers in this age have several places from whence they are receiving spiritual guidance, insights, and strength.

WHAT IS A STOREHOUSE?

A "storehouse" is where items are kept. It is a place where needed items may be secured. It takes many and varied storehouses to meet essential and desired needs each day. You have need of groceries, gasoline, hardware items, furniture, etc. You pay at the "storehouse" where the items are obtained. You do not pay for groceries at the hardware, or for gasoline at the doctor's office. You pay for what you receive where you receive it.

Some of the "storehouses" you use may be thousands of miles away. You order by mail and receive shipment. Even though not in the community, you pay the "storehouse" from whence you received the items or services."

SPIRITUAL STOREHOUSE(S)

It is obvious your "spiritual" storehouse(s) is where you secure your spiritual food. This is often elsewhere than at the church where you belong. Of course, you appreciate your church and receive much from it. However, many other ministries may also be of great help to you. Sometimes ministry received from other sources is more beneficial and helpful than what is received from your local church. Are not these sources of spiritual help storehouses of spiritual power and truth?

No local church can meet all your spiritual needs. It cannot provide Christian music and teaching 24-hours-a-day. It cannot provide for large inspirational conferences nor publish nourishing books and magazines. Many ministries are needed to meet all your spiritual needs. Thus, there are many "spiritual storehouses" from whence you receive. The ministries which are blessing you need and are worthy of your support from your tithes and offerings.

Give to wherever and whenever the Holy Spirit directs you! If you ask God for wisdom, He will not guide you to unfaithful ministries. Be sensitive to His leading!

P

FOURTEEN TENETS

There are basic tenets which serve as a foundation of our healing ministry.

The following fourteen will give you a better understanding of the approach and aims of Spiritual Healing:

1. ALL OF GOD

We believe all healing is of God.

2. DESIRES WHOLENESS

We believe God desires for us wholeness and health. Jesus spent much of His time here on earth healing the sick. He came to always do the Father's will and healing the sick was a major portion of His life of obedience.

3. MANY AGENCIES

We believe God uses many agencies for healing. These include medicine, surgery, psychiatry, physicians, prayer, confession, diet and exercise.

4. HUMAN VESSELS

We believe God works almost invariably through human beings to do His healing. We are to be willing vessels for His Will.

5. NOT MAGIC

We believe Spiritual Healing is not magic, hocus-pocus or sleight-of-hand. It is simply taking God at His word. In faith, believing, you make intercession for healing and thank Him for what is already taking place.

6. WITHIN THE CHURCH

We believe God's healing power operates within the Church which is the Body of Christ here on earth, but it is not limited to His Church.

7. RIGHTEOUSNESS

We believe physical health does not necessarily indicate righteousness, nor does illness necessarily indicate specific sins in a person's life.

8. PROMOTE HEALTH

We believe Christian witness and fellowship promote health and in many ways prevent illness by providing purposeful living and wholesome companionship. This results in proper stewardship of strength and health.

9. CHRIST'S MINISTRY OURS

We believe healing was an important part of Christ's ministry here on earth and is intended to be a part of His disciples' work in every generation.

10. NO FAILURES

We believe there are no failures in Spiritual Healing. No one can be brought into the presence of the healing Christ without being changed spiritually, emotionally, or physically. In some cases, they are changed in all three areas.

11. CHRIST LIVES

We believe Jesus Christ lives today in His risen power. He is the same today as yesterday and will be the same forever and ever.

12. SALVATION

We believe the word "salvation" means not only deliverance from sin, but also deliverance from physical and mental evils.

13. REVIVAL

We believe the revival of Spiritual Healing in the Church today will be the means of the greatest advance of Christianity in this century.

14. BELIEVE

We believe this is vital for both our present and our future.

CONCLUSION

In conclusion, I present the question to you. What do you believe?

Q

SOME BENEFITS OF A SPIRITUAL HEALING MINISTRY

Are there benefits derived from a healing ministry? Obviously, the answer is, yes! What then, are some valid reasons for the emphasis upon the Lord's desire for wholeness?

CONCERN

The ministry of healing helps to develop a fellowship of concern. It helps to bring together a fellowship of the concerned.

The healing services provide opportunity for the concerned to focus their prayers, affection, and love upon particular individuals. It is in such services that joy, sorrows, victories, defeats, and concerns become shared experiences. There comes a fuller realization that what happens to one, in a sense, happens to all.

REALITY

Another benefit of the ministry of healing is that it helps believers to be aware of the reality of Jesus's Presence. Our Lord is seen as being very near. His love is real. His concern is genuine. His power is present. His desire is wholeness.

Many testify that during the healing service they feel His presence and power as at no other time. "*Lo, I am with you always,*" is not simply a statement, but stark reality at these services.

WHERE THE ACTION IS

The healing service is not simply another service of theory and theology. Action is the keynote of it. People are praying and believing and when they do, something happens! Prayer is power. It does change you and others.

There may not always be phenomenal physical recovery at once, but there is always a deepening of the spiritual life, a gaining of insight, or recovery of strength. "The healing service is where the water hits the wheel," is an appropriate rephrasing of an ancient adage.

A change is inevitable in both the ones ministering and the ones ministered unto.

FIRST THINGS FIRST

The healing ministry brings a natural increase of interest in prayer. It helps individuals to realize prayer is not to equip you to do the work of the Church, but that prayer *is* the work of the Church.

Jesus said, "*Men ought always to pray and not to faint,*" Luke 18:1. The viewpoint of most Christians today is that Jesus said, "You ought always to organize, plan, and promote; and be busy beavers."

The ministry of healing will teach you to wait upon the Lord and to trust in His power.

INDIVIDUAL PARTICIPATION

People at the healing service do not remain passive in the pews. They are participants. Each has the opportunity to receive the laying-on-of-hands with prayer. They bring to the altar their concerns and the concerns they have for others.

Even if you choose to remain in your pew through the entire service, there is still a deep personal concern you feel for others.

In a sense, each one present is a link in the chain of power.

THE WHOLE PERSON

Another benefit of the healing ministry is that it gives opportunity to express the basic belief of the close relationship of the physical, spiritual, and emotional aspects of a person.

The Church is called to minister to the whole person. The ministry of healing offers the most balanced approach I know to the total needs of each person.

PREVENTION OF ILLNESS

The healing ministry provides guidance for a person to appropriate the strength to remain strong of body, soul, and spirit. It even helps to develop one's personality to the place where you can better cope with illness and other problems. Preventive medicine is in vogue today. It certainly should include trusting God!

R

HOW TO RECEIVE GOD'S BLESSING

Many are most anxious to receive all the Lord has in store for them. How can this best be done? May I offer the following suggestions?

I. SEEK GUIDANCE

Invite the Holy Spirit to guide you as you begin to prepare yourself to receive God's best. He may give you a Bible passage or message, a person, or an experience as part of the answer and comfort for your need:

"Likewise the Spirit also helpeth our infirmities: for we know not what we should pray for as we ought: but the Spirit itself maketh intercession for us with groanings which cannot be uttered," Rom. 8:26.

II. GIVE THANKS

Give thanks to God for what He has already done for you and your loved ones. Thank God for what the one in need has already meant to you. Count your many blessings:

"Be careful for nothing. But in every thing by prayer and supplication with thanksgiving let your requests be made known unto God," Phil. 4:6.

III. FORGIVE

Forgive everyone who has injured you in any way. Do all you can to be at peace with all. Even be willing to ask those you have injured to forgive you:

"And when you stand praying, forgive, if ye have ought against any, that your Father also which is in heaven may forgive you your trespasses," Mark 11:25.

IV. DETERMINE NEED

Seek to agree within yourself and with your family what is most needed at the time and why it is needed:

"Again I say unto you that if two of you shall agree on earth as touching anything that they shall ask, it shall be done for them of my Father which is in heaven," Matt. 18:19.

V. RELINQUISHMENT

Relinquish your life into God's hands. Let Him make His improvements in you. Be willing to exchange what you think is best for yourself for His best for you:

"And no one puts new wine into old wineskins, or else the new wine will burst the wineskins, and be spilled, and the wineskins will be ruined," Luke 5:37.

VI. OPEN TO GOD

Invite Jesus to come within you and support you while you are waiting for God's best. As a flower opens to receive light, rain, and air; may you open yourself to receive God's best:

"Behold, I stand at the door, and knock: if any man hear my voice and open the door, I will come in to him, and will sup with him, and he with me," Rev. 3:20.

VII. PICTURE THE BEST

I encourage you to make a picture in your mind of God's best coming to you:

"For as he thinketh in his heart, so is he. Eat and drink, saith he to thee, but his heart is not with thee," Pro. 23:7.

VIII. EXPECT THE BEST

Seek to begin each day thinking of what good thing the Lord has in store for you. Expect the Lord to bless. Do not dwell on the dreaded areas of your life, but on the blessed areas:

"Therefore I say unto you, what things soever ye desire, when ye pray believe that ye receive them, and ye shall have them," Mark 11:24.

IX. REST IN GOD

Learn to abide in His care. Rest yourself and your loved ones in the security of God's love which was with you when you were born, which is with you now, and which will be with you through all eternity:

"If ye abide in me, and my words abide in you, ye shall ask what ye will, and it shall be done unto you," John 15:7.

X. TURN TO GOD

Seek to always keep your heart and life turned in the Lord's direction. Prayer is the process by which you get yourself into alignment with the Lord to receive His best. Regardless of your circumstances, return unto the Father:

"I will arise and go to my father, and will say unto him, Father, I have sinned against heaven, and before thee," Luke 15:18.

XI. RELATE

Relate to what God has done for you in the past--that is faith. Relate to what He is going to do for you in the future--that is hope. Relate to what He is doing for you now--that is love:

"And now abideth faith, hope, love, these three; but the greatest of these is love," I Cor. 13:13.

S

A MATTER OF DEVOTION

I am often asked why I am so devoted to the ministry of healing. My response to this valid question is always the same.

"I am not devoted to the healing ministry. I am devoted to Jesus Christ."

DYNAMITE OF OBEDIENCE

I am not devoted to some program or to a plan. I am devoted to a Person. That Person is Jesus Christ.

My calling is not to meet some need in the world. I have been called to do the will of the Creator of the world. Doing His will issues forth the dynamite of obedience.

My pastoral ministry and that of any pastor is enriched by accepting all that Jesus has in store for His people. It is not that healing is my "bag," but rather that Jesus is my Lord.

I am called to be a pastor of a local congregation. If I am faithful to my calling, the Lord's message of wholeness will be my message. My ministry is not an emphasis upon healing so much as it is endeavoring to lift up our Lord in my parish. Healings are the natural result of obedience to our Lord. It is tangibly beholding His presence and power.

SUMMARY OF CHRIST'S MINISTRY

There are two places in the Bible where our Lord's ministry is presented in capsule form. Both instances present healing as a vital aspect of His ministry.

The first is when the disciples of John the Baptist ask Christ if He is truly the Messiah or should they look for someone else. Jesus replied by having them tell John what He was doing and what they had actually seen:

"...*Go and show John again those things which ye do hear and see: The blind receive their sight, and the lame walk, the lepers are cleansed, and the deaf hear, the dead are raised up, and the poor have the gospel preached to them...*" Matt. 11:2-5.

The second reference is Peter's summary of the ministry of Jesus. He is preaching to the Gentiles and wants them to understand the ministry of our Lord.

"*How God anointed Jesus of Nazareth with the Holy Ghost and with power; who went about doing good, and healing all that were oppressed of the devil; for God was with Him,*" Acts 10:38.

DEVOTION TO CHRIST

I want to present some reasons why devotion to Christ will lead to a ministry of healing. I feel they are worthy of your careful and prayerful consideration:

1. The very nature of Christ is a spirit of compassion. He desired wholeness for the afflicted and the oppressed. His very nature led Him to be constantly ministering to individuals in all areas of their life. He did not hesitate to bring healing to them.

2. Jesus' commission to His disciples included healing. They were to proclaim that the Kingdom of God was at hand, and they were to heal the sick.

His disciples were told to believe Jesus wanted the sick well and to tell the sick the Good News of wholeness (Matt. 10:1; Mark 6:7-13; Luke 9:1-6).

3. The early church leaders believed the Lord desired wholeness. The disciples did not proclaim or develop a program. They presented a Person, Jesus Christ.

A natural result of lifting up the Lord Jesus was the "signs and wonders." Signs and wonders were not the things the early believers followed, but signs and wonders followed the early believers. These were the proof of the full gospel being faithfully proclaimed (Rom. 15:18-19; Heb. 2:4; II Cor. 12:12).

THE REAL QUESTION

The real bottom line question for a believer is not "Why a healing ministry?" but rather "Why am I neglecting or ignoring the ministry of healing?" The answer to this piercing question will measure your devotion to the full ministry of our Lord Jesus Christ.

T

PROCLAIM ALL OF THE GOOD NEWS

The Christian faith has many facets such as teaching, preaching, prayer, social concern, healing, and evangelism.

It is peculiar, however, that the healing aspect has been so sorely neglected. It comprised such a large part of our Lord's ministry and that of the Apostolic Church. I am amazed at its neglect by the Institutional Church through the centuries.

TRUTH DEMONSTRATED

Jesus did not merely declare that the Kingdom of God is at hand. He demonstrated this truth. His miracles were evidence of the presence of God, evidence that He was the Son of God, the Messiah!

Even Nicodemus was reached through the healing ministry of our Lord. He was attracted by the miracles of our Lord. "...*no man can do these miracles that thou doest, except God be with him,*" John 3:2.

HARMONY OF THE GOSPELS

A harmony of the Gospels reveals the startling fact that approximately one out of every three incidents in the life of our Lord concerns healing.

From the beginning of His public ministry to His last hours, He worked miracles of healing (Luke 22:50, 51).

If so much of His ministry was that of helping others through healing, how can we neglect this message of hope?

POWER AVAILABLE

Centuries of neglect do not negate the fact that the power of Jesus Christ is available. Niagara Falis has existed for eons, but it was not until recently its great power was harnessed for the good of mankind.

Most Christians have sought to convert the unbeliever and to edify the believer through proper theology. Yet, it is evident a congregation is not presenting a complete ministry if healing is neglected.

Biblical preaching, prayer, sacraments, and evangelism cannot be substituted for the power of the Gospel. The evidences of the power are the miracles in our day.

PRECEDENT

The precedent for imparting wholeness was set by our Lord (Acts 10:38). The power is available (Matt. 28:18; John 14:12-14). The procedure is simply be-

lieving the Lord for great and marvelous things
(Matt. 17:20, 21).

PREACH ALL

Every Christian and every Christian congregation
is called to minister to the whole person. This must
include the proclamation and appropriation of our
Lord's healing power. The Great Physician is for our
day! You and I are called to proclaim all of the Good
News, not just selected portions of it.

U

A SYMBOL OF HEALING

This symbol of healing is an effort on my part to visually convey the message of wholeness.

I feel the Lord revealed to me the insights concerning the symbol. Our daughter-in-law, Patrice Bartow, did the art work.

The symbol imparts the concept that the Triune God is the agent of healing. Also that it is by faith we receive and impart the blessings and message of healing.

It is my prayer the symbol of healing will help implant upon your mind and heart the essential aspects of the Spiritual Healing Ministry. May you believe and receive the Lord's wholeness for you and yours.

The following is my interpretation of the symbol. You may have other insights as you observe the symbol in the light of what I have written.

THE CIRCLE

The circle of the symbol represents God the Father. He is over all and desirous of extending His healing, love, and mercy to all. It is His very nature to extend His wholeness to us.

He is more willing to heal than we are often willing to accept His healings (Ps. 34:8, 40:5; 86:15; Matt. 5:45; Luke 11:13; I Pet. 5:7).

THE SHIELD

The shield of the symbol represents Faith. Faith is the gift of God and so vital for an effective ministry of healing.

Because of my effort to teach faith is a gift from God, the shield is touching the circle and is being presented by the hands of the Lord Jesus (Eph. 2:8, 9; Luke 17:5; Gal. 5:6; James 2:17; I John 5:4).

THE HANDS

The hands holding and offering the shield of faith represent the hands of the Lord Jesus Christ. He is giving to you the faith to believe He desires the very best for you. The hands speak of the truth that the Lord completely identified Himself with humanity and continues to do so (Luke 2:11; Matt. 25:40; Acts 9:4; 10:38; Phil. 2:5-8).

THE DOVE

The dove of the symbol represents the Holy Spirit. The healing gift, message, and ministry are of divine origin and power.

It is the Holy Spirit Who enables you to behold the love and mystery of the Lord's tender care (Luke 11:13, 24:49; Acts 1:8; Rom. 8:11; John 16:13, 14:17).

THE HAND

The hand on the shield represents the one ministering. The hand is used to bestow a blessing upon the one for whom prayer is being offered. The hand issues forth from the hand of the Lord Jesus. It is touched by the dove which is symbolic of the power of the Holy Spirit working through the individual.

The hand is on the shield of faith and thus speaks of this vital ingredient. The shield is touching the circle which represents the Father. Thus the blessing is imparted in the Name of God the Father, Son, and Holy Spirit!

V

FAITH CLINIC

Jesus said, "*all things are possible to him who believes,*" Mark 9:23.

The Holy Spirit revealed to Paul, who wrote in his letters that a person's right standing with the Lord is possible through faith alone (Rom. 1:17, 5:1; Gal. 2:16; Eph. 2:8).

The writer of the book of Hebrews proclaims the only way to really please God is by faith. It is impossible to do so otherwise (Heb. 11:6).

THE IMPORTANCE OF FAITH

If faith is so important, isn't it absolutely essential that every person be specifically and creatively taught concerning faith? Faith is not a take-it-or-leave-it matter. Faith is the very foundation of our relationship to one another and to the Living God.

Faith can move mountains...the mountains of sin, the mountains of difficulties, the mountains of ruined relationships, the mountains of frustrated visions and shattered dreams. This truth needs to be shouted from the housetops because, in the life of most people, a chain of mountains exists which keeps them from the fertile valleys of fellowship and fruit-fulness toward the Lord. These mountains can only be scaled, made level, or removed by faith. There is no other road to victory.

CANTON'S FAITH CLINIC

I believe every community needs some place where individuals can be specifically taught concerning faith. We all need to hear again and again what faith is, how it is received, released, taught, and applied to the needs of life. We need to understand the difference faith makes in one's life, Who is the basis of faith and when faith can be relevant. All of this and more needs to be taught again and again unto those willing to receive this teaching.

I believe so strongly that faith is the key to a victorious Christian life, that I want to emphasize each week our Faith Clinic. The key to success in teaching and preaching is faith. The key to healing in body, soul, and spirit is faith. I believe that every city or area needs at least one "Faith Clinic." We designate ours as Canton's Faith Clinic. Your Clinic can bear your city or area by name.

CHARACTERISTICS OF
A FAITH CLINIC

What is the nature of a Faith Clinic? It is outwardly not much different than what our Spiritual Healing Services have been for years. However, there is more overt emphasis upon faith and its prime importance in the life of each person.

Some may say, "But hasn't faith always been taught in the churches and isn't it taught now, especially in a healing service?" I would have to answer, "Yes, to a degree." However, faith is not emphasized as it should be. Frequently, the faith which is proclaimed and believed still is not the kind of faith which releases the power of God for great things.

A Faith Clinic should constantly teach the what, how, when, where, and Who of faith. It should be a place where the practical results of faith are evident and where the preaching and teaching is accompanied by "signs and wonders," Rom. 15:18, 19; II Cor. 12:12; Heb 2:4.

CLINIC

The word "clinic" conveys the concept of practical application of the truths proclaimed. Clinic means "instruction of a class by treatment of patients in the presence of pupils." Isn't this the way a healing service should be conducted?

A clinic provides intensive training by qualified teachers and practical guidance by those successful in their endeavors.

Thus, there are baseball, football, basketball and medical clinics held throughout the nation. They all need some place where they can be taught the fine points of the game. They need a Clinic where they can have practical experience and guidance in their area of interest.

I see our weekly Faith Clinic as a time when individuals can zero in on this important facet of life. Our goal is to lead people to a greater life of faith and trust in the Lord. It is a service in which we give opportunity for faith to be released and the blessings of God received.

A Faith Clinic conveys the idea of action and results. We can grasp this in the area of medicine, and most communities have a place designated as a "Clinic" for the treatment of disease. One of the most famous is the Cleveland Clinic. Practical results are expected from these places. Is it too much to expect practical help from our exercise of faith? I think not! I am convinced we should believe for great things. Faith as a grain of mustard seed will accomplish much. The blending of the faith of many in a Faith Clinic will accomplish even more!

A FAITH CLINIC AND HEALING

Our Faith Clinic is sponsored by the Spiritual Healing Ministry and is our weekly healing service. This is because I firmly believe a Faith Clinic concept does not negate the emphasis upon healing, but rather accents it. Try it!

EMOTIONALLY INDUCED WHOLENESS

The letters "E.I.I." are often used to signify Emotionally Induced Illnesses. Many hospital beds are occupied by individuals who have "thought" themselves into a state of illness. In addition, many illnesses could have been prevented if individuals had a proper approach to life.

It is not difficult for me to convince individuals that illness is often emotionally induced. Most people are aware of problems of their own or others which are the result of wrong mental and emotional attitudes.

E.I.W.

I want you to consider what I term "E.I.W.," which stands for Emotionally Induced Wholeness.

The Lord desires your wholeness. It is important you believe this and trust Him for it.

Your mental attitude can help maintain wholeness and help restore it when illness does happen to come your way.

STEPS TO E.I.W.

I suggest the following tangible ways to help with your Emotionally Induced Wholeness:

1. Discipline yourself to begin each day visualizing yourself as whole. Use your God-given power of imagination to visualize the Lord Jesus being with you. See Him extending His wholeness to every aspect of your body, soul, and spirit.

Endeavor to repeat this procedure at least three times throughout the day. Often repeat the words of Jesus, "...*what things ye desire, when ye pray, believe that ye receive them, and ye shall have them,*" Mark 11:24.

2. If you have developed any type of illness, visualize yourself as whole. It doesn't matter if it be a specific organ of the body or simply a general illness. Visualize the healing power of the Lord flowing into the affected area and bringing wholeness.

I suggest visualizing wholeness and applying the Lord's healing laws by:

1. Seeing the organ (or whatever part is affected) as completely healed and in a perfect state--and thanking Him for it.

2. Seeing yourself doing things which you would normally do if you did not have the affliction.

3. Visualize yourself as in the perfect light and love of the Lord. This permits you to get your mind off of the problem and unto the Problem Solver. It keeps you from dwelling upon the affliction and inadequacy of yourself. It leads to concentration upon the Great Physician and His All Sufficiency.

Dwelling upon your pain or illness simply drives it deeper into the recesses of your mind and total being. Looking unto the Great Physician focuses power and attention at the proper place.

4. When you pray for others visualize them in the light and love of Jesus. Ask the one unto whom you are ministering with prayer to visualize himself in His light and love.

AS YOU BELIEVE

Dr. Carl Simonton conducted experiments on 152 patients he was treating with cobalt radiation. He instructed each patient to visualize what the cobalt was doing to the cancer. They were to picture the cancerous area as raw hamburger or raw liver with a vast army of millions of tiny white blood cells attacking the cancer cells and carrying them away.

The 20 patients who really applied his directions for visualizing wholeness were the only ones whose response to radiation was rated "excellent."

The 63 patients who were "good" in response to visualizing wholeness achieved "good" results from radiation. Those who were indifferent to blending the visualizing of wholeness with radiation treatment had only "fair" or "poor" results.

Dr. Simonton says, "I strongly believe that health is influenced by a patient's mental attitude." His conclusion is not new. Jesus knew the power of believing!

X

SPIRITUAL HEALING AND EVANGELISM

The Church throughout the world is being challenged to reach out as never before in the nineties. Evangelism is moving into the spotlight among major denominations. Where and how does healing enter into the evangelistic thrust of this new decade?

We hear alot about New Testament evangelism. What really was New Testament evangelism?

We usually think of evangelism as proclaiming the Good News concerning Jesus Christ and the world being reconciled unto the Father through Him, and it certainly is this; however there is more to it than merely proclaiming. What Good News does the New Testament record that should be proclaimed?

We usually think of evangelism as bringing individuals to Christ. How and why were individuals brought to Christ as recorded in the New Testament?

HEALING AND EVANGELISM

Emily Gardner Neal in her book, *The Lord Our Healer*, says, "The healing ministry has opened the way for a return to our once power-filled heritage.

6. *"And heal the sick that are therein, and say unto them, 'The kingdom of God is come nigh unto you,'"* Luke 10:9.

7. *"Verily, verily, I say unto you, He that believeth on me, the works that I do shall he do also; and greater works than these shall he do; because I go unto my Father,"* John 14:12.

How many times do we have to be told to heal the sick in Jesus' Name? If we are going to follow the New Testament teachings we will proclaim the ministry of wholeness.

FISHERS OF MEN

Matt. 4:19 tells us Jesus called Peter and Andrew to follow Him and He would make them fishers of men. They followed Him. How did He teach them to fish?

We have no record of Him giving them 14 lessons on friendly evangelism. There is no record of a long lecture concerning how you must be born again. There is no hint He gave them a crash calling program course.

Jesus taught His disciples to fish for men by revealing unto them how to heal through the power of God. They immediately beheld Him teaching, preaching, and healing.

Most Christians today spend their time teaching and preaching. Few Christians teach others to fish for men as Jesus taught them and include healing in their ministry.

Healing the sick, which was the heart of the evangelistic efforts of Jesus, has become heresy to many. This outlook has lead to many factions in the church, as teaching and preaching promotes pet doctrines and methods.

Jesus never concentrated on four spiritual laws, the Roman Road, nor two qualifying questions. He healed people. He did not lecture. He loved. He did not harangue the common people. He healed them. He caught thousands in His net as He fished for men as directed by His Father to do so.

Our world during the nineties will not be converted to Christ through pious teaching of so-called sound doctrine. It will only be reached as it sees the power of God being released through His Son the Lord Jesus Christ. His church must reclaim the proclamation and the power as recorded in Acts 3:6: *"Silver and gold have I none; but such as I have give I thee: In the Name of Jesus Christ of Nazareth rise up and walk."* When His Church does this, New Testament evangelism will be seen once more.

BORN AGAIN

Experiencing the New Birth is the first, essential part of being made whole in and through Christ. Let us look at some facets of this in relationship to evangelism.

Jesus certainly forgives sin (Mark 2:5). Jesus came as an atonement for our sins and to give His life for us as Saviour (Luke 2:11; 19:10; John 3:16).

However, isn't it interesting the message, "you must be born again," was presented to one man, at night, in private, and Jesus never did tell him to go tell everyone (John 3:1-21).

speak the Word with boldness. What did they ask for to enable them to be bold? It was for the Lord to continue to heal. *"And now, Lord, behold their threatenings: and grant unto thy servants, that with all boldness they may speak thy word, by stretching forth thine hand to heal; and that signs and wonders may be done by the name of the Holy Child Jesus,"* Acts 4:29, 30.

CONCLUSION

Our conclusion must include reference to the beginning of this chapter. Certainly New Testament evangelism included the healing of the sick. Individuals were brought to Jesus to be healed. He healed them. He instructed His disciples to do likewise. This commission to His followers has never been rescinded. May we be able to proclaim His message with boldness as we trust Jesus to stretch forth His hand to heal in our day and in our churches.

May we realize the miracles of Jesus were not only to prove Who He was, but were possible because of Whom He is! He is the Son of God unto Whom all power has been imparted (Matt. 28:18). He is the Son of God and our Saviour Who has given His power unto His followers (Acts 1:8). We are to witness in power unto the uttermost part of the earth!

Y

RESTING (SLAIN) IN THE SPIRIT

A woman exclaimed to her friend, "What happened to that lady? She must be sick! Why, she has fainted and fallen and that pastor has left her alone and is not even paying any attention to her!"

The above is part of the conversation my wife heard while sitting in the pew of a large Episcopal Church. The healing message had been presented and I was ministering unto those who had come forward. One of the women fainted away in the Spirit. What happened to her and others with a similar experience is a question often asked of me. The two women were disturbed because they did not understand. My desire is to help people understand "falling under the power of the Presence of God."

DESCRIPTION

What happens when a person "rests in the Spirit"? It is as if, in a sense, the functions of the body are shut off. The individual goes into a sleep-like experience.

Some believers have stayed in this state for a sustained period of time of up to several hours. The normal functions of the body simply do not function, but there are no ill effects. However, the average person remains in this "sleep" condition for only a few minutes, or 15 to 20 minutes at the most. Other terms used to describe this experience are "slain in the Spirit," or "falling under the power."

SOME EXAMPLES

Jo was within about five feet of me when I lifted my hands to minister unto her. She got no closer but fell to the floor as if she had fainted away. A few moments later she arose and returned to her seat.

It was not until the next day I learned of her condition. She had what three doctors had told her was an incurable bowel condition. She bled constantly and had become weak and emaciated. She pleaded with her husband to join her in praying she would die.

During this experience of "resting in the Spirit," she was immediately and wonderfully healed. She bore witness to this the next day and has continued to live a normal life. Praise Jesus!

Another exciting healing took place while Minnie lay on the floor at the front of our church. The ministry of the laying-on-of-hands resulted in her falling and being caught and gently laid on the floor. She lay there for several minutes while others continued to come forward for ministry.

The next day and ever since, she has born witness to a tremendous emotional healing which took place while she was "resting in the Spirit."

An interesting part of her experience involves her "loud crying out to God." She apologized for disturbing the meeting, but said she could not help it.

The unique fact is, no one heard anything from her! This experience of crying out in loud agony was all within her spirit. Those present never even knew such turmoil was taking place within her inner-most being. The Bible describes such "groanings in the spirit." What a difference this has made in her life!

Here is a miraculous experience which involved "resting in the Spirit." It was told to me some months after the incident:

Jim was in the midst of a divorce and planned to leave his wife in a few days. She was at her parents for a couple of weeks and his plan was to be completely moved out by the time she returned. She was very much aware of the tension and his intent. Alcohol abuse on his part compounded all the other problems.

I was asked to help minister at a meeting in a large restaurant in Youngstown, Ohio. Jim stopped because he saw all the cars and thought a party was in progress! To his dismay, he discovered it was a religious service. He stayed and, for some reason, came forward for laying-on-of-hands with prayer. Here is his story: "I felt something start to move up my arms and then all over me. I couldn't continue to stand and fainted away. When I awoke, I felt wonderful! I no longer hated my wife. I no longer had a desire for alcohol. I was a changed person. I don't know how it happened, but I certainly know it happened while I was unconscious!"

Jim later met his wife at the airport with enthusiasm and they are still together and living for Jesus and each other!

WHAT IS IT?

"Resting in the Spirit" is not easy to define. It is as if a "sleep" comes over the individual. The person often discovers it is impossible to remain standing. In most cases, they gently fall to the floor, but in some cases they almost crash.

Many refer to this experience as "being slain in the Spirit." There is nothing sinful about this description, but to me, it leaves much to be desired. It implies that maybe they have been killed or have been injured in some way. I much prefer "resting in the Spirit."

It is as if the person is overcome with the Presence of God and goes into a semi-conscious state. Most fall gently backward, others just collapse to the floor, and on occasion some fall forward. Regardless of how a person falls, it has been very meaningful to many.

BIBLICAL BASIS

The Bible certainly lends credence to the inability of men to stand in the Presence of the Living God. There are several incidents which should be prayerfully and carefully considered by those who accept and those who do not accept the experience of "resting in the Spirit."

OLD TESTAMENT/SLEEP

There are several references in the Old Testament which appear to support the fact individuals could not stand in the Presence of the power of the Spirit. There are also several references to a "deep sleep" coming upon an individual. The powerful Presence of the Lord left a person unable to remain mobile!

Genesis 2:21, "*And the Lord caused a deep sleep to fall upon Adam, and he slept: and he took one of his ribs, and closed up the flesh instead thereof.*"

The Lord's Presence overcame Adam and while in that state, Eve came forth.

Genesis 15:12, "*And when the sun was going down, a deep sleep fell upon Abram; and, lo, an horror of great darkness fell upon him.*"

I Samuel 26:12, "*So David took the spear and the cruse of water from Saul's bolster; and they got them away, and no man saw it, nor knew it, neither awaked; for they were all asleep; because a deep sleep from the Lord was fallen upon them.*"

Daniel 8:18, "*Now as he was speaking with me, I was in a deep sleep on my face toward the ground: but he touched me, and set me upright.*"

OLD TESTAMENT/FALLING

There are several references in the Old Testament where individuals fell before the Lord:

Judges 13:20, "*For it came to pass, when the flame went up toward heaven from off the altar that the angel of the Lord ascended in the flame of the altar. And Manoah and his wife looked on it, and FELL ON THEIR FACES to the ground.*"

It is not certain if they fell voluntarily or involuntarily. The inference seems to be the Presence was so great they could not resist the power and fell to the ground.

II Chronicles 5:13, 14, "*It came to pass, as the trumpeters and singers were as one, to make one sound to be heard in praising and thanking the Lord; and when they lifted up their voice with the trumpets and cymbals and instruments of music, and praised the Lord saying, 'For He is good; for His mercy endureth forever:' that then the house was filled with a cloud, even the house of the Lord ; so that the PRIESTS COULD NOT STAND to minister by reason of the cloud: for the glory of the Lord had filled the house of God.*"

Here there is no doubt but what the Presence was so great the leaders of worship could not stand. They were overwhelmed by His Presence.

Ezekiel experienced the Presence and rested in the Spirit:

Ezekiel 1:28, "*As the appearance of the bow that is in the cloud in the day of rain, so was the appearance of the likeness of the glory of the Lord. And when I saw it, I FELL UPON MY FACE, and I heard a voice of one that spake.*"

Ezekiel 3:23, "*Then I arose, and went forth into the plain: and, behold, the glory of the Lord stood there, as the glory which I saw by the river of Chebar: and I FELL ON MY FACE."*

It appears Daniel experienced being overcome by the Spirit of God.

Daniel 10:8-9, *"Therefore I was left alone, and saw this great vision, and there remained no strength in me: for my comeliness was turned in me into corruption, and I retained no strength. Yet heard I the voice of His words: and when I heard the voice of His words, then was I in a deep sleep on my face, and my face toward the ground."*

Most of the time the one who is "resting in the Spirit" can hear what is taking place. They are simply too weak to respond with the body. It is as if the outward person has been overcome, but the inward person is being ministered unto.

NEW TESTAMENT EXAMPLES

There are several New Testament references which allude to individuals being overcome with the Presence of the Lord:

Matthew 17:6, *"And when the disciples heard it, they FELL ON THEIR FACE, and were sore afraid."*

It is not clear whether this was an act of abject worship on the part of the disciples, or the result of the powerful Presence of the Lord. It appears from the fact that Jesus came and touched them (v. 7) that they were "resting in the Spirit."

Matthew 28:4, *"And for fear of him the keepers did shake, and BECAME AS DEAD MEN."*

The guards of the tomb were definitely affected by the Presence of the Lord. They were "resting in the Spirit" as the events of the resurrection unfolded.

Acts 2:13, "*Others mocking said, These men are full of new wine.*"

The men on the day of Pentecost were accused of being drunk. One of the characteristics of a drunk is inability to walk and stand properly. In fact, a person who is really inebriated will fall down and remain lying down.

I believe many were falling under the power on the day of Pentecost. This created the setting for the accusation of over-indulging. The gifts of tongues would not make them think the men were drunk. A drunk is not able to speak rapidly and fluently. In fact, a drunk is just the opposite. His speech is slurred and slow.

There is a possibility "resting in the Spirit" was experienced by the Apostle Paul.

Acts 9:3, 4, "*And as he journeyed, he came near Damascus: and suddenly there shined round about him a light from heaven: and HE FELL TO THE EARTH, and heard a voice saying unto him, 'Saul, Saul, why persecutest thou me?'*"

CHURCH HISTORY

The famous preacher of the 14th Century, Johannes Tauler, reports he "rested in the Spirit" while praying alone. He also reports many fell under the power during his revival services.

In fact, John Wesley, Charles Finney, George Fox and many other well-known evangelists had many fall under the power of the Lord in their meetings. This experience was not uncommon in their services.

The recent wave of charismatic emphasis has witnessed a renewal of this phenomena. It is one of the many signs and wonders revealed today as people seek to obey the Lord and to permit His Presence and Power to flow in and through them.

PRACTICAL INSIGHTS

There are some practical insights which I would like to mention at this time:

1. The experience of falling is not to be intentionally sought by the believer. It is an experience bestowed by the grace of God and not something to be falsely imitated.

2. The experience is not needed for healing of body, soul, or spirit to occur. Many are healed who have never fallen under the power.

3. A person who has "fallen under the power" is not necessarily more devout than one who has not. You do not base your relationship with God on how many times you have "rested in the Spirit." Your salvation and hope is in Christ Jesus and not a manifestation of His Presence.

4. The experience should not be initiated nor imitated by anyone or anything. A service should not be geared to working people up to the point where they are herded into this experience. It should come from God and not from our emotionalism.

5. A "catcher" should be present when a group is assembled and the power begins to fall. It is wise to

put forth every effort to keep anyone from getting hurt as they fall.

6. The success of any service should never be measured by how many fell under the power. The outward signs are not what we seek, but the inward healings of body, soul, and spirit.

7. Congregations should be carefully taught concerning "resting in the Spirit" so they are not frightened by the experience. Also they should not abuse or misuse this experience.

8. The pastoral leadership should set the pace of proper teaching and experiencing "resting in the Spirit." A pastor should not discredit the experience or make light of it, but at the same time the pastor must give guidance for the proper appreciation of the experience.

9. A person should not feel they are a "second-class" Christian if they have not gone down under the power. I have been prayed for by some of the greatest spiritual leaders of our day. However, I have never "rested in the Spirit." Many have gone down around me during these moments of ministry, but I have never even staggered. I can't tell you why I have not fallen. It is certainly not because I have intentionally sought to brace myself and refused to fall.

10. There are times when it is impossible to keep from falling. I have seen many people seek to resist the power. However, many of them have still gone down. It is certainly not because of any pressure from me or any effort on my part at our services prior to my even touching them. Many others go down when I have ever so gently touched them. I have never

pushed anyone down. The power is the Presence of the Lord and not me.

On one occasion a large man was helping me as the catcher. After all had been ministered unto, he started toward me for ministry. I lifted my hands while he was at least three feet from me. Even though he weighed well over 200 pounds, the moment I lifted my hands toward him, he was lifted about 6 inches off the floor. Both of his legs bent back and he flipped over and landed on his back. This man could not have been thrown this way by a strong man. It was the greatest demonstration of power in the area of falling under the Spirit's presence that I have ever witnessed.

11. Individuals should never base God's healing power on their "resting in the Spirit" experiences. The Lord is the healer regardless of how He may manifest Himself. I have witnessed many healings when it appeared nothing at all happened at the time of the laying-on-of-hands with prayer.

CONCLUSION

The conclusion of this entire matter for me is that the experience of "resting in the Spirit" should be seen as just one of God's varied experiences for His people. It should not be neglected or shunned, while at the same time it should not be overly promoted or advocated.

Z

MUSIC AND SPIRITUAL HEALING

Music plays a vital role in the life of almost every person. It is of special import in the church's ministry of healing.

MUSIC'S BENEFITS

First, music is a means of rejoicing before the Lord. There are many victories in a valid healing ministry and music provides an outlet to praise Him for the victories.

Second, encouragement is constantly needed in the face of great mountains to be crossed. Illness, financial problems, broken relationships, spiritual needs, and emotional trauma are areas of downers for many people. Such individuals need a time of inspiration and encouragement. This is especially true when there is no immediate healing of body, soul, or spirit. Music can enter into this situation and lift a person beyond their problems unto the Lord.

Music helps us to praise the Lord regardless of circumstances. The Old Testament prophet, Habakkuk, certainly stresses praise unto the Lord in all circumstances and at all times. It infers music was involved in rejoicing before the Lord. "*Although the fig tree shall not blossom, neither shall fruit be in the vines; the labour of the olive shall fail, and the fields shall yield no meat; the flock shall be cut off from the fold, and there shall be no herd in the stalls: (18) yet I will rejoice in the Lord, I will joy in the God of my salvation. (19) The Lord God is my strength, and he will make my feet like hinds feet, and he will make me to walk upon mine high places. To the chief singer on my stringed instruments,*" Habakkuk 3:17-19.

Third, music provides an opportunity for participation on the part of all. The people at a healing service, or any service, should not come to be entertained, but to be deeply involved. The singing of great hymns, gospel choruses, and spirit songs can all enhance involvement of the congregation.

Fourth, music provides a door for the use of special talent. Individuals can present special vocal numbers, play instruments such as the organ, piano, electronic keyboards, drums, guitar, trumpets and so on.

MODERN MUSIC

There has been alot of good, spiritual music written in our generation. It should be used.

The new music has been skillfully placed on backup cassettes and thus the average singer can have a fantastic orchestra for accompaniment, as well as harmonizing voices singing at different times throughout the number.

The electronic keyboard is a marvel of our electronic age. One or more of them can enhance your music program immeasurably. I am enthusiastic about the electronic keyboard for churches and especially to be used in the music area of the healing ministry. Below are just a few of the blessings of the electronic keyboard:

1. They are relatively easy to use. They can be played by less skillful musicians than is needed for an organ or the acoustical piano.

2. They provide a wide variety of sounds in a very small unit. For instance, they have organ, piano, strings, brass, percussion, wind instruments, along with many sound effects. All are reproduced to sound very authentic.

3. They are very portable. Since they only weigh a few pounds, they can be taken to any area of the church, as well as to a home or to a Nursing Home, etc.

4. They never get out of tune. Weather, moving around, or changes of the season will not affect the electronic keyboard.

5. Many of them are equipped for prerecording background music.

6. They are inexpensive. You can purchase many electronic keyboards for what you would pay for a good organ or piano. The average church could never afford the many instruments the keyboard will reproduce and blend together beautifully and easily.

OVERHEAD PROJECTOR

A service of praise and singing at the healing service will benefit from the use of an overhead projector. This provides the words for a variety of music without the use of several hymnbooks. It also frees the hands as they are lifted in praise unto the Lord.

COPYRIGHT

Today there are companies which care for any copyright privileges concerning music. Healing ministries and churches are urged to pay the nominal annual fee to receive proper permission to use music. It is not fair nor is it legal to reproduce music without the consent of the publisher. The convenience of having one company care for all of the music used is worth the small annual investment.

NEW SONGS

There are so many good writers today for those who want to sing praise songs and choruses unto the Lord. I feel the healing service is a wonderful place to keep on the cutting edge of Christian music.

I include a sample of music for our day. It is a contemporary arrangement of the Lord's Prayer. It catches the spirit of the nineties as it blends the timeless words of Jesus with modern concepts.

I appreciate the Lord's Prayer so much and have related a portion of it to each of the six steps of my Pattern of Prayer. I also suggest at group meetings during the 30-Day Prayer Pilgrimage that the Lord's

Prayer be used, as well as at other prayer times for individuals and groups.

The arranger, Steve Dallas, is a personal friend of mine. He is one of the most talented keyboard artists, vocalist, composer, transposer, choral arranger, instrumental and vocal teacher, and choral director I have ever known.

Mr. Dallas has a special skill at setting the scripture to music, as he had done with his classic oratorio, "THE TRUE VINE." This major work is a moving rendition of the 15th and 16th chapters of the Gospel of John.

You may write Life Enrichment Publishers for additional copies of the following arrangement and/or for the beautiful choral arrangement of the Lord's Prayer for your choir.

It is spiritually enriching to frequently pray the Lord's Prayer during private and/or corporate prayer time. How much more uplifting to sing it, or to hear it sung!

The text and score for Mr. Dallas's arrangement of the Lord's Prayer is as follows.

Matthew 6:6

(The Lord's Prayer)

Steve Dallas

© 1988 by Steve Dallas

IV

WHOLENESS

Satan may feel he can ultimately frustrate God's plans and the good of an individual. However, wholeness has been regained and we have the blessed hope for the future and forever of living and reigning with Jesus Christ.

I Corinthians 15 gives us the promise of sure victory. "For He must reign, till He hath put all enemies under His feet. The last enemy that shall be destroyed is death." (25, 26) In Him we will conquer death and not be defeated.

We sow an earthly body, we reap a spiritual body. We sow in dishonor, we are raised in honor. First we are earthy, then we become heavenly. And, just as we have borne the image of the earthly, we who are in Christ WILL BEAR the heavenly image, that of Jesus Christ our Lord. (42-49) What greater promise or hope could we have than to be like Him. Though this is a mystery to us, the promise is sure with God.

God has promised that in a moment we will be changed and we will no longer bear the pain and burden of this earthly life, but we will be given the wholeness of the heavenly life forever. Hallelujah!

THE PERFECT ENDING

The perfect ending of my HEALING HAND-BOOK fittingly deals with the perfect healing which awaits all believers.

SOURCE OF ILLNESS

We live in a world of sin and disease. No one escapes the consequences of the disobedience of Adam and Eve, nor the present negative influences of this imperfect world.

This world is too complex to know all the reasons for illness and disease. The following are some of the scriptural reasons for illness:

1. Lack of faith - Matt. 13:58
2. Known sin - Exodus 15:26
3. For the glory of God - John 11:4
4. In accordance with God's plan - Rom. 8:17-18; I Pet. 4:1-2, 19
5. Not discerning the Lord's body in the Holy Communion - I Cor. 11:27-31
6. Demonic attack - Matt. 12:22
7. Neglecting the laws of nature - Pro. 30:33
8. Lack of knowledge - I Cor. 13:9

9. For the works of God to be revealed - John 9:3
10. The natural body wears out - James 4:14,
    I Cor. 46-49

HOLY SOURCES OF HEALING

The scriptures do not leave us helpless in the face of illness and disease. The following are some of the scriptural suggestions to help restore and/or maintain wholeness of body, soul, and spirit:

1. Personal prayer - Job 42:5-6,10; James 5:16
2. Anointing - Mark 6:13; James 5:14-16
3. Laying-on-of-hands - Mark 16:17-18
4. Gifts of healing - I Cor. 12:9
5. His Word - Psalm 107:20
6. Prayer cloths - Acts 19:12; Pro. 4:20-22
7. Presence of a great believer - Acts 5:15
8. Worship - Psalm 32:7; Psalm 42:11
9. Music - I Sam. 16:14-23

AGENTS OF HEALING

There are three prime agents of healing as we travel through life. All of them enter into our experiences to some degree from time to time.

1. The nature of the human body - Pro. 17:22
2. Medical science - Matt. 9:12
3. God Himself through the release of His sovereign power - Psalm 103:2-5

WHEN ALL ELSE FAILS

I have presented the above to help make the point that all individuals are terminal cases in this world. The only people who will escape death are those alive when the Lord returns. Otherwise, there is no continual deliverance from illness in this life. Whatever the disease which takes us to the last enemy, death, must be faced. Satan thinks he will win the battle. The Good News is death does not win. Life does go on with the Lord! (I Cor. 15:51-58).

Some people would ask, "Won't a sick person and his/her loved ones lose their faith and turn their backs on the Lord if prayer is offered for healing and the person dies?"

This is a good and a natural question, but I have not witnessed that happening. I have seen far more people lose their faith and turn their back on the Lord because of lack of ministry on the part of the church rather than because of too much ministry.

Death is real. Death is certain. Death separates and death causes much grief and trouble. People understand they are not going to live forever. The ministry of wholeness simply keeps individuals living at their highest potential throughout their years. It does not proclaim nor guarantee life forever in this world.

DEEP APPRECIATION

Most people deeply appreciate the total ministry of wholeness for themselves and loved ones. The ministry of healing provides for a much better quality of life for individuals. It helps people to face the problems of body, soul, and spirit in a different way. Life becomes victorious instead of constantly defeating us when our hope is in the Lord Jesus and His healing power!

Let me present a couple of examples. I was called to go to Cheyenne, Wyoming to minister to a lady near death because of cancer. I made a hurried flight out and ministered unto her and the family, then flew back the next day.

I never knew this family prior to my responding to their call for ministry. The mother died a couple of days after I was there. Did the family react and say, "The anointing and laying-on-of-hands did not work. We are giving up on God." No! Just the opposite. They knew they had done everything humanly possible for their loved one.

The family members have become dear friends. In fact, a few weeks later the husband, two daughters, and two small grandchildren came to our summer healing conference at Westminster Church in Canton, Ohio. They stayed in our home. In addition, they brought a gracious memorial gift for the healing ministry. The gift was the result of their suggestion that in lieu of flowers, Memorial Gifts be given to the healing ministry.

Of course, they grieve and miss wife, mother, and grandmother. This reality is not denied. However, they are deeply appreciative of the healing ministry which presented all that the Lord has to offer. The woman had great peace prior to her death and actually sang and praised the Lord, though she was not a singer. The family knew she was in God's hands.

Another death occurred just prior to my writing this article which further illustrates the value of total ministry unto all.

A dear friend of our community recently died of cancer. Two of her children are members at Westminster. They love and undergird the healing ministry with their prayers and contributions. It was only natural they bring mother to the services. She and her husband are also among my closest friends.

The ministry of laying-on-of-hands, prayer, and anointing was extended to her as completely as we knew how to extend it. After a prolonged illness she died. Did the family react negatively toward the ministry of wholeness? No, a thousand times no! They are so grateful they did everything possible medically, spiritually, and practically.

This family requested Memorial Gifts be presented to the Spiritual Healing Ministry in lieu of flowers or to the Methodist Church to which she belonged. They did not become angry at the Ministry. They remain grateful for total ministry.

The above two families are also aware that the Lord is with them even as they are passing through the shadow of death. I am one who believes the believer who has died is not going through the shadow of death. The believer who has died in the Lord is not walking in the shadows, but in the light. The believer is not walking in the valley, but on the mountain tops. We who remain are going through the shadows and the valleys.

Those who remain must walk through the dark shadows and deep valleys of grief, sorrow, regret, resentment, loneliness, and many others. However, the Psalmist assures us the Lord will be there.

"Yea, though I walk through the valley of the shadow of death, I will fear no evil:for thou art with me; thy rod and thy staff they comfort me," Psalm 23:4.

I truly believe this verse is for those who remain following the death of a loved one or friend, rather than for the one who has died. We are the ones who truly need the comfort of the Lord. The believer is with Jesus!

O PERFECT DAY

Now we come to the climax of all of our efforts in the ministry of healing. It is the proclamation of the perfect day the Lord has for all of His children.

The perfect healing is the resurrection of the believer! It is the only way and the only time all illness, disease, and tribulations will be eliminated.

Throughout life we should live as close to the Lord as possible, faithfully pursue His methods for wholeness, and put our faith in Him. However, when life is over, we believe the Lord receives us unto Himself. This is the blessed hope of all believers.

Satan may feel he conquers through disease and death. We know differently. The Lord is the final conqueror!

Life with the Lord does not end at death for the believer, but it does change (I Cor. 15:1-58). The change is definitely for the better. The beloved Apostle John got a glimpse of life after death. It was so great he could not find the words to describe what was present. He ended up telling us what was not present, and that is enough to make us rejoice.

I close this book with the precious words from John's revelation:

"And I saw a new heaven, and a new earth; for the first heaven and the first earth were passed away; and there was no more sea. And I, John, saw the holy city, New Jerusalem, coming down from God out of heaven, prepared as a bride adorned for her husband.

"And I heard a great voice out of heaven saying, 'Behold, the tabernacle of God is with men, and He will dwell with them, and they shall be His people, and God Himself shall be with them, and be their God.'

" 'And God shall wipe away all tears from their eyes; and there shall be no more death, neither sorrow, nor crying, neither shall there be any more pain: for the former things are passed away.'

"And He that sat upon the throne said, 'Behold, I make all things new.'

"And He said unto me, 'Write, for these words are true and faithful.' And He said unto me, 'It is done. I am Alpha and Omega, the beginning and the end. I will give unto him that is athirst of the fountain of the water of life freely. He that overcometh shall inherit all things; and I will be his God, and he shall be my son,' " Rev. 21:1-7.

Indeed, we in the Spiritual Healing Ministry can proclaim in response to this revelation, there is perfect and everlasting healing for all believers. AMEN!

BIBLIOGRAPHY

Bartow, Donald W. - *Creative Churchmanship*

Bartow, Donald W. - *Personal Prayer Diary*

Bartow, Donald W. - *Leader's Guide for the 30-Day Prayer Pilgrimage*

Beuoy, Herbert - *The Heart Of A Healthy Body*

Ford, Peter S., M.D. - *The Healing Trinity*

Frost, Evelyn, Ph.D. - *Christian Healing*

Kelsey, Morton T. - *Healing and Christianity*

MacNutt, Francis - *Healing*

Neal, Emily G. - *A Reporter Finds God Through Spiritual Healing*

Neal, Emily G. - *The Lord Is Our Healer*

Pearson, Mark A. - *Christian Healing*

Peel, Robert - *Spiritual Healing In A Scientific Age*

Presbyterian Church - *Book Of Order; The Directory For Worship*

Presbyterian Church - *Life Abundant: Values, Choices Of Health Care*

Presbyterian Church - *The Person And Work Of The Holy Spirit*

Presbyterian Church - *The Relation Of Christian Faith To Health*

Ratcliff, J.D. - *Your Body And How It Works*

Samra, Cal - *The Joyful Christ, The Healing Power Of Humor*

Sanford, Agnes - *The Healing Gifts Of The Spirit*

Sanford, Agnes - *The Healing Power Of The Bible*

Shlemon, Barbara - *Healing Prayer*

Simpson, A.B. - *The Gospel Of Healing*

Tapscott, Betty - *The Fruit Of The Spirit*

Tillich, Paul - *The New Being*

Wagner, James K. - *Blessed To Be A Blessing*

Walsh, Tracy F. - *The Church's Ministry Of Healing For Young People And Children*

White, Anne S. - *Healing Adventure*

White, Anne S. - *The Transforming Power Of God*

Wilson, Michael - *The Church Is Healing*

INDEX

ISBN 0-938736-28-0